The Product Manager's Handbook

The Product Manager's Handbook

Third Edition

Linda Gorchels

McGraw-Hill
New York   Chicago   San Francisco   Lisbon
London   Madrid   Mexico City   Milan   New Delhi
San Juan   Seoul   Singapore   Sydney   Toronto

The **McGraw-Hill** Companies

Library of Congress Cataloging-in-Publication Data is on file.

6 7 8 9 10 11 12   DOC/DOC   1 5 4 3 2 1 0

Book p/n 0-07-145946-4
CD p/n 0-07-145947-2

Parts of
ISBN 0-07-145938-3

The sponsoring editor for this book was Roger Stewart and the production supervisor was David Zelonka. It was set in Fairfield Medium by Patricia Wallenburg.

Printed and bound by RR Donnelley.

 This book is printed on acid-free paper containing a minimum of 10 percent recycled, de-inked fiber.

Contents

Preface

Most business books deal with broad issues intended to appeal to as large a management audience as possible. Many are designed to be read leisurely on an airplane. This isn't one of them.

This is a book to challenge product managers to think differently about what their role is and how to do it better. Expect to find hands-on tools and templates, along with Business Briefs that help bring them to life. Expect to redefine your products and services using customer viewpoints in addition to your own. Expect to think more expansively about your competition, your customers, and your success factors. Expect to gain viewpoints well beyond my own.

I am fortunate to have a network of practitioners, academics, and consultants with relevant experience who have freely shared their unique perspectives. At the end of every chapter, an expert offers his or her ideas and knowledge related to a particular aspect of product management. Their insights and advice will sometimes support your predispositions and, at other times, make you rethink what you have been doing. And in all cases, you will be encouraged to pause, smile, or scratch your head at their opinions.

New to this edition is a CD containing the worksheets contained in the book. In addition, some templates and checklists are included—for a total of 20 items—to streamline your ability to benefit from the ideas and tools presented. All files are in Microsoft Word or Excel format, making it easy for you to refine and adapt to your unique situation.

Frequently Asked Questions

Q: *What is product management?*

A: A product manager typically is a middle manager charged with managing and marketing existing products—and developing new products—for a given product line, brand, or service. Other job titles could include brand manager, industry manager, or customer segment manager. (Note that the term product will refer to both products and services.)

Q: *What types of companies use product managers?*

A: Product managers are used in all types of companies, from consumer packaged goods to services (such as financial institutions) to industrial companies (such as original equipment manufacturers [OEMs], component suppliers, and after-market firms) to nonprofit organizations (such as hospitals).

Q: *What's the difference between product management and product development?*

A: Product management is the holistic job of product managers, including planning, forecasting, and marketing products or services. Product development is a corporate process of designing and commercializing new products. This book focuses on product management.

Q: *Who should read this book?*

A: This book is targeted most directly at existing product managers and customer segment managers (primarily in "nontraditional" roles beyond consumer packaged goods). However, it has been used effectively by people in all types of companies and industries. Many new product managers and directors or vice presidents of product management or marketing have found it valuable as well.

Q: *What will I learn by reading this book?*

A: You'll learn about different approaches to product management from different types of organizations, as well as ideas for getting work done through other functional areas. You'll learn how to strategically evaluate your product portfolio, walk through a typical corporate development process, and prepare for effective launch strategies. And finally, you'll learn various ways to add perceived value both to your product and to your effectiveness as a product manager.

Q: *How will I learn these skills?*

A: Several techniques have been used to help you in the learning process: (1) contemporary vignettes—referred to as Business Briefs—showing product management in action; (2) hands-on worksheets for the planning process, in hard copy in the book and in electronic format on the CD; (3) checklists at the end of each chapter for evaluating progress at every critical stage; and (4) expert interviews at the end of every chapter to stimulate different opinions, insights, and perspectives. For more information on learning product management skills, refer to the University of Wisconsin-Madison Executive Education Web site at http://uwexeced.com/marketing.

Q: *Is the book available internationally?*

A: Yes, the book has been translated into other languages and has had increasing international sales. Based on product management training I have conducted in Asia, the skills are highly transferable and appropriate.

Acknowledgments

Thanks to all of the product managers who have shared their ideas, offered suggestions, and challenged me over the past 20 years. And a special thanks to my network of colleagues—both those who were interviewed in this book and those who have given me fantastic ideas over the years. This book is for all of you.

Part One

Preparing Your Strategic Foundations

HELP WANTED

Business Strategist

Visionary with a genius for implementation. Must be both entrepreneurial and corporate-minded. Requires focus but with adaptability, not allowing fire-fighting to overtake strategy. Can work with people from all levels and cultures. Responsible for financial success of products with minimal authority. Experience required. Superhero cape with a red **S** optional. E-mail inquiries to …

Many people would be uncomfortable applying for this type of job. But the description fundamentally fits strong product managers. To be successful as a product manager, a host of business skills is necessary in addition to business- or product-related skills. Thinking long-term about the *future* revenue streams of a product, while simultaneously managing *current* revenue streams, is a critical balancing act. This first section addresses the strategic foundations of future revenue streams.

The first chapter provides a strategic planning framework for product managers. Chapters 2 through 5 cover specific knowledge areas that fit into this framework, including market segmentation, competitive intelligence, branding strategy, and financial and pricing analysis.

Chapter One

A Strategic Planning Framework for Product Managers

Why are you in product management? And why are you managing the specific product and services that you are? Hopefully, it's because you have a passion for your offerings and for the benefits these offerings give to customers. This chapter focuses on the characteristics of "heavyweight" product managers and provides a framework to turn their passion into business strategies.

Heavyweight Product Managers[1]

Heavyweight product managers are business strategists as well as competent follow-through individuals. They have to achieve profit through superior customer satisfaction with their products. And they must do this through people over whom they have no direct authority.

During the 1980s, product managers began appearing on the staffs of more and more automotive companies. The motivation for this change was the growth in international competition, the increasing complexity of the products, and more demanding, sophisticated customers. Product managers (called "large product leaders" at Honda and "program managers" at Ford) were challenged to create not only functionally superior cars, but also cars that are distinctive and embody a certain personality or "feel" that would be consistent with future customer needs.

This last aspect, bringing the customer into the mix, is the product manager's most critical role. The auto companies previously had used matrix structures, coordinator committees, cross-functional teams, and other structural mechanisms to improve product development, but these were frequently inward-focused and did not anticipate future customer desires. External integration is an important and difficult task of the development process: Unless a company makes a deliberate effort to integrate customers into the development process, it is likely to create products that are technologically advanced and perhaps offer good value but fall short of the expectations of sophisticated customers.

Ford is one company that had early success with the external integration organizational concept. The Taurus, introduced in 1985, was designed to be a family vehicle with sophisticated European styling, handling, and ride. Its success was due to Team Taurus, the cross-functional group responsible for this product. The effectiveness of the team became the catalyst for organizational change at Ford. Shortly thereafter, it formalized the "program manager" concept that evolved out of the Taurus experience.

The external integration structure reinforced cross-functional integration at both the strategy and operational levels. In particular, marketing people (led by the program manager) began to meet directly with designers and engineers. Previously, their involvement had been through reports and memos. The program managers themselves were given greater responsibility for product planning and layout.

As this organizational structure continued to grow, the strength of the program manager's position increased, as did the effectiveness of the product-development process. Several products that were developed out of this structure followed the market success of the Taurus: the Lincoln Continental, the Thunderbird Super Coupe, the Probe, and the Explorer.

As time went on, Ford management discovered that integrated development required more than a cross-functional team. It became clear that simply assigning a project leader to a team did not guarantee product integrity. The effectiveness of the program manager was the missing link.

When markets were relatively stable, companies could achieve product integrity through strong functional organizations. Now, however, the ability to achieve superior product integrity depends on the leadership of the product manager. The product manager becomes the thread tying all the pieces together, filling in the gaps and ensuring that the final product is consistent with the original product–customer concept, with a special effort placed on understanding what customer wants will be at the time a new product is introduced, rather than what they are right now. This person must be able to understand:

· What the product does (performance and technical functions);
· What the product is (configuration, component technologies);
· Who the product serves (target market); and
· What the product means to customers (character, personality, image).

Characteristics of Heavyweight Product Managers

Of course, not all product managers provide the same level of effectiveness. Kim Clark and Takahiro Fujimoto, in their *Harvard Business Review* article "The Power of Product Integrity," differentiate between "heavyweight" product managers and "their lighter-weight counterparts." According to their research in the automotive industry,[2] many product managers are functional workers, rather than cross-functional leaders. They lack influence outside their own functional area, have little or no contact with working-level engineers or with marketing, and act primarily as facilitators and coordinators. As a result, they spend much of their time going to meetings, reading reports, and writing memos.

Heavyweight product managers, on the other hand, function as the product's general manager. Clark and Fujimoto explain:

In addition to concept-related duties, the responsibilities
that come with the job include: coordinating production
and sales as well as engineering; coordinating the entire
project from concept to market; signing off on specification,
cost-target, layout and major component choices; and maintaining direct contact with existing and potential customers.
Heavyweight product managers have a broad knowledge of
the product and process engineering required to develop an
entire vehicle. Years of experience with the companies give
their words weight and increase their influence with people
over whom they have no formal authority.[3]

Honda's "large product leader" is such a position. It combines
the generation of a strong product concept with the ability to
carry it through development to the final product experience for
the end-customer. When the product manager for the Honda
Accord began the third-generation design, he was challenged
with maintaining the concept "man maximum, machine minimum" throughout the development process, while still repositioning the Accord to fit future customer expectations. Starting
with a series of small-group brainstorming sessions, the product
leader and his team decided to personify the car's message to consumers with the image of "a rugby player in a business suit." The
next step was to break this image down into specific attributes of
a car. Five sets of key words were chosen: *open-minded, friendly
communication, tough spirit, stress-free,* and *love forever. Tough
spirit* was translated into maneuverability in difficult conditions.
Love forever translated into long-term customer satisfaction.
Stress-free led to efforts in noise and vibration reduction.

To capture all these elements was a challenge for the
Accord design team. In an effort to allow maximum space and
visibility for the occupants, a low engine hood and a larger-
than-usual front window were part of the design.
Unfortunately, the large window meant that the car could get
uncomfortably hot in the summer unless a large air condition-
er was added, which required a large engine. And the large
engine was contrary to the desire for a low engine hood.

Rather than allowing this to develop into an either-or decision, the product leader reminded the team to look at their

work through future customers' eyes and to maintain the integrity of the initial concept. The result was the development of a new engine that was both compact and powerful.

As the Honda example shows, being market-oriented is a critical role for the talented product manager. However, as Clark and Fujimoto also point out, it requires more than that:

> It begins with customers, to be sure, since the best concept developers invariably supplement the cooked information they get from marketing specialists with raw data they gather themselves. But strong product concepts also include a healthy measure of what we call "market imagination": they encompass what customers say they want and what the concept's creators imagine customers will want three or more years into the future. Remembering that customers know only existing products and existing technologies, they avoid the trap of being too close to customers and of designing products that will be out-of-date before they are even manufactured.[4]

The product manager must juggle numerous details and ensure that the subtleties of a product concept are not lost in development and marketing. Although creating product and marketing plans is part of this effort, an essential task is the interpersonal communication of these somewhat intangible ideas. Daily communication with functional engineering departments during the design phase, and with plant personnel during the development phase, is a necessary role of the product manager. Similarly, product managers test-drive the vehicles and continually strive to attain strong product integrity:

> The product manager's job touches every part of the new product process. Indeed, heavyweight product managers have to be "multilingual," fluent in the languages of customers, marketers, engineers, and designers. On one side, this means being able to translate an evocative concept like the pocket rocket into specific targets like "maximum speed 250 kilometers per hour" and "drag coefficient less than 0.3" that detail-oriented engineers can easily grasp. On the other side, it means being able to assess and communicate what a "0.3 drag coefficient" will mean to the customers.[5]

Outstanding product-management organizations depend on consistency between the formal and informal organizational structure. Honda demonstrated this consistency in some important ways. Communication lines were open and direct, rather than indirect. Functional specialists were respected, but not put on a pedestal. And the product concept was infused throughout the product team.

Heavyweight product managers in other industries have some of the same characteristics as those in the automotive industry. As Jean LeGrand states, in her article in *Bankers Magazine*, "A Product in Need of Management," a successful product manager in the banking industry "must be a senior-level professional, widely regarded in the profession." This individual must understand "complex portfolio management programs and such quantitative models as cost accounting and return on equity (ROE) computations." And, as in the automotive industry, the position requires market knowledge and the ability to translate technical concepts into customer-appropriate terms.

In fast-moving consumer goods (FMCG) companies, product managers (frequently called "brand managers") are less likely to have industry experience, but rather, to have strong management and marketing skills, typically requiring an MBA. They are expected to create strong brand recognition for their products through their ability to command respect, maintain momentum throughout a product-related project, and motivate everyone toward the same goal. As with heavyweight product managers in other industries, the FMCG brand manager must strive for and champion product integrity.

A Planning Framework

No shortage of perspectives exists on planning approaches and frameworks. That's probably good, since product managers from different companies benefit from different "realities" in how they strategize. Business-to-business product managers need a strong understanding of how to help salespeople and distributors sell to commercial customers. Consumer product managers not only require a clear "brand manager" perspective of household buyers, but also must have the ability to motivate trade partners. Global product managers have different responsibilities, depending on whether they design products for foreign purchasers or accept existing products from their headquarters in another country to "glocalize" within their domestic borders. Many planning principles are common across all these situations, although the implementation of the principles might vary.

It's also worth noting that product managers may be responsible for many types of plans. One plan is based on longer-term strategies—generating a "vision" of what the product portfolio should be in the future—to ensure future cash flows for their product area. This plan might include various innovation and rationalization strategies. Those who are involved in new product development must create project plans to guide the development effort and launch plans to guide commercialization activities. And on an annual basis, product managers will develop marketing or business plans for the top products or, possibly, their entire product line. These types of plans identify tactics to improve sales and profitability, possibly incorporating revitalization and maintenance strategies for select products.

Figure 1.1 shows the relationships among product planning forces and the primary categories of product strategies. A knowledge of market and competitive trends, along with an understanding of the sustainable product, brand, and financial performance characteristics, yields the analytical foundation for the product vision and portfolio goals. The tools to conduct these analyses are described in chapters 2 and 3. Using the information to craft brand and financial (business) plans is described in chapters 4 and 5. Chapters 6 through 10 provide more ideas to implement innovation, revitalization, maintenance, and rationalization strategies.

Determining the vision and strategy of the overall company is a basic part of this analysis (Figure 1.2). The vision is the mental picture of what the company will be in the future: the products it will offer and the markets it will serve. The corporate and divisional strategies are the general plans needed to move toward this vision. The product plans and marketing tac-

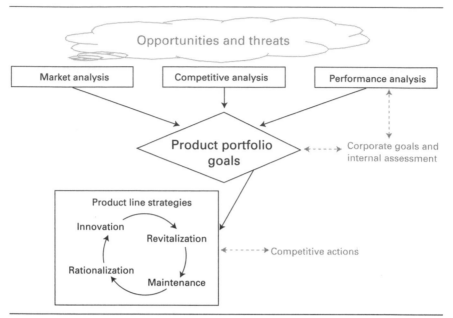

Figure 1.1   Product planning forces.

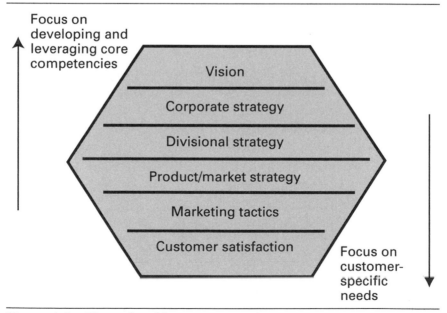

Figure 1.2   Hierarchy of business strategies.

tics should be consistent with the vision and strategies and move the company closer to superior customer satisfaction. The vision and corporate strategies are broad, with a focus on developing and leveraging core competencies. The product-specific strategies and tactics focus on customer-specific needs.

The vision should highlight the core capabilities that the company has or is willing to develop. For example, Komatsu, a Japanese manufacturer of earth-moving equipment, had a vision of beating Caterpillar. The company's strategies specified the skills it needed to acquire and the products it needed to develop to move toward that vision (see Business Brief 1.1, Komatsu's Long-Term Marketing Challenge).

The corporate assessment also looks at the general culture of the company, the strengths that provide the core competence, the weaknesses that must be minimized, and the role a product or product line plays in accomplishing the corporate strategy. The *culture* refers to how a company operates: its philosophies, management style, and structure. A product manager cannot impact the culture in the short term, but must rather understand and attempt to work within the culture.

Business Brief 1.1   Komatsu's long-term marketing challenge.

Komatsu, a Japanese manufacturer of bulldozers, developed a strategic vision of being a global player in earth-moving equipment—in essence, a vision of beating Caterpillar. This required a series of short-term plans that focused on the immediate problems and opportunities Komatsu had to respond to in the process of achieving its long-term goal.

In the 1960s, Komatsu was about one-third the size of Caterpillar, limited to one product line (small bulldozers), and scarcely represented outside of Japan. When Caterpillar threatened Komatsu in Japan, Komatsu's short-term objective was to protect its home market. The strategies used to accomplish this were product improvements, cost reductions, and new-product development through licensing agreements. In the early 1970s, Komatsu's challenge was to develop export markets. Since it was not yet strong enough to compete head-to-head with Caterpillar, it chose markets where Caterpillar was weak. Then, in the late 1970s, Komatsu felt prepared to compete against Caterpillar in the U.S. market.

continued on next page

Business Brief 1.1   continued

Komatsu's Long-Term Vision: Beat Caterpillar

Related short-term activities to move toward the vision:

Date	Corporate Challenge	Activities
Early 1960s	Protect Komatsu's home market against Caterpillar	Licensing deals with Cummins Engine, International Harvester, and Bucyrus-Eric
Mid-1960s	Begin quality improvement efforts	Several quality and cost-reduction programs
1960s to early 1970s	Build export markets	Komatsu Europe established service departments to assist newly industrializing countries
Late 1970s	Create new products and markets	Future and Frontiers program to identify new businesses based on society's needs and company's know-how
		Enters U.S. market

Note how the company stated a long-term vision or direction (become a more dominant global player than Caterpillar). Then, on a shorter-term basis, it focused on those problems and opportunities present at that time that might affect its ability to move toward its vision. The corporate challenges represented the shorter-term objectives of the marketing planning process.

In other words, they focused on the steps that needed to be taken at the current time to move closer to the future picture of the company. Finally, the activities column listed a brief summary of the action program or the tactics necessary to address the corporate challenges.

Source: Adapted from Gary Hamel and C.K. Prahalad, "Strategic Intent," *Harvard Business Review* (May–June 1989):63–76.

Examples of business culture include the *innovative, fast-paced organization* on one hand or the *conservative, "blue-chip" organization* on the other. The management style may be autocratic or democratic, and will have a resulting impact on a product manager's effectiveness.

Product managers often are uncertain about how their products contribute to the attainment of corporate goals (beyond revenue). To be sure, it's not an easy question to answer, but it must be considered. If the company is changing its position from economy products to more quality products, this change will impact the strategies of its product managers. Hyundai, for example, has declared that it would be the industry's top-quality producer, displacing Toyota, by 2008. Although a difficult goal, Hyundai has made progress: In 2004, it tied with Honda on J.D. Power & Associates Initial Quality Survey, jumping from 10th to second place.[6] From a strategic perspective, product managers must consider these linkages (Worksheet 1.1).

Several questions must be asked as part of this assessment, to help identify the key strengths and weaknesses of management, core competencies, the planning process, and other functional areas.

Worksheet 1.1   Linking product strategy to corporate strategy.

1. Describe the corporate vision, strategies, and core competencies that might affect the product programs:

2. List the strengths and weaknesses of the company that could directly affect the product or product line:

   Strengths:

   Weaknesses:

3. Describe the role your product/line plays in accomplishing the corporate strategy:

Management

1. Who are the actual movers and shakers within the company? Which ones should be part of a new-product venture?
2. Who is responsible for the budgeting process?
3. Does the company have any unusual business practices that are different from the competition?

Distinctive Competencies

1. What capabilities form the core of the firm's reason for being?
2. Are the various products produced by the firm leveraging these competencies effectively? How can product managers leverage the capabilities of other parts of the company?

The Planning Process

1. What is the basic approach to tactical and strategic planning?
2. Is it more likely that the company will grow by acquisition, penetration of new markets, or increased market share?
3. To what extent are documented objectives used in planning?
4. Where is the emphasis placed for the development of new products (e.g., product-line extensions, new applications, new-product ventures, etc.)?
5. What are the plans for global or international growth?
6. What significant new products are under development?

Other Functional Areas

1. What is the background of the research and development manager?
2. What is the overall caliber of the research staff?
3. What is the company's technical position?
4. Does the company have idle plants and excess capacity?
5. What is the major research and development thrust?
6. How is research and development organized?

After thinking more carefully about these questions, test your company's strategic IQ by completing the assessment in Worksheet 1.2.

Worksheet 1.2 Assessing your company's strategic IQ.

Read each of the following questions; evaluate your firm on a 1–5 scale (for questions 1–10) or a 1–10 scale (for questions 11–15), with 1 = Poor and the top value (5 or 10) = Excellent.

_____ 1. The company has a directional vision or "picture" of what it will look like in the future.

_____ 2. The strategic vision is stated concisely to avoid overloading the organization with competing (and possibly conflicting) initiatives.

_____ 3. Strategic thinking (broad-based, unrestricted) coexists with strategic planning (narrower and more detailed in focus).

_____ 4. The company emphasizes leveraging its resources to move toward an ambitious vision, rather than restricting its vision to fit current resources.

_____ 5. In making outsourcing, divestiture, and product-elimination decisions, the impact of the decision on distinctive competencies is considered.

_____ 6. In making acquisition decisions, the impact on core capabilities is considered.

_____ 7. A competitive focus is present throughout the organization, and a widespread use of competitive intelligence exists.

_____ 8. The company uses competitive innovation at least as frequently as (if not more frequently than) competitive imitation.

_____ 9. Key members in all departments throughout the company are aware of market trends that could impact the strategy.

_____ 10. The strategic plan plays an integral role in the development of annual marketing plans.

Note: The next five questions are worth 10 points each.

_____ 11. The company has studied its historical track record to truly understand the abilities and processes that drive its competitive edge.

_____ 12. The company strives for a portfolio of competitive advantages, in addition to a portfolio of products.

_____ 13. Annual plans do not simply project the past and present into the future, but rather describe what must be done (perhaps differently) next year to move closer to the strategic vision.

_____ 14. The company strives to transform its key processes into strategic capabilities that consistently provide superior value to the customer.

_____ 15. New products developed indicate that the company knows what customers want before customers know it themselves.

_____ Total (100 points)

Your Strategic Product Vision

Earlier, in the Komatsu example, we looked at a long-term vision statement for a company and saw how it related to short- and medium-term strategies. Product managers should have similar vision statements (or goals) for their areas of responsibility, tied to the corporate vision. Samsung's vision to move from laggard to leader in consumer electronics has a significant impact on the firm's products (see Business Brief 1.2). What would you like your product offering to "look like" 3 or 5 years into the future? What new products, services, or technologies do you expect to exist? Will you be serving the same customers, or will you have added new segments? How large will your product offering be (in terms of market share, volume, or product categories)?

Sometimes it's useful to think in terms of writing a future (and somewhat hypothetical) annual report just for your area of responsibility. If you are responsible for new product devel-

---

Business Brief 1.2   Samsung's vision.

The Korean company, Samsung Electronics, is reinventing itself from a me-too producer of electronics to a designer of "cool gadgets." Yun Jong-Yong, Samsung's chief executive, has a vision "to be the Mercedes of home electronics." To accomplish this, Samsung is striving to keep its product designs at the leading edge, without losing relevance to the users.

Designers work in three- to five-person teams from various specialties, a departure from the historical top-down tradition. Many of the new designs come from outside the company and build on a commitment to customer research and testing. In 2004, Samsung won five citations in the Industrial Design Excellence Awards (IDEA)—more than any American or European rival—and 33 total awards in top design contests in the United States, Europe, and Asia. The designs have increased brand value and market share.

While some analysts question whether Samsung has the breadth and depth to achieve its vision, there's no question they've made progress toward it in the last 5 years. The future will depend on their ability to continue to anticipate customer demands and maintain an advantage over the competition.

Source: Adapted with permission from David Rocks and Moon Ihlwan, "Samsung Design," *BusinessWeek* (December 6, 2004):88–96.

opment, envision the new products that will be part of your portfolio. If you are not responsible for new products (e.g., your job is a "downstream" position focused on supporting the sales effort), envision the competitive position your product will have in the future. Commit this vision to paper. As you work through the analyses in subsequent chapters, the vision may need to be "tweaked" or adapted—but that shouldn't be a major stumbling block for a heavyweight product manager!

A common challenge for multiple-product managers is balancing the demands of the complete portfolio versus individual products, and the demands of new versus existing products. If the number of products is small, set objectives for each one. If the number of products is too large for that to be practical, at least three approaches are possible. One is to identify the key products (similar to identifying the key accounts in your customer base). Then develop individual goals for those products and a broad, overall objective for the remaining products. A second approach is to group products by customer segment or application (if relevant), and establish goals on that basis. The third approach is a combination of product and market goals.

In any event, be prepared to make changes in emphasis dictated by changes in the marketplace. PepsiCo, for example, has decided to shift its flagship brand to Diet Pepsi, rather than regular Pepsi, as obesity concerns and aging Baby Boomers have impacted sales. Although the company isn't about to drastically cut marketing expenditures on the main product, it plans on doubling its marketing spending on Diet Pepsi.[7]

Checklist: A Strategic Planning Framework for Product Managers

· Heavyweight product managers function as the product's general managers and should be knowledgeable about their product and market requirements; competent in business, financial, and strategic skills; and capable of working through other people.

- Product strategies should be consistent with corporate visions.
- Since corporate culture and management style impact a product's potential success, product managers should be aware of these impacts.
- Product managers should establish long-term goals for their product offerings.

Interview with Paul Baumgart, General Manager, Respiratory Care, Information Technologies Division of GE Healthcare

Q: *What was the career path that took you to your current position?*

A: After obtaining my MBA, I joined the company in a financial analyst role, then went through a number of positions in product management, sales management, and corporate accounts, which led to a Marketing Manager role for a business segment, and eventually, the commercial marketing responsibility for the full product portfolio in North America. Subsequently, I have worked in Business Development, as a VP of Sales outside of the healthcare industry, then joined GE Healthcare in a commercial (Downstream) market management position. When GE acquired the company where I had spent my first 20 years in the industry, I took on an Integration Manager job, and that led to the opportunity to take on global responsibilities for our new Respiratory Care business.

Q: *Tell me about your biggest successes.*

A: Several come to mind. And I will take the liberty to define success along different dimensions and mention only three.

First, in the mid-1980s and 1990s, I became quite active in market development efforts to influence and support the world-wide movement to upgrade the quality and standards of anesthesia and monitoring systems used in the operating room. As Director of Corporate Accounts, I worked closely with the leadership of a large, proprietary, for-profit, healthcare system, and worked with them to set up an asset management approach to the challenge of addressing new technology and emerging industry standards in nearly 700 operating rooms spread around the country. The result was a significant sale of our products, while at the same time helping the customer to position itself as a leader by being one of the first multihospital organizations in the U.S. to completely address the new emerging standards for anesthesia equipment safety and intraoperative monitoring. I eventually went on to apply this same approach in a number of major international opportunities.

Second, recognition by the customers I have served in my career is a highly cherished success. In 2004, I was elected to the Board of Directors of the Anesthesia Patient Safety Foundation (APSF), an organization that has made a significant difference in the quality and safety of anesthesia care since its founding in 1984. As a marketing manager in this industry, the customer relationships I have built, the industry-thought leaders I have had access to, and the constructive interactions I have had with competitors under the umbrella of the APSF has added immeasurably to my own knowledge and credibility, both internally and externally.

One other success relates to the number of people who I have had the opportunity to coach and mentor in various positions, who have now moved on to take on significant leadership roles and establish their own track record of success. Communication skills and leadership style are two of the most important traits needed to be successful in a marketing career. It is the power of cross-functional teams working together to solve problems and exploit opportunities that drives commercial success and strategic and tactical agility. I have been blessed with the opportunity to work with some amazing people, and I take great pride in watching people who have been part of my teams soar on to greater heights.

Q: *What was most and least satisfying about your product management jobs?*

A: Anyone who has been a product manager for more than 6 months knows that the job is complex and multifaceted. Success comes from strategic grounding, being incredibly skillful at managing the 4 Ps and the tactical elements, and ultimately, at being able to "grunt" out the details required to ensure programs and plans are executed properly. Long hours spent building product configuration guides, managing pricing and price increases across many hundreds of item numbers, and reading through detailed product specifications are among my least satisfying parts of the job. Working with a team to develop a marketing strategy from a blank piece of paper and following it through program development, roll out, and launch, and seeing success in the form of measurable market share gains and sales success creates an unbelievably satisfying feeling. Also, being associated with the healthcare industry, I can make a clear connection between products I have helped to bring to market and what I view as truly meaningful improvements in the quality of healthcare not only in the U.S., but all over the world.

Q: *Customer knowledge is critical for product managers. What have you observed as the biggest mistakes product managers make in learning about and segmenting customers?*

A: A couple things come to mind. The first is a tendency sometimes to want to believe customers are more homogenous than they actually are. To an engineer or manufacturing operation, the ideal product has one version—one size fits all—and it may be unpopular for the product manager after successfully launching a new product to come back and say now we have to change this or that about it to meet the requirements of another segment that may have gone unrecognized in the product development process and early stages of specification creation. You really have to make sure that, in the early stages of defining the specific customer needs, you canvass a broad enough cross-section of the targeted customers to determine if differences exist in the specification due to co-existing segments. To sales representatives, there are 100 different product requirements. The product manager has to sit between the operations forces trying to create one product and the sales force trying to create 100, and determine the true nature of segmentation that does exist. And in determining that, be able to translate those differences into product features, pricing, packaging, services, and other requirements for the product. A common mistake for new product managers coming into their roles from a sales background is being unable to break loose from their previous customer-centric view of the world and become a little more "market-centric." Too many product variations can be as harmful to the business, in terms of cost burden and support requirements, as having only one. Being able to establish clear segmentation will help to add clarity to product specifications, define the bundle of services and product attributes that must be included in the offering, and also identify those segments that, for whatever reason, you choose as a business not to serve. Learning to say "no" as a product manager is just as important to the profitability and success of a business—maybe even more so—than knowing when to say "yes."

Q: *Do you think B2B product managers face different customer-analysis challenges than do B2C product managers?*

A: My opinion is yes. In B2B, product managers may tend to be more closely involved with specific customers, specific transactions and sales situations, and have more direct contact with customers, as well as the direct sales channels and resellers. That level of customer intimacy might actually hamper one's ability to stand back and try to take a more macro view of the market as a whole. However, that same level of customer knowledge, if managed within a broad marketing perspective or framework, will allow you to develop some pretty accurate assessments of customer needs and wants, as well as an awareness of fundamental differences that might exist within your customer base and that point to the presence of distinct segments. In B2B product marketing, you are typically dealing with a lot fewer numbers of customers than in consumer-oriented businesses, so B2C will need to rely much more heavily on more formal methods of market research and larger sample sizes to get meaningful data on which marketing plans and product specifications can be based.

Q: *What is the best advice you ever received?*

A: One piece of advice is from a former boss of mine: You can't draw a straight line from one point. The other is from Steven Covey: Begin with the end in mind.

Q: *What advice can you provide to today's product managers?*

A: Try to always maintain a "fresh set of eyes" and a conscious effort to maintain an unbiased objectivity when looking at your markets. It is easy to get so close to your products and your customers that you might miss a new, emerging segment, or a budding trend that will evolve in a way that may cause the industry or the market to become redefined. As a product manager, we all tend to think about our products, and certainly most of what we do, by definition, is centered on taking care of the "widget." One way to try to keep an eye on new developing concepts, segments, and trends is to stop thinking only about the product and start thinking instead about what it is your product or service does. For example, if you are selling drill bits, realize that your customer is buying the ability to create a hole. Thinking about the business from the product point of view or from the customer's-need point of view will give you two entirely different perspectives. I think the latter view gives you much better staying power in the market.

Notes

1. The section on heavyweight product managers was adapted from Kim B. Clark and Takahiro Fujimoto, "The Power of Product Integrity," *Harvard Business Review* (November–December 1990): 107–118; Christopher Power, "Flops," *BusinessWeek* (16 August, 1993): 76–82; and Jean E. LeGrand, "A Product in Need of Management," *Banker Magazine* (November–December 1992): 73–76.
2. Although the product managers in the automotive industry described in this section were generally part of engineering, most product managers in other industries are in marketing, marketing/sales, or product management departments.
3. Clark and Fujimoto, 108.
4. Clark and Fujimoto, 109.
5. Clark and Fujimoto, 110.
6. Anonymous, "Hyundai Steers for the Top," *Wall Street Journal* (April 27, 2005): B3.
7. Chad Terhune, "In Switch, Pepsi Makes Diet Cola Its New Flagship," *Wall Street Journal* (March 16, 2005): B1.

Chapter Two

Trend-Spotting, Research, and Customer Segmentation

The planning described in the previous chapter will not be effective without good information. Gathering information is a time-consuming process, and product managers must balance the need for intelligence with the challenge of information overload. It's not an easy balance to reach. The ability to segment and target customers has grown increasingly more sophisticated with the growth of technology. So, product managers must stop thinking that their job is to sell products. Rather, their job is to help customers *buy* products. Since different customers have different needs and expectations, product managers must clarify what these differences are, as well as the significance of these differences in their plans.

The cornerstone of an effective business strategy is the ability to attract and retain high-profit customers. More focus should be placed on growing customers, rather than on just growing product sales. Product managers must have a clear-cut understanding and appreciation of the market(s) for their products. These markets could include existing customers as well as potential customers, singular clients as well as groups or segments, and individuals using your product as well as those

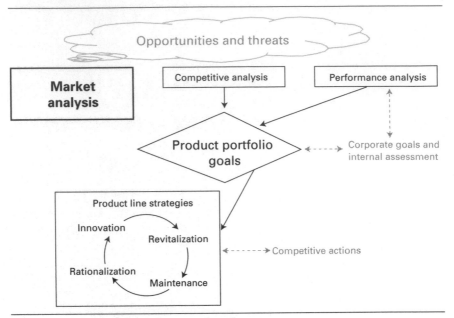

Figure 2.1   Market analysis in the planning process.

influencing its purchase. This chapter focuses on the issues involved in analyzing your markets and establishing plans to maximize their profitability—the market analysis piece of the planning process (Figure 2.1).

Trend-Spotting and Customer Research

Product managers, whether they are involved in brainstorming new product ideas or crafting innovative, go-to-market strategies for existing products, must be adept at spotting and capitalizing on trends. It is far too easy to get caught up in the business of day-to-day firefighting and lose sight of what's happening all around us. Trend-spotting can be a full-time job. Therefore, product managers should determine which trends they will *actively* seek out, and which they will *opportunistically* evaluate. Create folders (virtual or actual) with labels of the key trends you want to follow. For example, a technology product manager may follow wi-fi, convergence, and programmable logic trends. A foods product manager may follow obesity, labeling, and regulatory trends.

Sometimes, it is helpful to ask colleagues to help with this project. Establish a Trend Analysis Group (TAG) team and have each colleague agree to feed you information on a particular trend. Also create a folder labeled *Opportunistic,* in which to collect random thoughts and insights. File articles, customer data, channel and sales insights, various downloads, and random ideas in these folders. Then develop the discipline to review the information on a routine basis.

Numerous trends could put pressure on product strategies. For example, Hewlett-Packard has discovered a cross-current of trends affecting its printer business. Most existing PC owners already have printers, so the market for new sales is expected to be virtually flat. Competitors have become more aggressive, causing HP's market share to drop. Meanwhile, a new industry of cartridge refillers has emerged, hurting HP's ink sales. Although HP's printer division is still significant (accounting for 73% of its earnings in 2004), this mix of trends cannot be ignored and will require efforts in new product development.[1]

Technology trends provide both opportunities and threats. Nanotechnology, while still at the fuzzy front-end of innovation, has the potential to impact a multitude of industries.[2] The Web provides an overwhelming amount of data, but also can provide opportunities. As more and more hospitals curtail visits by pharmaceutical sales reps, product managers are turning to the Web for possible solutions. Online detailing, product Web sites, and e-mail marketing are expected to receive increased spending.[3]

Monitoring demographic trends and shifts also can highlight the need for new products, language modifications, and/or marketing strategy changes. Although it has been standard to focus on youth for most new consumer products, many companies have started to reach out to older adults. Proctor & Gamble has identified about 30 products that it can market directly to people 50 and older, and Sony has increased advertising to make its high-end gadgets more appealing to the 50 to 64 age group.[4] The aging of the global population also results in physical challenges to traditional car design, and the

Japanese have begun to incorporate features to address these challenges (see Business Brief 2.1).

It is absolutely critical that product managers stay on top of trends that could affect their markets, their product, their competitors, and their technologies. As always, some prioritization is helpful. Categorize the trends in terms of probability and significance (Figure 2.2). *Probability* refers to the likelihood that a trend will happen within your current planning cycle. *Significance* refers to the positive or negative impact the trend could have on your product strategy. Focus first on trends that have the highest probabilities and significance factors.

Business Brief 2.1   Japanese car options for the elderly.

With the dramatic increase in the percentage of elderly in the populations of virtually all developed countries, demand will be growing for many related products and services. Japan has noted that by 2010, one-fourth of its population will be over 65 years of age, and it has begun to address the issue. At the 31st International Home Care and Rehabilitation Exhibition in Tokyo, 'Elder Car' options were displayed next to booths showcasing adult diapers and home elevators.

A subsidiary of Nissan Motors offers wheelchair ramps for vans, as well as products for smaller cars, including swivel seats and a motorized crane to lift a wheelchair into and out of a trunk. Toyota is exploring "barrier-free cars," and has developed a car seat that doubles as a wheelchair. Even Ford Motor Company has developed a full-body jumpsuit that restricts movement, to help designers understand the limitations of old age. The jumpsuit comes with glasses that simulate weaker eyesight.

The current market for these types of vehicles is less than 1% of all automobiles sold. Many are adaptations of vehicles designed for the handicapped. Most car companies are taking a cautious, wait-and-see approach to the issue, due to concerns such as product liability. However, the demographic trend is real and could have a significant impact on future product demands.

Source: Adapted from Jathon Sapsford, "Japan's Auto Makers Ply the Aged with 'Elder Car' Options," *Wall Street Journal* (November 5, 2004): B1–B3.

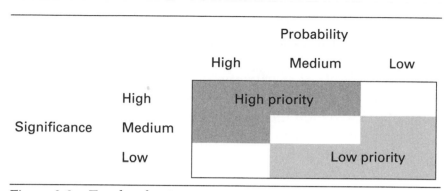

Figure 2.2   Trend evaluation matrix.

Research Projects

Gathering customer information is generally a responsibility of marketing research, so this is simply a primer to overview definitions and jargon.[5] We'll start by differentiating primary, syndicated, and secondary research. *Primary research* refers to surveys, focus groups, and other methods designed to gather information for a stated purpose. The sample is selected and the questionnaire is designed specifically for that purpose. *Syndicated research* often refers to a "shared cost" study, in which a firm may insert a question or two into a generic study. The sample and questionnaire are not specifically focused on that firm's goals, but are used when the sample is deemed "close enough." Syndicated research also includes warehouse and retail sales data compiled by companies such as A.C. Nielsen. *Secondary research* refers to an analysis of census data, trade association statistics, and other previously compiled and published data.

Research also can be categorized into qualitative, quantitative, or experimental. *Qualitative research,* such as focus groups and case studies, attempts to provide richer, deeper answers and insights, but it does so at the expense of being representative—the results cannot be statistically projected to the overall customer base. Because the sample size is necessarily small, it might not be representative of the population; also, the fluidity of the questions challenges a statistical analysis of results.

Quantitative research is essentially at the opposite end of the continuum from qualitative. It requires a questionnaire with carefully worded, closed-ended questions and a true probability sample. Both these requirements are necessary to project the results from the sample to the population (from which the sample was drawn), with any statistical confidence. In reality, most customer research incorporates some aspects of both qualitative and quantitative research.

Experiments are used less frequently than qualitative or quantitative research when compiling customer information. Consumer product managers may use market tests or in-store tests to determine which package design or advertising message "pulls" better than another. In setting up a market experiment, the researcher strives to select similar groups of customer (controlling for as many extraneous variables as possible), and then gives each group a different package design (or price, ad message, or other variable). The comparative reactions to the variations of this one factor are measured and used as a basis for decision making.

If a product manager does not have the skills, access, or funds for a comprehensive customer research project, a few alternative approaches are possible.

- Split the research into several small projects that focus on the most critical questions but are more affordable.
- Share the cost with another product manager who needs information from the same set of customers.
- Find a college marketing research class that will take it on as a semester project.
- Hire an intern with the right skill set to conduct the research.
- Determine if a secondary research project (perhaps conducted by consultants in your industry) provides information that can augment what you already know.

The techniques described so far are primarily "formal" research projects. Product managers also can obtain much information using informal techniques. These include customer visits, trade show conversations, suggestions and comments made to customer service reps, user group input, complaint letters, product repair records, blogs, dealer/distributor/rep advisory councils, and other person-to-person sources.

Preliminary Customer Segmentation Questions

Market analysis refers to studying current and potential customers for a product or product line. Start by asking yourself some basic questions about existing customers.

1. Is there a group of heavy users of the product(s)? What percent of the purchasers do they constitute?
2. Is the primary target market growing, stable, or declining?
3. Under what circumstances do customers purchase the product(s)?
4. How and why is geographical coverage limited?
5. What percentage of customers are national accounts? International?
6. Are most customers new or repeat buyers?
7. Are the customers the end-users? If not, what information is available about the end-user?
8. Are the customers progressive? Traditional? Passive?
9. How sensitive have customers been to past price changes?
10. Does the customer base consist of a few large customers or many small buyers?

Now, if you haven't already done so, put current and potential customers into categories or segments. The segments are groups of customers with common demographics, common needs, and/or common uses for the product. The process of segmenting allows the marketer to get closer to the customer by focusing on the requirements of smaller groups. Although there had been a lot of press lately on one-to-one marketing, most product development efforts require a minimum market size beyond one (as defined by segmentation parameters) to be profitable.

It's important to break a total market into submarkets for a variety of reasons. First, it helps provide a better understanding of the aggregate market, including how and why customers buy. Second, it ensures a better allocation of resources, because the benefits that specific groups are looking for are better understood. This should make it possible to build competitive features or services into the product offering. And finally, segmentation enables the company to exploit opportunities by uncovering hidden niches.

To begin the segmentation process, use factors most appropriate for your industry (Table 2.1). Consumer product companies use demographic variables, such as age and family status, or psychographic variables, such as attitudes and lifestyles. The objective of classifying customers into groups is to find similarities in the way they might respond to your product strategies.

> Understanding what connects people to each other in the category decisions they make and the brands they choose is far more revealing than determining how they differ. And usually, what connects them is their mood and frame of mind, not their demo- or psychographics. A 19-year-old female bicycle courier from Toronto and a 58-year-old male farmer from Saskatchewan have nothing in common: different demographics, completely different lifestyle, and likely different values. But they both love Kraft Dinner, vote NDP, shop at discount stores, get their news on the Internet, and go to Vegas.[6]

Table 2.1   Segmentation Factors

Type of Factor	Consumer	Product-Market Business-to-Business
Demographic	Age, sex, race Income Family size Family life cycle stage Location	Industry (NAICS) Geographic location Company size Functional decision maker Profitability
Psychographic	Lifestyle Attitudes	Risk categories Psychology of decision maker
Application/ use of product	Frequency of purchase Size of purchase How product is used	Application Importance of purchase Volume, frequency
Benefits (possibly beyond the product)	Emotional satisfaction	Support requirements Service requirements Relationships

Industrial product companies use the North American Industry Classification System (NAICS),[7] company size, or functional titles. Many companies evaluate the end-use of the product as a segmentation variable. For example, a product manager for nylon might break segments into end-use groups such as menswear, tires, and upholstery. Most B2B segmentation is multilevel. For example, a supplier of products to hospitals might first look at different company types, such as teaching hospital, community hospital, owned specialty practice, home health business, outpatient clinic, foundation, or company-sponsored facility. At a second level, segments of business units exist within hospitals, such as oncology, pediatrics, telemetry, cardiac services, behavioral lifestyle, general surgery, obstetrics, case management, rehabilitation, and emergency. And finally, specific functional titles could represent different needs, such as physician, nurse manager, nurse, and so forth. It's worth noting that the different personalities and interests of people within the same function may suggest a different level of interest in your products and services.

Service companies use intensity of need, risk categories, or distance from the company. Lifestyle differences might also be the basis for segmentation. Aramark, in studying customer segments for its hospital food-service, identified five categories of health care workers based on individual insights. Banks build models of propensity-to-buy among customers (see Business Brief 2.2).

After identifying segments that have different needs, examine the product's performance in each segment. What is the average order size, the share of segment sales, and the revenues generated? The example in Table 2.2 shows four identifiable market segments. The *Negotiator Segment* consists of the largest companies with special demands and the market power to negotiate for those demands. In rating the importance of six purchase criteria on a scale of 1 to 5, with 1 being "low importance" and 5 being "essential," price has an importance level of 4, quality/features is rated 1, delivery 3, installation 1, manufacturing/engineering support 1, and sales coverage 2. Based on industry data, the company estimates the overall sales in the

Business Brief 2.2   Market segmentation for service operations.

Aramark spent several months researching customers in an effort to improve their retail food-service operations for hospitals. The research consisted of focus groups, interviews with 700+ health care employees, and 40,000 "customer insight surveys." Based on the research, they identified five categories of health care workers: Healthies, Loyals, Bringers, Refuelers, and Skippers.

- *Healthies*—Health is a deciding factor in what they eat
- *Loyals*—Satisfied with hospital dining
- *Bringers*—Brown-bag lunch crowd
- *Refuelers*—Eat on the go
- *Skippers*—Avoid hospital food due to their negative opinion of it

As part of the research, Aramark estimated the percentage of customers falling into each segment, a ranking of targets, and the best way to develop a strategy to reach them.

More and more community banks are also segmenting customers based on a variety of criteria beyond traditional demographic variables. These companies typically analyze the profitable customers in their own databases and match the information with data from the outside to develop models of potential.

About five years ago, Commercial Federal began using predictive modeling, scoring customers on their propensity to buy certain products. Now, its monthly mailings (about 33 a month, promoting everything from checking accounts to home equity loans) are triggered by propensity scores based on factors like a maturing loan or a customer's anniversary with the thrift.

Segmentation marketing works by analyzing the characteristics of customers who have bought certain types of products. To determine likely prospects for a home equity line of credit, for example, a program would examine the thousands of such customers in a bank's database. It would then apply standard methods to develop a model for identifying prospects with the same characteristics.

Similarly, Tri-Tech Corporation, an electrical components distributor, decided to segment its customers according to how they wanted to buy from Tri-Tech. "Now, field reps call on the customers who want an in-person sales process, and the telesales people handle customers who want to order products via the phone or Internet." This type of segmentation process is particularly suited to the needs of a distributor.

Source: Anonymous, "Aramark HMS: Hospital foodservice customers ready for their close-ups," *Nation's Restaurant News* (April 4, 2005): 16. Chris Costanzo, "Finer Customer Segmentation Paying Off," *American Banker* (December 14, 2004): 6A. Andy Cohen, "Addressing their Needs," *Sales and Marketing Management* (July 2004): 18.

Table 2.2   Segmentation by Key Buying Factors

	Negotiator Segment	Big-Lot Segment	Solutions Segment	Custom Segment
Common purchase-decision criteria	Category killer Standard products Large purchases Strong price negotiators	Large customers Very price sensitive Standard products Large purchases	Solution-seekers Modified-standard products Medium-size lots Moderate price sensitivity	Nonstandard motors Special features Small lots Price often secondary
Price	••••	•••	••	•
Quality/features	•	••	•••	••••
Delivery	•••	••	••	•••
Installation	•	•	•••	••
Marketing/engineering support	•	••	•••	•••••
Sales coverage	••	••	••	•••••
Size and share	$89 million 13%	$113.4 million 31%	$69.3 million 30%	$66.6 million 25%
Average order size	$1,500 Industry: $15,000	$6,998 Industry: $5,000	$2,345 Industry: $2,000	$923 Industry: $3,000

Key to importance of buying factors: Low •   ••   •••   ••••   ••••• High segment are $89 million, with an industry-average order size of $15,000. Its share of this market is 13%, with an average order size of $1,500. By studying all the information, it appears that the company is most successful with the *Big-Lot* and *Solutions* segments. In both situations, a significant market share exists, and the order size is greater than the industry average.

After listing potential ways of segmenting the market, including both old and new market segments, the next step is to reduce the number of categories into a manageable number (3 to 7). First, eliminate any segments that the firm cannot serve, for whatever reason. Then examine the remaining segments in terms of fit with company resources, fit with long-term strategy, cost to reach, and risk to serve. Rank these segments so that the greatest proportion of resources will be devoted to the most important segments.

One way that product managers approach this is to simultaneously evaluate the attractiveness of different markets and determine their firm's ability to satisfy the needs of those markets. All customers are not created equal, and trying to build loyalty among all customers can be detrimental to the health of a firm. Product managers must determine *which* customers offer the best future return on investment. For mass-market products (e.g., fast-moving consumer goods—FMCG), profiling heavy users and developing a plan to appeal to them is common. The profile might include standard demographic variables such as age, sex, income, geographic location, marital status, and family size, as well as psychographic characteristics, such as perceptions of oneself and desired personality characteristics. For industrial products (e.g., capital equipment), customers requiring specific applications or uses may be more profitable than others, and may therefore be considered the "best" customers.

Market and Customer Analysis Process

Let's use the example of a hypothetical food service company called Progressive Foodservice, Inc. that sells food items to two major market categories: food service distributors and operators, each of which may be further segmented. The food service distributors consist of full-line distributors, specialty distributors, and buying groups. The food service operators consist of commercial operators (lodging, fast-food, restaurants, cafeterias, caterers, and retail hosts) and noncommercial operators (health care, educational institutions, airlines, and vending). Starting at the highest level of segmentation, the first step is to determine what needs are distinctly different among the segments. Assume that the full-service distributors and distributor buying groups are interested in centralized purchasing, volume buying to get a discounted price, and specialized distribution specifications. The specialty distributors, who carry a specific line of products or target a specific type of account, are interested in unique products and possible merchandising support to reach their customers.

For those sales made directly to food service operators, rather than through distributors, customers also have varying needs. Within the commercial group, fast-food restaurants demand just-in-time shipments of food products at the lowest possible price. The remaining commercial operators (to varying degrees) desire menu support and presentation ideas. The noncommercial operators are interested in consistent inventory replenishment and long shelf-life products. After studying these needs, Progressive recombined the markets into five broad need segments, then looked at two things: how attractive the segments are as a whole, and whether the firm had any competitive advantages in addressing the segment needs.

To determine market attractiveness, Progressive examined market size (the total number of customers in each segment), the growth rate, the strength of competition, the price sensitivity of the customers, the revenue and profitability of existing customers in these segments, and similar variables. Then, it rated each segment on a 1 to 5 scale, with 1 being "unattractive" and 5 being "highly attractive." General distributors (segment A) were rated 3, specialty distributors (segment B) were rated 4, fast-food chains (segment C) were rated 2, commercial operators (segment D) were rated 3, and noncommercial operators (segment E) were rated 1. Note that some blurring of customers and noncustomers occurs at this time, since we don't want to limit the analysis to what is happening now, but rather keep in mind the potential for growth. Compare the size, purchase volumes, and growth rate for each segment in the entire market with the size, purchase volumes, and growth rate for the respective segment of existing customers. Ask questions during this analysis:

- What is the demand in each segment for the product?
- What is the product's penetration?
- How many prospects are there in segments that purchase only competitive products? Why do they purchase only those products?
- Are you gaining or losing share?
- Do you participate in the most profitable segments in the industry?

Summarize the information in a table similar to that shown in Table 2.3.

To determine whether it had any competitive advantages in addressing the segment-specific needs, Progressive honestly appraised its own competencies and rated its ability to satisfy the needs of the segments. Again, using a 1 to 5 scale, Progressive rated itself 1 if strong competitors existed with significant abilities to satisfy the specific needs, 3 if it was at the same level as the competition, and 5 if it was significantly superior to the competition. Progressive's competitive ability-to-serve ratings are shown in Table 2.4. The "Requirements to Satisfy Needs" column highlights improvements or changes Progressive would need to make to address the needs of each of the five identified segments. The ratings identify how well Progressive can meet the needs, when compared with its competitors.

Combining the information on market attractiveness and ability to serve yields the matrix shown in Figure 2.3. For example, the General distributors segment has a "3" for market attractiveness and a "3" for ability to satisfy needs, placing it right in the center.

Table 2.3 Attractiveness Ratings of Market Segments for Progressive Foodservice, Inc.

Market Segment	Percentage of Company Sales	Percentage of Industry Sales	Characteristics of Market Attractiveness (size, growth rate, purchase volumes, etc.)	Rating (1–5)
General distributors	39%	27%	Top five play a pivotal role in the industry. Price is a driving factor.	3
Specialty distributors	14%	13%	Showing growth due to special food-service demands of aging population.	4
Fast-food chains	16%	22%	Approaching saturation of our type of product. Heavy competition and price pressure.	2
Commercial operators	22%	30%	Pockets of rapid growth (e.g., retail delis) due to dual-income families. Strong potential for our type of product.	3
Noncommercial operators	9%	8%	Static or declining potential.	1

Table 2.4 Ability-to-Serve Ratings for Progressive Foodservice, Inc.

Market Segment	Needs	Requirements to Satisfy Needs (product, skill set, locations, costs)	Rating (1–5)
General distributors	Centralized purchasing; volume buying at discounted price; specialized distribution specifications	Improved carrier terms, established extranet	3
Specialty distributors	Unique products; merchandising support	Commitment to R&D and new product development	4
Fast-food chains	Just-in-time shipments at lowest possible price	Shared cost shipping services	2
Commercial operators	Menu support; presentation suggestions	Consulting chef de cuisine on call; test kitchens; educational CD-ROMs	4
Non-commercial operators	Consistent inventory replenishment; long shelf-life products	Product development efforts on extending shelf life	1

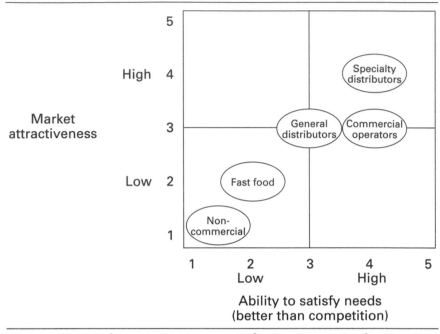

Figure 2.3   Market attractiveness matrix for Progressive Foodservice, Inc.

All else being equal, the best target market(s) would be in the upper right-hand quadrant, where a company has determined it has a highly attractive customer segment and a high competitive advantage in serving the segment. As expected, other considerations must be addressed. First, there may be no segment that falls solidly in this quadrant. In that case, a firm might target the most attractive segment that exists and determine what products and skills it would be necessary to develop to shift the segment to the right. Second, there may be a segment in the upper right quadrant having relatively little future profit potential compared with other segments. To help visualize this, the circles can be adjusted in size to represent the potential opportunity in that segment. Third, a segment in the upper right quadrant could already be dominated by the company, with little to be gained by increased resources. In that case, allocating sufficient marketing dollars to customer retention may be appropriate, with more resources being diverted to other promising segments. To help visualize this in the matrix, it is useful to draw the circles as pie charts, with a distinction between attained market and future potential. Finally, some segments that appear to be less attractive on an absolute basis might indeed turn out to be quite attractive if they are underserved by the competition.

To compile this information, both internal and secondary (published) sources are necessary. (Worksheets 2.1 and 2.2 help with this process.) From an internal perspective, sales records should be correlated with demographic characteristics to determine which variables relate most closely to profitability. Does company size, geographic location, type of application, or any other variable help "predict" sales? Once these variables are identified, you can extrapolate them to noncustomers to estimate market and growth potentials. The "deliverable" from this step of the analysis is a "knowledge chapter" in the product fact book, summarizing the drivers of loyalty and defining profitable customer segments.

Worksheet 2.1   Attractiveness Ratings of Market Segments

Market Segment	Percentage of Company Sales	Percentage of Industry Sales	Characteristics of Market Attractiveness (size, growth rate, purchase volumes, etc.)	Rating (1–5)
Segment A				
Segment B				
Segment C				
Segment D				
Segment E				

Worksheet 2.2   Ability-to-Serve Ratings by Market Segment

Market Segment	Needs	Requirements to Satisfy Needs (product, skill set, locations, costs)	Rating (1–5)
Segment A			
Segment B			
Segment C			
Segment D			
Segment E			

It's worth noting that, as companies design and implement new services to satisfy customer expectations, their processes usually become more complex and costs usually increase. Conventional cost-accounting methods do not properly identify differences in cost-to-serve. They fail to identify some of the post-production costs that are caused by addressing segment-specific needs. As will be discussed in Chapter 5, it's important to recognize that costs are not just uncontrollable occurrences, but rather are caused by measurable factors that can be managed. Therefore, an understanding of segment reporting and possibly activity-based costing must be part of the product manager's repertoire of skills.

Once these two worksheets are completed, the product manager can create the visual matrix described earlier for Progressive Foodservice, Inc. The information then can be used to identify primary and secondary target markets, their needs, and the issues a firm will need to address to satisfy the

Worksheet 2.3   Market Attractiveness Matrix

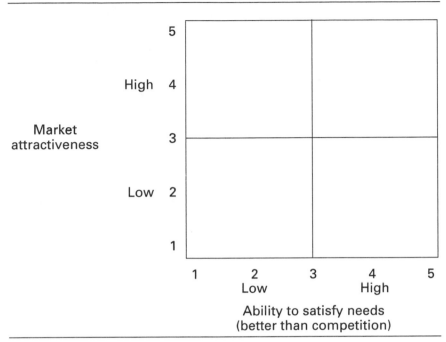

needs (see Worksheet 2.3). Note that the prior example blurred the distinction between a channel customer and an end-customer. While not "pure" or "ideal," it is real. Some product managers will refer to the channel as their customer and the end-user as a consumer, which is logical if going direct is not an option and there is no either-or proposition. In many circumstances, understanding the needs and expectations of the channel customer is critical for survival. P&G, for example, relies heavily on its relationship with Wal-Mart (contributing 17% of sales or $8.7 billion in 2005).[8] The companies share data and plans and link their computer systems for efficiency.

Balancing Customer Retention and Customer Acquisition

Once the profiling of the target market is completed, the next question is how to grow customer equity. (See Figure 2.4.) This could involve one or a combination of (1) increasing the profitability of existing customers, (2) attracting new customers

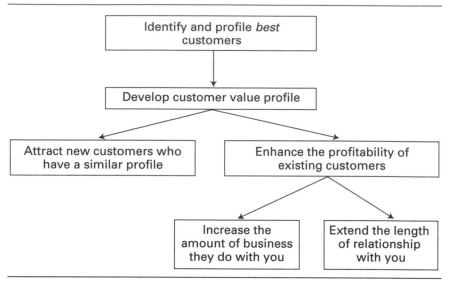

Figure 2.4   Customer analysis flow chart.

with the potential for future high-value business, or (3) "firing" low-potential customers. To increase existing profitability, invest in the highest-value customers first. How can add-on sales and cross-selling (of even other product managers' products!) increase customer equity? (Don't let a product or brand management focus hurt this effort. Remember that brands don't create wealth; customers do.)[9] What behaviors do you want to change in the market to increase its profitability? What behaviors do you need to change in your own company to increase profitability?

Database programs can help product managers understand the specific needs of segments and subsegments. Product managers should try to determine what activities would be necessary to get existing customers to increase the amount of business they do with the firm, to get "good" customers to become more loyal, and to get secondary customers converted into primary customers. Then, by taking advantage of flexible manufacturing and delivery, they can provide cost-effective offerings tailored to each group—offerings such as product features, price discounts, service arrangements, and purchase warranties. This approach has been used by industrial firms, by service-sector companies, and by resellers such as wholesalers and retailers. A Canadian grocery store chain, for example, analyzed a "typical" store with around 15,000 households, annual revenues of $25 million, and an operating margin of 2%.

> First, the company segmented the customer base surrounding the store into three categories: primary shoppers (those who give the store 80% or more of their grocery business), secondary shoppers (those who spend more than 10% but less than 50% of their grocery budget at the store), and nonshoppers.
>
> Second, the company calculated the impact on the store's profitability of small improvements in the behavior profiles of existing customers. Given the fixed cost structure of a grocery store, the contribution margin from each additional dollar spent by a customer can earn ten times the store's net profit margin. Thus, the company found that even small improvements in one of many customer behaviors led to very significant profitability gains. Expanding the customer base by 2% with primary shoppers, for example, would increase the store's profitability by more than 45%. Converting just two hundred secondary customers into primary customers would increase profitability by more than 20%. Selling one more produce item to every customer would increase profitability by more than 40%. Persuading every customer to substitute two store-brand items for two national brand items each time they visited the store would increase profitability by 55%. . . .
>
> Rather than focusing directly on these opportunities, though, the company, like most other organizations, had been paying attention to more traditional objectives, such as productivity, market share, and quality. As a result, it had overlooked the possibility of closing this full-potential gap by optimizing customer value exchanges.[10]

Firing Your Customers

A particular challenge that many product managers face is saying "no" to an unprofitable customer (or even an unprofitable segment). All companies have customers who demand special services (with no additional revenue generated), who demand "rock-bottom" prices for everything, or who require changing the basic product or service to fit their unique needs. When this is the case, only a few options are available: raise the price, reduce the cost of servicing the customer, or discontinue doing business with the customer.

Raising the price to compensate for the value being supplied is the most obvious solution. However, this may be difficult at best. The customer must perceive and believe in the competitive value, and if the customer is not part of the target market, a good "fit" might not exist between their needs and your firm's capabilities. That leads to the second option: reducing the cost to serve. It's crucial that the product manager clearly understands the total costs "caused by" the customer (see Chapter 5 on contribution reporting). Figure 2.5 provides an example format for including both direct and indirect revenues and costs by customer. Only by understanding the true costs can an effort be made to reduce them.

Discontinuing business with a customer may be a last, but necessary, resort. Typically, it happens indirectly through the

---

Customer: Akins, Inc.
Industry: Semiconductor machinery manufacturing

Product	Product revenue	Product cost	Contribution
Total			
Other customer revenue +			
Other customer expenses −			
Total contribution =			

Figure 2.5 Customer profitability analysis.

changing of policies or raising of prices. However, before this happens, ask a few questions:

· Does this customer bring in business simply by being a customer?
· Will this customer grow into a strategic customer in the future?
· Does the customer absorb overhead that would need to be allocated elsewhere if the business relationship is ended?

Provide an honest appraisal of the situation, and be prepared to say "no" if necessary.

Checklist: Trend-Spotting, Research, and Customer Segmentation

· Establish folders for key trends that you want to actively follow, as well as opportunistic trends that you may want to consider for future actions.
· Set up a trend analysis group (TAG) team to help monitor trends.
· Segment customers based on variables most relevant to your product and strategy.
· In profiling "good" customers, consider factors such as profitability, market size and growth rate, reference value for other customers, and level of price sensitivity
· Evaluate your ability to satisfy customer needs better than the competition can.
· Combine market attractiveness and ability-to-serve evaluations to prioritize market segments and customers.
· Have a balance between customer acquisition and customer retention.
· In developing strategies, decide what you want various customer segments to do as a result of your marketing efforts.
· Practice the art of saying "no" by designing policies and products specifically for targeted customers.

Interview with Art Weinstein, Nova Southeastern University

Art Weinstein, Ph.D., is Professor and Chair of Marketing at Nova Southeastern University, Fort Lauderdale, Florida. He is the author of *Handbook of Market Segmentation: Strategic Targeting for Business and Technology Firms*, 3rd Edition, Binghampton, NY: Haworth Press, 2004.

Q: *Segmentation and customer analysis are skills that brand and product managers always want to hone. What have you observed as the biggest mistakes product managers make in segmenting and studying their customers?*

A: Product managers tend to do what their name implies—manage products, rather than manage customer needs. As a result, they tend to be well entrenched in the established market, rather than venturing out into the emerging market or even the imagined market. These latter two arenas are mastered by few companies, although Apple has done this effectively, at times. In addition, product managers sometimes focus exclusively on their target market and fail to learn why noncustomers do not respond to their strategic marketing initiatives.

Q: *Do you think B2B product managers face different customer analysis challenges than do B2C brand managers?*

A: Yes, there are four major differences between consumer and B2B markets. First, the area served by industrial marketers is typically larger than the one served by neighborhood retailers or personal and professional service firms. It is common for the industrial firm to conduct business regionally and internationally, as well as via the Internet. Despite this larger trade area focus, the customer base is generally highly concentrated. Second, most industrial sales are larger than those in consumer markets. Dependency on a smaller core of customers can lead to variations in revenues and profits due to customer acquisition or defection, derived demand, changes in macro-environmental conditions, global terrorism concerns, etc. Third, B2B markets are characterized by complex decision making. This means multiple buying influence; demanding, smart, and rational customers; and longer buying cycles. Finally, industrial customers get "closer" to the product manager, since personal selling is still a dominant strategy. Trade journals, associations, and directories offer solid market intelligence. And, B2B marketers are using databases, direct and group e-mails, online chats, and mobile telecommunications to stay well-connected with clients.

Q: *What changes in segmentation do you expect over the next 5 years?*

A: Product managers should be aware of the new segmentation challenges that have emerged. Six priority areas include: (1) improving levels of segmentation sophistication within the organization, (2) building innovative segmentation models to gain a competitive edge, (3) responding to the segment-of-one buyer, (4) replacing static segmentation with dynamic segmentation (re-segmenting markets on a regular basis), (5) focusing on the customers' customers and new types of value chain players, and (6) extending segmentation from the transaction to the relationship.

Q: *What is the best advice you ever received with regard to segmentation?*

A: The two most memorable thoughts about segmentation were as follows. First, a high-tech consultant once told me that almost all marketing and research problems are segmentation problems. Recognize the strategic significance of segmentation in all marketing initiatives (including product strategy) and plan accordingly. Second, an astute B2B executive noted that one cannot have effective segmentation unless the "right" relevant (pre-segmented) market is defined. Follow-up research in this area revealed that the five key variables are customer needs, customer groups, technologies, competition, and products.

Q: *What tips can you give product managers about market segmentation?*

A: Commit to segmentation-driven product development and management, open the lines of communication regarding this activity throughout the organization (production, R&D, marketing, etc.), have a marketing information system/research function in place, be sure the segmentation approach fits the organization's mission and needs, provide appropriate personnel and financing for the segmentation initiatives, and get help (consulting, research, syndicated products, training, etc.) when needed.

For further information, contact Dr. Art Weinstein at: art@huizenga. nova.edu. Or visit http://home.bellsouth.net/p/PWP-artweinstein.

Notes

1. Peter Burrows and Ben Elgin, "Why HP is Pruning the Printers," *BusinessWeek* (May 9, 2005): 38–39.
2. Numerous trend-watching publications follow nanotechnology. *The Futurist* (a publication of the World Future Society) has covered it in several issues. One such article is "Molecular Nanotech: Benefits and Risks," by Mike Treder, *The Futurist* (January-February 2004): 42–46. This was also the *BusinessWeek* cover story in the February 14, 2005 issue.
3. Rich Tomaselli, "Pharma Replacing Reps with Web," *Advertising Age* (January 24, 2005): 50.
4. Kelly Greene, "Marketing Surprise: Older Consumers Buy Stuff, Too," *Wall Street Journal* (April 6, 2004): A1–A12.
5. For more information on a step-by-step process for managing a marketing research project, refer to Linda Gorchels, *The Product Manager's Field Guide* (McGraw-Hill, 2003): Chapter 4.
6. Liz Torlee, "The Perils of Segmentation," *Marketing* (Aug 23–Aug 30, 2004): 31.
7. Industries were previously grouped according to the Standard Industrial Classification (SIC) codes. Refer to www.census.gov for the translation to NAICS.
8. Sarah Ellison, Ann Zimmerman, and Charles Forelle, "P&G's Gillette Edge: The Playbook It Honed at Wal-Mart," *Wall Street Journal* (January 31, 2005): A1–A12.
9. Refer to Niraj Dawar, "What Are Brands Good For?" *MIT Sloan Management Review* (Fall 2004): 31–37 for a discussion on replacing brand management with customer management.
10. Alan W. H. Grant and Leonard A. Schlesinger, "Realize Your Customers' Full Profit Potential," *Harvard Business Review* 73: 5 (September–October 1995): 61–62.

Chapter Three

Competitive Intelligence for Competitive Strategies

A critical aspect of a product manager's job is to objectively define the product's strengths and weaknesses against the competition *as perceived by the market,* and to use that knowledge to implement competitive strategies successfully. To be able to implement competitive strategies on an ongoing basis, you must have access to an ongoing stream of information about the competitive environment for your product and the impact it has on your ability to compete. The process of collecting and analyzing this information is called competitive intelligence (CI) or business intelligence. This is the competitive analysis piece of the planning process (Figure 3.1).

Competitive Analysis

The competitive analysis is a summary of information compiled from electronic, published, and human sources (Worksheet 3.1). Annual reports, newspaper articles, Google searches, trade shows, sales staff, government and trade association reports, and informal conversations with customers can provide much of the necessary information. This type of CI is an important part

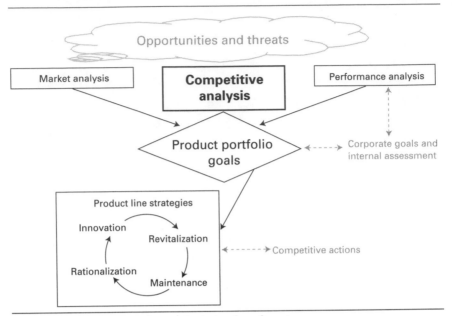

Figure 3.1   Competitive analysis in the planning process.

of a product manager's job, and it provides some of the foundation concepts for competitive strategy and product positioning. Here are a few questions to consider as part of the analysis:

1. To which competitors have you lost business, and from which have you gained business? (This is an indication of the competition from the customer's perspective.)
2. Where (in what regions, applications, industries, etc.) is competition the strongest? Why?
3. What are the corporate competencies of the companies that own competing products? What is the relationship between the competencies and the products?
4. What are the list prices of the competing products? The actual prices?
5. What is the market perception of the competing products? Awareness level? Customer loyalty?
6. Are there any specific product features that are "best-in-class," against which your product should be benchmarked?
7. Is the competing product a small percentage of its company's business, or is it the main product of the company? How

Worksheet 3.1   Competitive Analysis

General Information for Fy____

Division: Group: Product Line: Market:

	Your Product	Product A	Product B	Product C	Product D
Sales volume (units)					
Sales revenue ($)					
Profit					
Market share					
Target market(s)					
General product strategy					
Product differentiation					
Customer image					
General price strategy					
Average/list price					
General promotion strategy					
General distribution strategy					
Sales force size					
Sales force strengths					

important are the sales to the competitor, and how much is the company willing to invest to protect these sales?

Establishing a Competitive Intelligence Process

A number of reasons exist why a product manager should be aware of the competitive arena. It can help you anticipate marketplace shifts. It can help you anticipate the actions or reactions of specific competitors, or identify new competition. It can help you learn from the successes and failures of others. It can help you learn about new technologies, processes, or events that could change your product strategies. It can help you craft tools and approaches to be used by the sales force or marketing communications people.

Let's say a salesperson reports to you that a competitor dropped the price of a product competing directly with your highest gross-margin item. Before dropping your price to match, ask yourself whether *this* competitor offering *this* price drop could affect your ability to compete. If the answer is "yes," you should do a bit of "sleuthing" to answer the following questions:

· Is the price drop an apples-to-apples comparison, or have select features or services been modified?
· Is the price drop sufficient to overcome customer inertia to change?
· If so, does the competitor have the capacity to handle increased demand without damaging customer satisfaction?
· Is the price change restricted to one territory or account, or is it across-the-board?

You should consider analogous questions when *initiating* a product or marketing change, and anticipate the potential competitive response to your actions. Failing to do so can put you at a competitive disadvantage. When Bristol-Myers launched Datril (emphasizing savings of a dollar compared with Tylenol), it seemingly did not anticipate the speed and strength of response from Johnson & Johnson. J&J used CI to identify the projected entry strategy, and it was able to blunt the Bristol-Myers campaign effectiveness through a media strategy of its own.[1] Similarly, when Corel purchased the WordPerfect suite in the mid-1990s, it attempted to use a low price to compete directly against the Microsoft Office Suite, but did not have the ability to compete long-term in a price war against Microsoft.

Who Are Your Real Competitors?

A starting point for developing a CI process is to determine which competitors to study continuously and which to study episodically. It is impossible to gather everything about all competitors on an ongoing basis. As mentioned in the previous chapter on trends, it is important to prioritize. You might miss some information by restricting your focus, but the greater manageability provided by restricted focus will yield more actionable data.

Start with a deceptively simply question: "Who is your competition?" Many of you will answer the question with "it depends." That's a valid answer. That's why it may be useful to look at competition from a variety of perspectives. The key competitors are most often (but not always) the *direct competitors* offering a similar type of product or service—competing packages of toothpaste (e.g., Crest versus Colgate) or equipment (e.g., Caterpillar versus Komatsu). To compete at this level, the product manager must articulate specific feature advantages over the main competing products.

Another level of competition is category competition. Whereas a few identified competitors may be categorized under direct competition, when dealing with *category competition*, you might be competing against dozens of companies that comprise your category or industry. For example, the manufacturers of component parts for industrial equipment might compete with a number of local, privately owned shops. Here, product managers are challenged to position their products as best in the *category*.

A third level is *substitute competition*, in which the customer obtains functionality without using the product of *any* company in the category. Some companies may choose to manufacture the product or perform the service themselves. For example, a bank might choose to self-insure rather than use the products of a private mortgage insurance company. Several industries are jumping on the do-it-yourself bandwagon (see Business Brief 3.1). Or a new industry (such as satellite TV) may try to displace an existing industry (like cable TV). In these situations, product managers must demonstrate to customers

Business Brief 3.1   Do-it-yourself competition.

Given the weak financial status of the airline industry, many airline companies are making parts for themselves, rather than purchase them from suppliers—especially parts that are replaced repeatedly. Continental Airlines makes tray tables and window shades in its Houston facility, saving $2 million annually. It also molds its own plastic toilet seats for $88 versus a $719 OEM price, and makes bathroom mirrors for $460 rather than the $3,000 it was quoted. American Airlines makes an aluminum part, which it had previously purchased, for $5.24, saving the company $170,000 per year.

Rising health care costs also are resulting in some DIY efforts in corporations. Since 1990, Quad Graphics has increasingly handled its own primary care. It employs its own internists, pediatricians, and family practition-ers—26 in all. It owns a laboratory, pharmacy, and rehabilitation unit, and contracts with local hospitals for advanced care. Quad Graphics spent $6,000 per employee on medical costs in 2004—20% less than the average competitors in its home state of Wisconsin. Perdue Farms, Sprint Corporation, and Pitney Bowes run their own medical centers. Toyota Motor Company, Kohler Plumbing, and Miller Brewing are considering this approach.

While many companies are increasing their outsourcing of many tasks in an effort to save money, others are taking the opposite approach, as demonstrated here.

Source: Melanie Trottman, "Nuts-and-Bolts Savings," *Wall Street Journal* (May 3, 2005): B1–B2. Vanessa Fuhrmann, "One Cure for High Health Costs: In-House Clinics at Companies," *Wall Street Journal* (February 11, 2005): A1–A8.

either the risk of staying with their current approach to addressing their needs, or prove their products offer a definite superiority over the current approach.

Another example of substitute competition is caused by technology convergence and disruption. The Apple iPod, for example, sparked a mini-revolution by allowing music to be purchased through Internet downloads rather than through retail CDs. But it is also now facing competition from wireless companies that are encouraging their customers to use their cell phones to download songs over the air.

A fourth type of competition is *budget competition*. This is perhaps the most challenging for product managers, because it is the least tangible. A customer may choose to buy a new software system instead of investing the money in a new product. Similarly, a homeowner may decide to buy hardwood floors rather than a new hot tub. Although product managers cannot design a strategy to convince customers to buy their products before spending money on *anything* else, it's important to at least be aware of this level of competition and adjust forecasts accordingly.

The final type of competition is *organizational competition*. For many B2B products and for many services, customers make purchase decisions based not just on a product's features, but also on the services and incentives they get from a specific competitor, a potential *bundle* of products they might have access to, or the relationship they have established with the firm. In these cases, the product manager must work collaboratively with others in the organization to establish a sustainable advantage on a corporate-wide basis. Each of these categories of competition are listed in Table 3.1.

Note that different markets may perceive different competitors, and the product manager must decide how to best position his product, based on the importance of the market–competitor combination. Sometimes, separate strategies must be developed. For example, a consumer packaged-goods product manager may need to have a marketing strategy aimed at competing against other directly competing products at the consumer level, while simultaneously competing against other organizations (with different value propositions) at the channel level.

Remember that customers consciously or subconsciously make purchase decisions by comparing among what *they* perceive to be competitors. Determining whom your customers perceive as your competitors provides a clue to their price sensitivity. These key competitors should be regularly tracked to identify strategy shifts that might require a change in your pricing or marketing strategy. Several methods may be used to identify whom customers perceive as your competitors. For consumer products, purchase data from syndicated sources, such as Nielsen, can be used to determine brand-switching behavior. This helps identify who you have lost business to or

Table 3.1   Types of Competition

Type of Competition	Today	Future Impacts	Implications
Directly competing products	List competitors and specific product features.	What percent of competition does this represent, both today and in the future? For which customers?	How can you establish differential advantage against these products?
Category	Describe the category and the companies and products within the category.	What percent of competition does this represent, both today and in the future? For which customers?	How can you position your offering as best in category?
Substitutes	Describe the actual "need" the products and services provide with their functionality.	What percent of competition does this represent, both today and in the future? For which customers?	How can you influence the perceived risk of customers shifting from one substitute to another?
Budget	Highlight potential resistance of customers to spend money on your type of product or service.	What percent of competition does this represent, both today and in the future? For which customers?	How can you encourage shifting of budgetary expenditures to your product?
Organizational	Explain the "augmented" product provided by competing companies.	What percent of competition does this represent, both today and in the future? For which customers?	How can you develop collaborative efforts to better position your company over competing companies?

gained business from—a behavioral indicator of perceived competition. Another approach (that can be used for services and business products, in addition to consumer products) is similarity assessments. Using this approach, customers are given either the products or product *cues* (such as literature or product names on 3×5 cards) and asked to divide them into groups based on similarity.

On the other hand, the competitive set in which the customer places you may not fit your *desired* position. You might want to be perceived as a higher or lower price-point competitor, or as a niche player. In that case, you must examine the companies in the *desired* competitive set and decide whether you can reposition what your customers believe, or whether you should add a new brand. The California wine industry offers an example of each approach. Glen Ellen and Gallo decided to move from the low-end ("popular") price category of wines to the faster-growing premium segment. Gallo made the transition by creating a new brand, Turning Leaf, and pricing this new brand at the premium-category price point. Glen Ellen is attempting to make the transition *without* a new brand by focusing on its brand heritage, wax seal, and upgraded product quality.[2] In both cases, the higher price points position the wines against new competitors.

Regardless of your situation, reduce the number of competitors you *continually* obtain information about to a manageable few. (The companies in this "manageable few" may vary as competitors enter and exit a market, so don't be afraid to change as conditions dictate.) Other competitors should be studied periodically or on an as-needed basis.

What Do You Need to Know?

Not all snippets of information are equally valuable. What is your competitive edge? What knowledge about the competition might help you protect your edge? If your competitive edge is superior delivery, stay abreast of competitive delivery standards that could threaten this advantage. If your differentiation is technological support, monitor competitive support activities that could have a negative impact on your position. Your goal is to avoid surprises that might force you into price competition. That being said, most product managers are understandably concerned about obtaining competitive price and cost information. (Just remember that if the only competitive data you gather are prices, you may be forced to compete solely on price.)

Many competitive prices are available through the public domain. Except in closed-bid situations, most companies are able to get competitive price lists from trade shows, the sales force, common customers, or the Internet. Although this may not be the "actual" price that customers pay, you may still be able to glean information by tracking the price list over time, looking for changes. A *change* in the published prices should trigger some additional evaluations on your part. Is the price change related to other factors, such as an organizational restructuring or a change in capabilities? These factors are frequently part of a shift in strategy.

Several factors could signal a potential shift in strategy: a change in management, a change in capabilities, or a change in mission statement. Let's examine each of these three factors, starting with a change in management. If a competitor has a new management team, it may signal a new direction (especially if the old management team was ousted by the board). The current management team may have been hired to repeat accomplishments achieved for a prior employer. By studying the strategic direction at the previous organization, you can assume similar potential strategy changes in the new company.

A change in capabilities could arise from a new location, additional investment in R&D, or increased staffing. By piecing together this information from industry journals, trade associations, help-wanted ads, and personal sources, you can estimate what effect this could have on your competitor's *future* strategy. Help-wanted ads not only alert you to what your competitor's strategy requires in terms of future staffing (e.g., competence in a particular scientific field or increased emphasis on customer service), it may also provide more knowledge about the company, since it is trying to "sell" itself to prospective employees.

Finally, a change in mission statement also can suggest a new direction. For example, the revised wording of a firm's mission statement from "to be the premier customer-driven real estate company in the U.S." to the statement "to be the premier customer-driven real estate *services* company in the U.S." highlights the increased importance of services in its new strategy. Most of this type of information is appropriate for organizational competition, and can be compiled in a form similar to Worksheet 3.2.

Worksheet 3.2   Competitive organizational profile.

	Your Company	Company A	Company B	Company C
Mission				
Core competencies				
Description of organization and officers				

R&D
  Philosophy, thrust
  #, experience of
    employees
  Patents				

Production capabilities
  Av. labor rates
  Max. capacity
  % of use
  Min. production
    for BE
  % outsourced				

Personnel
  New Layoffs
  Turnover
  % union				

Facilities
  New locations
  Closed locations				

Apparent strategy				

Monitor account-specific activity. Competitors may be offering special incentives to major accounts. Promotional blitzes may indicate a renewed emphasis on certain products or market segments, or it may be a direct attempt to shift a key account away from you.

How Do You Get Started Using "People" Sources?

Start your CI activities by determining whom your key competitors are and what the competitive edge is that you want to defend. Focus on the types of data most relevant to helping you make sound decisions and the types of data that have helped you make decisions in the past. Never lose sight of the fact that you are not simply collecting random pieces of information about the competition, but rather specific pieces of information that help you in the race to provide more value to your customers—and more quickly—than your competitors.

The type of information collected might encompass product design, branding, services, pricing, and a host of other variables that, in total, comprise your competitive edge. Protecting your edge requires a "real-time" stream of knowledge about the changing competitive landscape. The sales force is perhaps the most significant fund of information on an ongoing basis. Sales staff have the most direct contact with customers, and consequently have customer feedback on the competition that is both real and perceptual. However, since their primary job is to sell, it's important to be meticulous about their involvement in CI activities.

To be successful in collecting information from the sales force, you must prove to both the sales reps and their managers that the process has value to them. That means a certain amount of homework is necessary. Find out what information is already available internally from sales. Call reports, won–lost reports, and sales records can be analyzed to look for red flags and trends. A competitive move in one territory may seem insignificant until added to information from other territories, or when examined as part of a larger global rollout strategy. Then, by augmenting these findings with public data (from published sources and industry analysts), you may be able to offer the sales force tips on competing more successfully.

After completing this homework, it's time for face-to-face contact with sales. (No amount of corporate posturing, e-mails, or dictates will replace it.) Take the time to introduce yourself to sales staff and learn about their customers. Demonstrate your commitment to share vital information that will help them close sales. Learn about "their" world. By initiating the information-sharing process, you will encourage reciprocity on the part of sales by demonstrating "what's in it for them." Be prepared to work through sales administration, marketing, or other departments as necessary to coordinate these efforts.

Once sales staff trust that sharing information with you will indeed help them to be more successful on the job, you must decide on the best way to handle the data collection and dissemination. Ask sales to forward to you any price lists or customer input they receive on policies as they relate to your products. But don't limit the request to pricing information.

Most marketers appreciate the importance of using trade shows to gather primary research on the competitors and their activities. However, a process is not always in place to make this more effective. Sales staff and other employees can gather better CI at trade shows if asked to do so and if provided with specific goals. Develop a checklist of issues you would like explored at the trade show and provide "assignments" to the booth staff. For example, you might want to learn about an announced price cut by Competitor A, a proposed product launch by Competitor B, and a change in promotional positioning by Competitor C. Assign each of these issues to an individual to explore, both while staffing the booth and while walking the floor. Check back with these people at the end of the day or at the end of the show.

New-product sales training can be another subtle forum for planting the seed of information gathering. A portion of the training might also include a motivational explanation of the need for and use of market intelligence by product managers, and how providing this information can help the sales staff. A standard intelligence report form can be built into a call report, designed into the menu system on a computer, or included as part of the expense form. Because this information typically comes into sales management or sales administration, a process must be established to send a copy of relevant product-related data to the appropriate product manager. The type of information useful for submission might include:

· New-product announcements by competitors
· Effective and ineffective approaches to selling a product
· Changes in competitive strategies
· Unusual product applications by customers, especially if they indicate a trend
· Perspectives on market trends that might affect company strategy

How Do You Put the Pieces Together?

It's useful to break the CI-gathering process into three categories: continuous, periodic, and project-based. *Continuous* CI focuses on the most direct competitors (or industries, technologies, etc.) that you want to monitor on an ongoing basis. These should include the aspects of the external environment that might have the biggest potential impact on your ability to compete in the marketplace. Having a stream of information from the sales force (as mentioned earlier) is part of continuous data collection, but it doesn't need to stop there. After defining the type of information that you need, and the periodicals, journals, newspapers, and Web sites that you want to monitor, set up an automated CI alert program. Many proprietary services such as Factiva, Dialog, and Lexis/Nexis offer electronic alerts, but if your company does not subscribe to these services, more basic alerts may be set up with Google or Yahoo.

Although you cannot monitor everything all of the time, you should conduct periodic CI on the less direct competitors or trends to determine whether anything has changed. *Periodic* CI can be conducted monthly, quarterly, or annually, depending on the rate of change in your industry. The value of a periodic search of information is that it may highlight unexpected changes that could shift the priorities for your continuous data collection process.

Project-based CI, as the term implies, is conducted on an *as-needed* basis, similar to a marketing research project. When continuous or periodic data collection uncovers some unexpected findings, you are ready to launch a new product, or you need specific insights for a new strategy, it may be necessary to launch a specific, in-depth analysis of the issue.

Analyzing Competitive Information

One of the main goals of analysis is to forecast what competing companies are likely to do in the future. If you are competing in an oligopolistic industry, your concerns may be with the actions of individual competitors. How will they respond to the RFP you are bidding on? When will they launch a superior product? On the other hand, if you are competing against numerous competitors in more of a "pure competition" environment, you may be more concerned with the macro movements in the industry.

CI requires a balance between competitor data and customer data. It's risky to be too focused on one, if it causes the neglect of the other. Information on both is necessary to be truly market-oriented (Figure 3.2). But just gathering market-oriented data and other forms of business intelligence is not

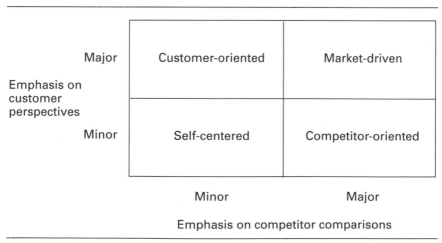

	Minor	Major
Major	Customer-oriented	Market-driven
Minor	Self-centered	Competitor-oriented

Emphasis on customer perspectives

Emphasis on competitor comparisons

Figure 3.2   Being market-driven requires a balanced perspective.

enough—product managers must use the information to improve competitive strategies. Otherwise, says Rebecca Wettemann, vice president of research at Nucleus Research in Wellesley, Massachusetts, "it's like having a bank account with millions of dollars in it but no ATM card. If you can't get it out, and can't make it work for you, then it is not really useful."[3]

At the most basic level, comparing the relative strengths and weaknesses of product features can help a product manager establish positioning strategies, marketing communications, and sales-support materials. As mentioned earlier, the Apple iPod is facing competition from the wireless networks. Although they are not direct competitors in the "purest" sense, they pose a potential threat to the iPod's future ability to compete. Technological advances in storage, compression, and battery life have made it easier to receive and store music by phone. Therefore, it makes sense for Apple to compare the iPod with products in this category of competition, as shown in Table 3.2.

Beyond performing a product-by-product comparison, Apple also will need to look at trends and abilities in the overall telecom industry. As of this writing, Verizon Wireless, Sprint, and Cingular Wireless are expected to launch services for downloading music by the end of 2005. Apple has also partnered with Motorola to introduce the Rokr, a handset that plays music from its iTunes music store.[4] While they aren't going to cause an overnight sensation in wireless music, they do have a few advantages. Perhaps the biggest advantage is the fact that a quarter of the world's population (1.4 billion people) have cell phones. Another advantage is the simplicity of billing—the music downloads could simply be added to the monthly charges.[5]

Pharmaceutical companies are faced with competitive challenges as they try to anticipate the emergence of generics after the expiration of product patents. Product managers must monitor CI on the manufacturers of generic products. They can then create models (perhaps as Excel spreadsheets) to estimate the impact of sales or market share loss to the competition under varying scenarios, as well as estimate the likelihood of these scenarios occurring.

Table 3.2   How iPod's Phone Rivals Stack Up

	Price	Pluses	Minuses
iPod	$99 to $449	Apple offers three levels of devices—the iPod, mini, and Shuffle—which can store between 120 and 15,000 songs.	Doesn't do downloads over the air, make calls, or take pictures.
Samsung SGH-1300	$450 to $500	A 3-gigabyte hard drive that can store 1,000 songs, scroll-wheel navigation, and iPod-quality sound.	Won't hit key U.S. market until end of 2005 at the earliest, keypad buttons may be too cramped.
SonyEricsson W800 Walkman	$300	Funky design, capacity for at least 250 songs, battery life similar to the iPod mini, and sharp 2-megapixel camera.	Can't connect to some online music stores, let alone handle wireless music downloads.
Motorola E6801	$400 to $600	Memory card storage of up to 600 songs, stereo-quality speakers, can handle MP3s and popular music file formats in Microsoft and RealNetworks.	Boring gray design in a clunky shape and a low-quality camera.
Nokia 7710	$500 to $600	Wide, bright color screen, stores different types of music files, expandable memory can store 300 songs.	No keypad, stylus only. Risk of face sticking to screen during calls.

Source: Condensed from Roger O. Crockett, "iPod Killer," *BusinessWeek* (April 25, 2005): 59–61.

Checklist: Competitive Intelligence for Competitive Strategies

· Determine the impact of competitors in each of the five categories.
· Establish an ongoing CI process for the key competition from this analysis.

· Develop strong relations with sales to contribute to the process.
· Focus on information that affects your ability to compete.
· Use CI to create and update strategies.

Interview with Timothy J. Kindler, President, Society of Competitive Intelligence Professionals

Tim Kindler is the Director of Corporate Competitive Intelligence at Eastman Kodak Company, and he has been a member of the Conference Board Council on Competitive Analysis since 1998.

Q: *In a nutshell, could you describe the Society of Competitive Intelligence Professionals and what resources it might provide for product managers?*

A: The Society of Competitive Intelligence Professionals (SCIP) is the global not-for-profit membership organization for people involved with the development and use of competitive intelligence (CI). Established in 1986, today SCIP has more than 3,000 members and more than 50 local chapters and affiliates around the world.

Regardless of whether a person is involved full-time in competitive intelligence or as part of a separate functional job (as is the case with product managers), SCIP provides training opportunities, a toolkit of processes and analytical techniques, a Code of Ethics, and a network of other CI professionals with whom to share best practices.

Q: *What is your perspective on ethics in competitive intelligence?*

A: Despite the occasional eye-catching headline and characterization in the press of CI being a cloak-and-dagger operation, in reality CI is nothing more than a derivative of basic business analysis. An ethical approach to CI is critical. A company's reputation is valuable, perhaps even its most valuable asset. When considering improper and unethical CI activities, the downside is clearly far greater than the upside. A company might use the SCIP code of ethics as a foundation, perhaps supplemented by additional company-specific items.

Q: *Competitive intelligence is a skill that product managers always want to hone. What have you observed as the biggest mistakes product managers make in CI?*

A: From my standpoint, the biggest mistake made by product managers is to underinvest in CI. (It should be noted that this mistake is not limited to product managers.) The reasons behind the underinvestment in CI include constraints on resources (time, people, funding) and a perceived lack of need ("I already know my industry.").

The underinvestment can take multiple forms. Managers either do not do CI at all, or have the CI performed in a minimalist, cursory fashion. A view of the competition must be more than a paragraph or two in a business plan. Many product managers no doubt take the proper approach. Those who do not, however, run a greater risk of encountering unexpected events.

Q: *Do you think B2B product managers face different challenges than B2C product managers in gathering information about competitors?*

A: No. At the core, the foundational aspects of competitive intelligence are end-market agnostic. The tools and resources available for gathering information, as well as those for analyzing the information to create intelligence and insight, can be employed regardless of whether you are in a B2B or B2C environment. Sources may be different, and each environment may have some nuanced advantages, but in the grand scheme of things the work is far more similar than dissimilar.

Q: *What changes in CI philosophies, strategies, or concepts have you observed over the last 5 years?*

A: The most pronounced change in CI over the past 5 years has been the growth in the profession, driven by active CI participation by many companies today. To support this transition, more extensive course offerings at both the undergraduate and graduate levels are sprouting up in business schools. Although not yet at a point of equivalent standing with disciplines like accounting, marketing, and finance, CI is becoming a mainstream function in many corporations. That said, the economic pressures of the last few years have certainly impacted CI activities inside companies. On the one hand, more intense competition and financial pressure increases the need for CI services. At the same time, the need by many companies to cut costs puts many staff functions, including CI operations, at risk for downsizing or elimination.

Q: *What changes in CI philosophies, strategies, or concepts do you expect over the next 5 years?*

A: Moving into the future, I see two overriding trends in the realm of CI. First, as the profession continues to mature, the output of those performing CI work will continue to shift from more rudimentary analyses and fact finding to highly complex, holistic, forward-looking analyses. Second, the role of the full-time CI analyst inside a company, while not going away, will be supplemented by that of the part-time CI analyst. The part-timers are people who perform CI as part of their other functional specialties.

Q: *What is the best advice you have ever received?*

A: "Don't do anything that would get you on the front page of the *Wall Street Journal.*" By this I mean, be very careful that all intelligence activities are legal and ethical. Don't risk damaging your own reputation or your company's reputation.

Q: *What advice can you give product managers about CI?*

A: Just do it!!! Most companies today face an increasingly competitive and highly dynamic landscape. Now more than ever, knowing what the competition is doing—and planning to do—is key to success. At the same time, business teams all too often can be bogged down on internal issues without fully and appropriately integrating the external environment. Having a fact-based understanding of the competition—overall strategy, management tendencies, organization structure, and incentive systems, financial position (overall and product specific), core competencies, IP (intellectual property) position, manufacturing capabilities, product portfolio, go-to-market strategy and tactics, alliances and partnerships, strengths and weaknesses—helps to provide forward-looking and actionable intelligence to decision makers so that the external perspective is not lost. Keep in mind that CI means more than just understanding competitors. CI analysts complement competitor-specific insights with an awareness of other external issues (economic, geopolitical, legal/regulatory, technology trends, channel structure, etc.). This holistic view helps with go-to-market strategies and ultimate competitive advantage.

More information about the Society of Competitive Intelligence Professionals can be found at http://www.scip.org/.

Notes

1. John A. Nolan, "It's the Third Millennium: Do You Know Where Your Competitor Is?" *Journal of Business Strategy* (November/December 1999): 11–15.
2. Theresa Howard, "Glen Ellen Reformulates to Go Upscale," *Brandweek* (May 1, 2000): 78.
3. Julie Schlosser, "Looking for Intelligence in Ice Cream," *Fortune* (March 17, 2003): 115.
4. Nick Wingfield, "New Apple-Motorola Cellphone May Be Just the Overture," *Wall Street Journal*, Sept. 8, 2005: B1.
5. Roger O. Crockett, "iPod Killer," *BusinessWeek*, April 25, 2005: 61.

Chapter Four

Branding Strategies

Is there any difference between a product manager and a brand manager? Well, yes and no. At one end of the continuum, the term *brand manager* is commonly used in the consumer arena to designate those people who manage related products (such as toothpaste or detergent) under a specific brand umbrella (such as Crest® or Wisk®). The emphasis is on positioning the brand name in the minds of the end-users (and possibly the channel), so that a consistent brand identity can be created. At the other end of the continuum, the term *product manager* is commonly used in business-to-business (B2B) situations to designate the individual who is actively involved in ideation and product development (often working closely with engineering), and who sometimes has a product line that may or may not have product brand names that are separate from the company brand. However, substantial overlap occurs in the middle of this continuum. This chapter focuses most heavily on branding strategies in the overlapping middle.

This chapter, along with Chapter 5, comprises the performance analysis phase of planning, as indicated in Figure 4.1.

The Basics

Those product managers who are not in "traditional" consumer packaged goods occasionally feel that brands are irrelevant to

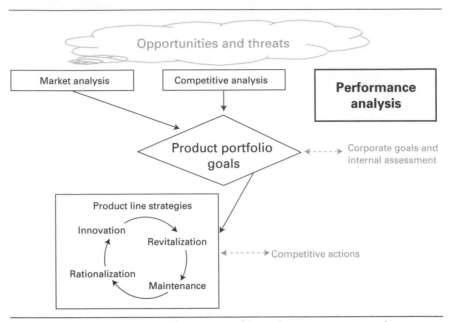

Figure 4.1   Evaluating performance of branding strategies in planning.

their industries. That may be due to a common perception that a brand is somehow simply a marketing "gimmick" (a charge that may be true for some products). Nevertheless, a brand identity can simplify customer-buying decisions, because the brand serves as a form of identification that connotes a specific level of quality, price or value, and support.

The term *brand* has been defined differently by a range of experts and organizations. The American Marketing Association defines a brand as: "a name, term, design, symbol, or any other feature that identifies one seller's good or service as distinct from those of other sellers ... A brand may identify one item, a family of items, or all items of that seller."[1] Kevin Lane Keller, a noted branding guru, argues, "a brand is a product ... that adds other dimensions to differentiate in some way from other products designed to satisfy the same need. These differences may be rational and tangible ... or more symbolic, emotional, and intangible."[2] Interbrand, an international consultancy specializing in brand strategies, defines a brand as "a mixture of attributes, tangible and intangible, symbolized in a trademark, which, if managed properly, creates value and influence … [F]rom a marketing or consumer perspective [value] is *the promise and delivery of an experience* … Brands offer customers a means to choose and enable recognition within cluttered markets."[3]

From these definitions, it's clear that a brand encompasses a holistic set of tangible and intangible attributes, the embodiment of a promise customers perceive as being made to them. As such, a brand is a sort of *executive summary* or *stereotype* that customers use to make purchase decisions. Just as people form stereotypes (good and bad) of sports figures, politicians, and geographic locations, they form stereotypes of products, services, and companies. Product managers should strive to understand and administer their brand's stereotypes. Ask yourself four fundamental questions:

1. What *image* do customers have of your brand?
2. What value (*brand equity*) does this image have for customers?
3. How do target customers perceive this brand image compared to the competition (*brand positioning*)?
4. Is the customer perception what we *want* it to be, and is it consistent with our goals (*brand management*)? See Table 4.1.

What Image Do Customers Have of Your Brand?

Regarding the first question, the brand image is the customer's perception of your products, services, and company.

Table 4.1   Fundamental Brand Issues

Brand Issue	Description	Product Manager Concerns
Image	Customer's perception	Define rational and emotional cues
Equity	Relevance and importance	Define why customers should *care*
Positioning	Image vis-à-vis the competition	Define your differential advantage
Management	Ongoing strategies	Define future plans

This image is developed through customer experience with the product (or service or company), through marketing activities controlled by the company, and through interactions that customers have with sources of information outside of the company. Think about the following corporate brands: Apple Computer Inc., Harley-Davidson Motor Co., and Samsung. Apple is generally looked at as "the company that defines high-tech hipness."[4] Harley-Davidson has an "outlaw" aura of rugged individualism and a sense of freedom.[5] Samsung has been transforming itself into a designer of state-of-the-art cool.[6]

Now think about how customers might describe offerings in *your* industry or product category. Some of these descriptors might be rational (such as *fast response* or *complete product line*), whereas other descriptors might be more emotional (such as *friendly* or *trustworthy*). Similarly, the descriptors could be positive or negative. Assess what descriptors customers would use to depict your product(s). Keep in mind that the image may be different for customers than for noncustomers, and even between different groups of customers.

What Value (Brand Equity) Does This Image Have for Customers?

The second question assesses the value customers place on the image just described. How *relevant* and *important* are these images? Customers may have a solid image of a product, but may or may not feel it is relevant to their needs, or that in some other way it is not of value to them. This is the concept of customer-based brand equity. Maintaining relevance in changing markets can be challenging. Let's return to Harley-Davidson. The individualistic image has been highly relevant for the "dreamer" sub-segment of baby boomers. However, the median age of Harley buyers has been slowly rising, and Harley is challenged with making its brand and products relevant in new and meaningful ways as it pursues younger male buyers and female customers. Think of your product's image. How relevant and important is this image to your customers?

What Is the Positioning Compared to the Competition?

The third question addresses the brand's position vis-à-vis the competition. How distinct is the brand image? Both Apple and Harley-Davidson are cult brands that have been quite successful in distancing themselves from the competition and creating brand loyalty. Samsung also has been quite effective in establishing an image, but maintaining it over time will require keeping competitors at bay. If a product manager has one product under one brand umbrella, the brand positioning and product positioning are the same. When a product manager is responsible for several products, all products might share the "essence" of the same brand image, individual products might have separate positions that remain consistent with an overall brand image, or specific products might have distinct brand identities. This is discussed further in the section on designing a brand strategy.

Is the Customer Perception What You Want It to Be?

The final question on brand management involves the ongoing *strategies* that a product manager uses to establish and manage a competitively different brand image that is valuable and relevant to a significant market. Decisions have to be made on line extensions, on matching brand value to specific customers and market segments, and on ensuring the product can deliver on the brand promises made. In Apple's example, the introduction of products such as the iPod, the iPod Shuffle, the iPod nano, and the Mac Mini require an examination of the relationship between the corporate brand and the individual product brands. For Harley-Davidson, it's important to understand the relevance that different market segments may place on brand values. And finally, in Samsung's case, continued investment in product design will be necessary to maintain its position against Sony, Motorola, and emerging competitors.

Designing a Branding Strategy

In designing a branding strategy, product managers must determine the relative importance of the company's image versus the product's image in the purchase decision. Does the customer select a product independent of knowledge of the company, or in large part because of it? Many B2C products will have brand names that are separate from the company name, whereas many B2B and service-sector products will incorporate the company name in some manner. (Yes, there are exceptions to this statement.) The relative emphasis placed on the company name should be driven by the customer decision process. Ask yourself what percent of the purchase decision for a given product is the result of customer familiarity with the company (or possibly business unit or division) name, and what is the result of the product? If several of these factors influence the purchase decision, the product manager may need to build (or borrow) equity from several different structural hierarchy levels.

The corporate image or reputation is governed by factors beyond the control of most product managers. The resulting corporate brand is typically the responsibility of corporate communications. At this level, communication is with all shareholders (customers, suppliers, employees, stockholders). The image of the product, and the responsibility for product brands, rests with product managers. Here the communication is aimed at end-customers and the channel.

Brand Hierarchy Relationships

Whenever a product brand is linked to the company, product managers must evaluate the influences of one on the other. Although they may or may not be able to change or control the corporate (or divisional) reputation, understanding it will be necessary to properly position their product(s). Products geared toward a specific industry may find difficulty gaining widespread acceptance, if the corporate umbrella brand is not perceived as "fitting" that industry. Low-priced products may be perceived as inconsistent with a company believed to be the "BMW" of the industry (or vice versa). Flashy products may strain a conservative corporate image. On the other hand, product managers who can leverage a corporate image to facilitate product marketing benefit from a strong company position.

Let's use a university example to demonstrate the hierarchy. The University of Wisconsin-Madison recently pursued an effort to better link the "corporate" (university) brand to the "business units (colleges, athletics) brands as well as the "family" (department) brands. The image of UW-Madison, as a land grant, Big-Ten institution, is one of research and forward-thinking *sifting and winnowing*, as well as dedication to athletics. The top-level brand promise states "UW-Madison provides a comprehensive educational environment in which intelligent, spirited students and scholars can work together to create change that influences Wisconsin and the world." The next level of the brand would include, for example, the School of Business. The School also strives to fulfill the image and brand promise of research and change that influences Wisconsin and the world, and it does partly through its "family" brands, such as the Executive Education Center, the Small Business Development Center, the Family Business Center, and other centers. These family brands target specific types of customers (family business owners, small business personnel, or corporate managers and executives) with specific product offerings (e.g., seminars on product management, small business fundamentals, etc.) The university, the schools, and the centers are *endorsing* brands for the specific seminar products. In this case, the managers of these products rely heavily on the endorsing brands for positioning, even though specific product characteristics and marketing parameters play a role.

In another example, Apple Computers is the corporate endorsing brand for products such as the iPod family brand. Within this product family, the iPod is the full-featured product and the iPod Shuffle is the entry-level *flanker brand*. Because Apple has a premium image, the marketing of the iPod Shuffle has to be handled carefully to avoid damaging either the family brand or the corporate brand. On the other hand, the premium image added prestige and credibility to the launch of the Shuffle product.

When the corporate name is a potential hindrance, sometimes business unit or family brands emerge as endorsers to a product brand. For example, when Cascadian Farms, a supplier of cereals and other products to natural foods retailers such as Whole Foods, was acquired by General Mills, it was clear that the GM image did not add value to the target customers. To this organic customer segment, the heritage of Cascadian Farms had more equity than the image of General Mills. Therefore, its cereal boxes identify the product (e.g., Oats & Honey Granola), with Cascadian Farms as the sponsoring company.[7]

Beyond determining whether the corporate brand should be an endorsing brand, with the products being sub-brands, a product manager will need to evaluate a host of other factors. What is the core positioning for the brand or product (as viewed by customers), and what do you want it to be? Can and should the brand be extended to other products or categories? Might a different brand be justified—or even required—to create a new position or appeal to a new segment?

Core Positioning

The brand should be positioned to take advantage of your customer-valued strengths, while being different from the competition. Companies can consider many approaches, including price-value positions, usage positions, user-focused positions, alternative positions, secondary association positions, or attribute positions. The positioning can apply to a brand or to a brand–product combination (Table 4.2).

Price-value positions run along a continuum from premier to mass market. A premier position is typically held by a market leader whose products have a higher price (and presumably higher quality) than the competition. Prestige products such as Rolex, and market leaders such as Caterpillar, are examples of premier brand positions. At the other end of the continuum, mass market brands rely more on efficiency (e.g., Wal-Mart) or economy (e.g., Suave). If a product manager is going to compete at more than one price-value position, consideration should be given to a dual or flanker branding strategy, in which different brands are used for different positions.

Usage positions are directly linked to applications or the way a product is used. Although not entirely by strategy, Apple computers were historically perceived as the computers for

Table 4.2   Positioning Approaches

Positioning Approach	Comments	Examples
Price-value	Establishes unique prestige or economy, and may facilitate a good-better-best strategy or product range	Toyota Lexus vs. Toyota Camry
Usage	Highlights product applications	Excedrin (for migraines)
User-focused	Can be directly related to segmentation	JC Penney ("middle market")
Alternative	An anti-category position (that is sometimes short-term as competition in the anti-category increases)	Organic Choice (Scotts' new brand of organic fertilizer)
Secondary association	Focuses on "borrowing" meaning from a location, person, or another product	BMW (German engineering) Affinity credit cards (co-branded with an association, company, cause, etc.)
Attribute	Emphasizes specific features or benefits	Nexium (the purple pill) Dell (customization) FedEx (guaranteed delivery) Tums (with calcium)

graphic design, whereas PCs were more IT focused. Excedrin® established a position as *the* pain medication for migraines. Genetic reagents may be positioned for pure research versus applied research functions.

Sometimes relevance is established (or implied) by positioning products toward *Users*—certain types of individuals (e.g., do-it-yourselfers, parents), or experts (e.g., professional golfers, engineers), or industries (e.g., water purification industry, hospitals). Brands may be associated with the type of individuals (or companies) the target customers *aspire* to be like. Nike, for example, is a brand that appeals to aspiring athletes. Harley-Davidson appeals to a rebel's self-image (see Business Brief 4.1).

Brands use an *alternative* approach when they establish themselves as anti-category products. During the 1970s, 7UP

Business Brief 4.1   Harley Davidson: The great American comeback brand.

In one of the August issues every year, *BusinessWeek* publishes Interbrand's annual ranking of the world's most valuable brands—and Harley Davidson is a consistent entry. But that hasn't always been the case. In 1975, when Jeffrey Bleustein joined the company as engineering vice-president, the product was notorious for shoddy workmanship. Bleustein (who later became CEO) and his colleagues restored quality and introduced new models. In 2005, Harley had racked up 19 years of unbroken gains in earnings and sales.

Harley's success as a cult brand has been driven by the unshakable loyalty and advocacy of the Harley Owner's Group (HOG)—a 650,000-member club that lets folks "feed one another's rebel self-image." The brand image is one of rugged individualism, of freedom and rebellion, of a "little bit of bad." It is connected to American culture and values, beginning historically with its production being devoted to supplying U.S. and Allied troops during World Wars I and II. The company has reinforced this cult brand image with "360-degree marketing." They attempt to create a sense of community— an extended family, of sorts— through HOG events, plant tours, races, and bike rallies.

But continuing the success of the brand is a challenge. The median age of new Harley buyers increased to 46 in 2003, up from under 45 in 1997. Demand among the core Baby Boomers is cooling off. Now, the brand must be extended to new markets and/or new products. To reach new markets, Harley is trying to make the brand and products relevant in new and meaningful ways to "dreamers" who may some day buy a Harley. Women have grown from about 5% to 10% of the retail buyers, and sales to Gen Xers are growing. The company has developed a branded driver's education training program called Rider's Edge. Dealers customize the program to appeal to their local market. Revenues also are generated through licensed items, from leather pants to Harley-themed Barbie dolls. Harley-Davidson now has an advisory board of brand marketers that looks at "brand" from a total business perspective.

Source: Adapted from Joseph Weber, "He Really Got Harley Roaring," *BusinessWeek* (March 21, 2005): 70; Dale Buss, "Can Harley Ride the New Wave?" *Brandweek* (October 25, 2004): 20; Diane Brady et. al., "Cult Brands," *BusinessWeek* (August 2, 2004): 66; James Speros, "Why the Harley brand's So Hot," *Advertising Age* (March 15, 2004): 26.

branded itself as the *uncola*, a soft drink that was the antithesis of the cola product category. Satellite television signal providers advertise themselves as alternatives to cable TV. It's worth noting that this approach might be successful in the early stages of the product life cycle—and can occasionally provide a continued first-mover advantage in, say, new technologies—but the entrance of competition into the "anti" category might reduce the effectiveness of this approach.

Secondary associations provide another potential basis of positioning. Product managers sometimes "borrow" meaning from a geographic location, a spokesperson, or even an object. Switzerland, as the home of Swiss watches, conjures an image of precision. Germany is noted for automotive performance. The Napa Valley is associated with wines. Products originating from such locations can sometimes benefit from an association with these strengths. In other situations, products attempt to establish a connection with relevant locations or other factors to build a base for a secondary association. Athletes (e.g., Tiger Woods for Nike Golf), politicians (e.g., Bob Dole for Viagra), and actors (e.g., William Shatner for PriceLine) lend specific characteristics to the products they endorse.

Positioning by *attribute* refers to establishing a differential identity on the basis of some unique product or service feature or benefit. For example, if your product is the *only* one in the category to offer a titanium shaft, or a blue-tinted lens, or some other special feature, it might be possible to position on that basis, if for some reason the competition will not copy that feature *and* if that attribute is visible and relevant to your target customers. Positioning on the basis of a benefit (as is the case for Volvo with safety) is a similar approach but the attribute is less tangible.

Several do's and don'ts apply positioning. *Do* position from strength. Without it, you have no ability to protect your difference from the competition. *Do* reinforce the positioning through all marketing. If your various customer touchpoints provide contradictory cues, the image becomes diluted and the market confused. *Do* be consistent. Think of the brand positioning as a long-term investment.

On the other hand, there are things to avoid. *Don't* try to be everything to everybody. This requires focus and discipline, because the temptation exists to stretch your funds as far as possible. Unfortunately, a lack of focus confuses customers to the point of pushing them toward the competition. Even though a position will not appeal to all customers, as long as it fits a large enough segment, you will have an edge. *Don't* use different positionings for the same target market. If your product appeals to distinctly different customer groups that don't overlap, it's possible to position the offering differently. But if significant overlap is present, the brand image becomes convoluted. *Don't* position on price, unless you have a true cost advantage. Even with a cost advantage, this position can be dangerous if a future new technology obsoletes your efficiencies. *Don't* position on a promise you can't fulfill. This is consistent with the first *do* of positioning from strength. Be sure you can follow through on your promises to customers.

Brand Extensions

When product managers add more products to their portfolio of offerings, they may need to evaluate both the fit of the products and the fit of the brand. As always, the moves should be logical from a customer perspective. For example, when dealing with technology products, the brand goes beyond a traditional promise of quality and carries over to line extensions. Customers want to know that complex products made by the same company work well together—quality is not enough in and of itself. That's why Sony, Apple, and Samsung opened "brand showrooms" to allow customers to experience the breadth of the product line.[8]

How far can a brand be extended before it dilutes its identity with customers and risks becoming meaningless? What are the advantages and disadvantages of extensions? How should brand extensions be executed? When should flanker and dual branding strategies be used? These are difficult questions for product managers. While no concrete answers exist, product managers should at least give careful consideration to the questions.

Given the expense of establishing a strong brand awareness, companies are always tempted to leverage the brand by extending it to product variants in the same product line (e.g., a different flavor, a different size, or a different color), or even to different product categories (e.g., extending the Jell-O name from instant gelatin mix to frozen pudding pops). To the extent that the essence of the brand (e.g., freshness, on-time delivery, fun) fits the new product, it can work. Daimler-Chrysler's Jeep introduced the Kolcraft Jeep Cherokee All-Terrain Stroller in 2001. The brand concept extended well, and the product sold briskly—even prompting a copycat entry from Ford's Land Rover. The stroller won the number 2 spot in the August 2004 "Top Branding Extensions" survey conducted by TippingSpring, a New York branding firm. Apple got the number 1 spot for its iTunes online music store brand extension.[9]

Of course, brand extensions incur certain risks. The new product may be perceived as significantly different from the original product, causing confusion in the marketplace. Also, if the new product fails, a negative attitude carry-over to the first product may occur.

Therefore, companies frequently try to benefit from a known brand, while still keeping individual products somewhat separated. McDonald's carries its promise of speed and convenience to numerous products, and links them with a common naming mechanism of the *Mc* prefix (McMuffin, McNuggets, etc.). Similarly, Hewlett Packard extended its printer family brands through use of the *Jet* suffix (OfficeJet, DeskJet, LaserJet), and Sony extended its portable music players brand through the use of the *man* suffix (Walkman, Discman).

In cases where significantly different value propositions are inherent in the products, it may be worthwhile to use separate brands. Product managers offering good-better-best product lines might opt for different brands to represent each line. Or, if two similar products are offered through different value channels (e.g., a big-box retailer and a value-added reseller), a dual branding strategy might be employed.

Brand Elements and Programs

Once a strategy for hierarchy and positioning is developed, it must be implemented through the selection and application of various brand elements. This may include (but not be limited to) creating brand names, defining the logo and related brand elements, and establishing the communications program to accomplish your branding goals. As mentioned earlier, customers form an impression of a brand from a variety of touchpoints, not all of which can be controlled by a product manager. Nevertheless, a product manager should strive to control brand communications whenever possible.

Kevin Lane Keller has identified five criteria to use to evaluate various brand elements: memorability, meaningfulness, transferability, adaptability, and protectability.[10] *Memorability* refers to the inherent ability to be remembered and facilitate recall at time of purchase. *Meaningfulness* is the trait of being descriptive and/or persuasive, of capturing and enhancing the intangible characteristics of the brand. *Transferability* relates to the extent to which the brand element can be extended to different products, categories, or geographic markets. *Adaptability* suggests the ability to update the brand element over time, to remain relevant to the market without losing the long-term equity already established. The final criterion, *protectability*, refers to the extent to which the brand element can be protected either legally or competitively. These five criteria provide a checklist for product managers to use when beginning a new branding effort, or when evaluating changes to an existing brand.

Brand Elements

What impact do brand names have on product success? That's a difficult question, because a synergy exists between the two. Before the *first* purchase of a new product, the product's name has not yet established value in the customer's mind. After purchase, however, the product name becomes important and is, in effect, the reflection of a successful product. Chemical product brands such as Teflon, Skydrol, Plexiglas, and Roundup are all long-established, highly successful products with significant sales volume. The memorability of their names, once successful purchase and use experiences happened, helped gain future sales. In the absence of a name, little leverage is gained in introducing related products, and even small changes in formulation, design, or function might prompt competitive bidding.[11]

Brand names can come from a variety of sources. Some are current usage words, such as People® or Oracle®, or word combinations such as Hamburger Helper® or Janitor-in-a-Drum®. These are easy to spell, pronounce, and remember, but should not be descriptive of the category in which the products reside, especially if the category descriptor has been in common usage for a considerable time. Hybrid words, such as ThinkPad® or AquaFresh®, are intended to be more descriptive of a product's benefits, and they overcome some of the difficulties encountered with registering common usage words. However, the escalation in the number of hybrids registered has reduced the pool of potential brand names using this approach. *Neologisms* are brand names that are meaningless in and of themselves, such as Tylenol® and Pepsi®. These types of brand names will be distinct, but will require more marketing communications efforts to establish a meaning in the customer's minds. Regardless of the method used to brainstorm names, the most common goal is to find a brand name that communicates the positioning and fundamental benefits of the offering to target customers. When seeking new brand names, it's important to conduct a thorough search of existing brands to avoid infringing on another company's trademarks.

Numerous trademarkable brand elements exist beyond brand names, including logos, symbols, characters, packages, slogans, and jingles. These elements are used to stimulate brand awareness, establish a differential and memorable identity, and/or communicate a solid value proposition. Many product managers complain about the "logo cops" when their corporate marketing communications department enforces consistency in the typography, layout, and color of logos. Rather than fight the efforts, product managers should work within the guidelines and strive to draw benefits from the corporate brand for their product brands.

Characters are sometimes used to reinforce a brand's rational or emotional attributes. The Maytag repairman was used to communicate a message of reliability. The Keebler elves established a brand personality of magic and fun. Crest has revived its Crest Kid with the same theme of *no cavities* (see Business Brief 4.2). Slogans (such as GE's Imagination at Work) also are used to strengthen a brand image or promise. Product managers should consider the best ways to incorporate these into their product's marketing program.

Business Brief 4.2   Character icons must remain relevant.

Companies generally attempt to keep their brand icons consistent. But that's not always possible or advisable. Sometimes change is necessary to be relevant to new audiences or expectations.

Dell began phasing out "Steven" (Dude, you're getting' a Dell) in 2002, when it was determined that the message of customization was not clear enough in the marketing communications and was not relevant to their primary business target. Although the character had high recognition, the approach was not as effective in cementing the brand position as desired. Similarly, Aflac insurance has launched a campaign "that partly muzzles its web-footed friend and instead seeks to better define what the company does." Customers said they remembered the duck and related it to some type of insurance, but weren't sure what Aflac could do for them.

P&G, while retaining the "Look Mom—no cavities" theme for Crest, has moved from the Normal Rockwell image of the 1950s to a Cuban-born girl named Enya Martinez. The modern-day Crest Kid is reflective of the surge in the Hispanic population in the United States.

Other icons have also had updates and make-overs. Aunt Jemima, the matriarch of pancakes and syrup, received a new hairstyle and modified dress in 1989. The Brawny man—the 1970s plaid-shirted muscleman on Georgia Pacific's paper towels—received an extreme make-over in 2004, being "replaced with a dark-haired younger character who might even be labeled a 'metrosexual.'"

Source: Brian Steinberg, "P&G Brushes Up Iconic Image of 'Crest Kid' in New Campaign, *Wall Street Journal* (March 29, 2005): B9. Suzanne Vranica, "Dell, Starting New Campaign, Plans for Life without Steven," *Wall Street Journal* (October 16, 2002): B3. Suzanne Vranica, "Aflac Partly Muzzles Iconic Duck," *Wall Street Journal* (December 2, 2004): B8. Claire Atkinson, "Brawny Man Now a Metrosexual," *Advertising Age* (February 16, 2004): 8.

Marketing Program

Regardless of the specific brand elements used in contributing to a brand image, the related marketing program is even more critical. A strong product strategy is at the heart of a successful marketing program. The product portfolio must consistently deliver on both the tangible and intangible promises of the brand. The perceived value will depend partly on the correct pricing strategy. The channel used to deliver the product to customers must offer the appropriate identity and support. And finally, the marketing communications must promise only what can be provided on a consistent, ongoing basis.

Coca-Cola discovered the risk of running an advertising campaign that was in conflict with its long-term brand identity. Long identified with touch-feely commercials such as "I'd like to Teach the World to Sing," Coca-Cola wanted to be daring in 2000. It decided to test a new agency with an "edgy" campaign that turned its traditional "warm & fuzzy" image on its head. One commercial aired a crotchety grandmother in a wheelchair who goes ballistic at a family reunion when there is no Coke. Another presented friends fighting at a high school reunion for the same reason. Consumers and bottlers wrote in to complain that the ads were mean-spirited. The ads disappeared after a few weeks, scrapping a $72.9 million campaign.[12]

In general, the marketing program should be consistent with the desired brand identity and positioning discussed throughout this chapter. However, product managers should continually challenge the status quo and decide whether the old rules still apply. Periodically visit Interbrand's Web site (http://www.brandchannel.com) to read the various features and papers that provide diametrically opposed ideas. Some just might work for you.

Checklist: Branding Strategies

- Remember that a brand is a stereotype or executive summary in the minds of your customers.
- Strive to understand your image, equity, and positioning, and then manage these aspects of brand over time.

- Don't underestimate the value of your corporate brand.
- Position your brand on strengths that are relevant and valuable to customers and different from the competition.
- Carefully evaluate risks and benefits before extending a brand.
- Maintain brand consistency in your marketing program.

Interview with Scott Davis, Senior Partner, Prophet

Scott Davis is the author of *Brand Asset Management: Driving Profitable Growth Through Your Brands*, and co-author of the best selling book, *Building the Brand-Driven Business*. Scott writes an ongoing column for *Advertising Age's Point*, is an accomplished lecturer and speaker, and is an Adjunct Professor at Northwestern University's Kellogg School of Management.

Q: *In a nutshell, could you describe Prophet?*

A: Prophet is a global consultancy that helps companies grow and transform by getting the most out of their brands, their marketing investments, and their people. Our philosophy is that a brand is just as much of an asset to an organization as its people, equipment, and capital, and, as such, the brand needs as much nurturing and investment as any other asset to grow its value over time. We have a solid track record of turning existing brands into category leaders and in helping companies across industries build their brands in order to increase profitability and create a true competitive advantage.

Q: *Branding is a skill that brand and product managers always want to hone. What have you observed as the biggest mistakes product managers make in branding?*

A: For all of the talk about branding, I think that what it's all about is still a fuzzy concept, even to product managers who should know better. It's often mistakenly viewed as being all about the look (logo design) or about the messages, and typically is still very inwardly focused. "This is what we think our brand means to our customers." In fact, a brand is about the relationship customers have with it, and the associations they assign to it, all of which is fostered and developed before, during, and after the purchase.

Q: *Do you think B2B product managers face brand challenges different from those of B2C brand managers?*

A: These days, the distinctions between the brand challenges grappled with by B2B and B2C marketers are blurring. B2B marketers are exploiting many of the same nontraditional levers (e.g. blogs, e-mail, and the like) as B2C marketers. Both must deal with far better informed and skeptical customers due to the Internet and other cultural phenomena. And the trends toward "mass customization and individuality" mean that B2C players must think like their B2B counterparts in some respects in developing more customized and individualized offers to their customers.

Q: *What changes in branding philosophies, strategies, or concepts do you expect over the next 5 years?*

A: I don't know that we'll see "changes," per se, but we will see a continuing evolution. First, the holistic view of brand will continue to become more widely adopted. By this, I mean that powerful brands are built from the inside out—the way its promises and representations are upheld and supported in every corner of the business. It's not just marketing that's the keeper of the flame; it's the retail clerk, the call center operator, the installers, and service technicians. As more and more businesses realize this, they're going to become increasingly focused on training all their employees to better uphold the brand values in their day-to-day dealings with all of the organization's stakeholders. Second, it will no longer be acceptable for brand to rest isolated in the marketing silo. The integration of brand strategy with business strategy will become a corporate imperative, and the most meaningful measures of a brand's success and power will be tied to its ability to move the needle on business growth and profitability.

Q: *What is the best advice you ever received with regard to branding?*

A: Probably to not die on a sword about using the word "brand." In some companies, the word "brand" has developed a bad reputation. It's important to go with what works in your organization—our promise, our identity, our customer contract, our purpose, etc. And it's important to remember that externally, a strong brand helps to simplify the customer decision-making process. For example, when two products are virtually the same, without a strong brand, the default will always be price. Furthermore, if you don't take the time to build your brand, others will build it for you (i.e., customers, competitors, influencers, etc.), and likely in a way that you would not agree with.

Q: *What advice can you give product managers about branding?*

A: There is a fine line between having a product with a name versus having a product that is attached to a strong brand. Your world of possibilities is greatly expanded if you have the latter. Don't be consumed just with facts and reports. Take the time to figure out customers' true expectations and feelings about your brand and then integrate the two to drive out meaningful insights that will serve as the platform for future growth initiatives.

Notes

1. From the glossary on the American Marketing Association Web site, http://www.marketingpower.com/.
2. Keller, Kevin Lane, *Strategic Brand Management* (Prentice-Hall, 1998): 4
3. From http://www.brandchannel.com/education_glossary.asp.
4. Beth Snyder Bulik, "Apple Hires HP Star to Bring Stronger Marketing Punch," *Advertising Age* (Vol. 76: 8, Feb. 21, 2005): 4.
5. Joseph Weber, "He Really Got Harley Roaring," *Business Week* (March 21, 2005): 70.
6. David Rocks and Moon Ihlwan, "Samsung Design," *Business Week* (December 6, 2004): 88–96.
7. Kevin Helliker, "In Natural Foods, a Big Name's No Big Help," *Wall Street Journal* (June 7, 2002): B1+.
8. Anonymous, "Leaders: Brand New; Consumer Electronics," *The Economist* (January 15, 2005): 10.
9. Todd Wasserman, "Marketers Extend Kudos to Jeep, Apple," *Brandweek* (October 11, 2004): 4.
10. Keller, Kevin Lane, *Strategic Brand Management* (Prentice-Hall, 1998): 132.
11. Steve Butler, "Product Range Brands: A Frequently Overlooked Source of Value in the Chemical Industry," *Chemical Market Reporter* (December 9, 2002): 26.
12. Betsy McKay & Suzanne Vranica, "How a Coke Ad Campaign Fell Flat with Viewers," *Wall Street Journal* (March 19, 2001): B1–B4.

Chapter Five

Financial and Pricing Performance

To be able to make sound decisions, a product manager needs to establish a framework of financial plans, budgets, and controls related to his products, services, and customers. The starting point is a foundation of financial and managerial accounting that allows the product manager to better understand the profit contribution of his offerings, so that decisions on product rationalization, pricing, and product-line management can be made. From a broader financial perspective, a product manager should understand the key ratios and concepts that are drawn from an understanding of financial statements.

Basic Financial Concepts

General Cost Classifications

In manufactured product environments, two major cost classifications exist—manufacturing and nonmanufacturing—each of which has subclassifications. *Manufacturing costs* include all those related to the transformation of raw materials into final products, including direct materials, direct labor, and manufacturing overhead.

- *Direct materials*, such as wood in tables and steel in cars, become an integral part of the finished product and can be considered direct costs. Other materials, such as glue, may be more difficult to link to individual units of production and may be classified as indirect materials to be included in overhead.
- *Direct labor* includes the labor directly traceable to the creation of products. Research and development, support-staff time, and other labor not directly related to manufacturing are included in indirect labor.
- *Manufacturing overhead* includes all costs of manufacturing, excluding the direct material and direct labor costs described above. Included in this category are items such as indirect material, indirect labor, heat, light, and depreciation.

Nonmanufacturing costs include the marketing, sales, administrative, and support costs unrelated to the production of products. These are typically included on the selling, general, and administrative (SG&A) expenses line of an income statement. Historically, the nonmanufacturing costs have been less significant than the manufacturing costs for most products. However, the growth of service industries and the emergence of various technologies have reversed the relative weight of these costs in most companies.

- *Marketing and selling* costs include advertising, shipping, sales commission, and salaries.
- *Administrative expenses* include executive, organizational, and clerical salaries.

Both manufacturing and nonmanufacturing costs result from the normal operation of a business. In addition, other expenses may be incurred, such as the purchase of an asset, that are charged to the income statement for the period, even though they are not operating expenses. These costs are presented in the simplified income statement in Figure 5.1. The cost of goods sold includes the direct material and labor as well as manufacturing overhead. The data are frequently derived

Sales
– cost of goods sold

Gross profit
– operating expenses

Net income from operations
+ other income
– other expenses

Net income before taxes
– income taxes

Net income

Figure 5.1   Simplified income statement.

from *standard costs* and are a combination of fixed and variable expenses. (Standard costs are predetermined cost amounts that represent what cost *should* be under the most efficient methods of operation; in other words, they are benchmarks for measuring performance.) Similarly, the overhead expenses (comprised of the nonmanufacturing or SG&A expenses) may be a combination of fixed and variable costs.

The income statement resulting from the above process of listing costs provides a historical review of the results of operations. It does not necessarily provide the information for planning and improving the decision-making process of product management. To provide this type of information, it is necessary to distinguish between the variable and incremental costs associated with products, to better understand their contributions to overhead and profit.

Concepts of Segmented Reporting

Variable costs are those that vary in direct relation to the activity level. If activity level doubles, variable costs double in total. This is true because the cost per unit stays approximately constant over a relevant range of activity. Direct materials and direct labor are variable production costs, and sales commissions represent a variable sales expense. In addition, step-variable (similar to incremental or semifixed) costs may exist. Setup time, seasonal labor, and similar activities related to the amount of business can be considered variable to that piece of business. *Fixed costs*, on the other hand, do not change, regardless of changes in the level of activity. Since fixed costs remain constant in total, the amount of cost per unit goes down as the number of units increases. It is sometimes said that variable costs are the costs of *doing* business, whereas fixed costs are the costs of *being in* business.

Once costs have been separated into fixed and variable elements, it is easier for product managers to determine the contribution of different products or customer segments. It is also easier for companies to evaluate the performance of several product managers. A comparison of a traditional income statement (using historical cost information) and a contribution income statement (separating fixed and variable costs) is shown in Table 5.1.

Note that, in Table 5.1, the top line (sales revenue) and the bottom line (net income) are the same using both approaches.

Table 5.1   Traditional Income Statement Versus Contribution Income Statement

Traditional			Contribution		
Sales		$17,000	Sales		$17,000
less cost of goods sold		11,000	less variable expenses		
			var. production	$,5000	
			var. administrative	$2,200	
			var. selling	$500	$7,700
Gross margin		$6,000	Contribution margin		$9,300
less operating expenses			less fixed expenses		
administrative	$2,000		fixed production	$4,000	
selling	$3,000	$5,000	fixed admin.	$1,500	
			fixed selling	$2,800	$8,300
Net income before taxes		$1,000	Net income before taxes		$1,000

However, using the contribution margin approach, it becomes clear that these particular sales contribute $9,300 to fixed costs (prior to break-even) and profit (after break-even is achieved). This concept of contribution reporting can be applied to business units, departments, product managers, product lines, customers, or similar units of analysis. When applied to these segments, direct costs and common costs must be understood.

Direct costs are those that can be identified directly with a particular unit of analysis (i.e., product manager, product, customer, etc.) and that arise either because of the unit or because of the activity within it. *Common costs* are those that cannot be identified directly with any particular unit, but rather are identified in common with all units. The common costs (most likely fixed costs) cannot be allocated except through arbitrary means. An example of contribution reporting is shown in Table 5.2. Note that this example presents an income statement constructed for the product managers as if they were businesses. In this example, company revenues are $900,000, of which $500,000 come from Product Manager 1 and $400,000 come from Product Manager 2. They contribute $80,000 and $170,000, respectively, with $160,000 in overhead not allocated to either. The $400,000 revenue of Product Manager 2 comes from a standard model ($150,000) and a custom model ($250,000) contributing $70,000 and $140,000, respectively. Product Manager 2 has $40,000 of fixed expenses not related directly to either product. The custom product receives $180,000 from contractors and $70,000 from residential customers to generate its $250,000 in revenue. The segment contributions are shown without an arbitrary allocation of the $10,000 of fixed costs for the custom model that aren't directly related to either customer group.

Cost Drivers

Before a product manager can price a product or evaluate a product line, she must understand what the cost drivers are for the various products and customers. Some customers require additional expediting charges, others require special shipping and handling, while others expect free services. To determine

Table 5.2   Contribution Reporting

	Units of Contribution Analysis		
	Total Company	Product Manager 1	Product Manager 2
Sales	$900,000	$500,000	$400,000
Less variable expenses			
cost of goods sold	400,000	270,000	130,000
other variable expenses	100,000	70,000	30,000
Total variable expenses	500,000	340,000	160,000
Contribution margin	400,000	160,000	240,000
less direct fixed expenses	150,000	80,000	70,000
Product manager margins	250,000	$80,000	$170,000
less common fixed expenses	160,000		
Net income	$90,000		
	Product Manager 2	Standard Model	Custom Model
Sales	$400,000	$150,000	$250,000
Less variable expenses			
cost of goods sold	130,000	50,000	80,000
other variable expenses	30,000	20,000	10,000
Total variable expenses	160,000	70,000	90,000
Contribution margin	240,000	80,000	160,000
less direct fixed expenses	30,000	10,000	20,000
Product margins	210,000	$70,000	$140,000
less common fixed expenses	40,000		
Net income	$170,000		
	Custom Model	Contractors	Residential
Sales	$250,000	$180,000	$70,000
Less variable expenses			
cost of goods sold	80,000	60,000	20,000
other variable expenses	10,000	3,000	7,000
Total variable expenses	90,000	63,000	27,000
Contribution margin	160,000	117,000	43,000
less direct fixed expenses	10,000	7,000	3,000
Customer segment margins	150,000	$110,000	$40,000
less common fixed expenses	10,000		
Net income	$140,000		

the true financial contribution, each of these costs should be allocated to the particular product or customer.

Financial Statement Analysis

As suggested earlier, financial statements are historical documents indicating what happened during a particular period. This perspective helps a product manager judge past performance through the use of ratios. In addition, by comparing changes in the statements over time, it is possible to identify performance trends and use the information for subsequent decisions.

Investment Decisions

Directly or indirectly, product mangers may be involved in capital budgeting decisions in the preparation of investment proposals for new products, new markets, or new business ventures. The most common methods of evaluating different proposals are average rate of return, payback period, present value, and internal rate of return.

The *average rate of return* is the ratio of the average annual profits to the investment in the project. Using this method, the product manager prepares a forecast of the improvement in profit over a number of years from a given investment. The total profit is divided by the number of years to give an average annual profit; this then is expressed either as a percentage of the original investment or as a percentage of the average investment per year. Assume the following stream of profits from, for example, a new product:

- Year 1: $100,000
- Year 2: $200,000
- Year 3: $300,000   Average: $240,000
- Year 4: $250,000
- Year 5: $350,000
- Total: $1,200,000

If the initial investment was $1 million, the average annual profit would be the $240,000 as a percent of $1 million, or

24%. Alternatively, the $240,000 could be expressed as a percentage of the average investment for each of the 5 years. In either case, the rate would be compared to hurdles used by the company or to industry norms.

The *payback period* is calculated by determining the length of time (number of years) it takes to recover an initial investment. In the above example, the investment of $1 million is paid back during the fifth year. After 4 years, the cumulative profits are $850,000, with the remaining $150,000 being earned sometime during the final year. Here again, the payback as an absolute value is less important than looking at the relative values of different projects.

The *present value* (or net present value) refers to the value of future cash inflows compared to the current outflow of the initial investment.

The *internal rate of return* is the interest rate that makes the present value of all projected future cash flows equal to the initial outlay for the investment. In other words, it is the rate that makes the net present value (NPV) equal zero. The calculation is somewhat complex mathematically, and since it is a value that would be provided by your financial group, the definition should be sufficient for our purposes.

Pricing Policies and Performance Improvement

An important part of a product manager's marketing function is pricing a product to balance profitability and customer satisfaction. For existing products, the seven-step process (shown in Figure 5.2) described in this chapter provides the basic considerations for setting prices and making price changes. The seven steps involved in setting price are:

1. Define business objectives and price management structure.
2. Profile customer segments and assess value.
3. Determine competitive price position.
4. Gauge relevant costs.
5. Stay within legal guidelines.

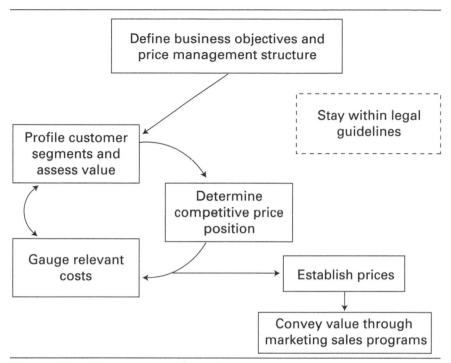

Figure 5.2   Pricing process flow chart.

6. Establish prices.
7. Convey value through marketing and sales programs.

Define Business Objectives and Price Management Structure

The first step, defining business objectives, was probably accomplished during the strategic overview described in Chapter 1. The corporate direction might specify a premium position or a mass-merchandiser/discount approach. These obviously have direct impact on the pricing. When setting the price, it is necessary to know if a product is a cash cow, is being used to enter a new market, or requires a specific ROI. On the other hand, in a decentralized organization, the corporate position might have minimal impact on product planning, and price will play a neutral role.

Avoiding price wars might be part of a corporate pricing strategy. For many companies, this can be done only by reducing the cost of producing products, as Heinz Pet Products chief Bill Johnson found out. After facing intense price pressure from the competition, Johnson decided that meeting price cuts, without also lowering the internal cost structure, would be deadly.

> "We decided to run pet foods assuming the price war would never end," he says. To do so, he turned the pricing equation on its head. "Instead of calculating out what it cost to make cat food and price accordingly, we asked ourselves what did consumers want to pay," Johnson explains. His team decided that today's finicky customers would pay between 25 cents and 33 cents per 5 1/2-ounce can, tops. Johnson then went to work rationalizing processes to hit that target. Step one was identifying his company's competitive advantages: strong brand equity, cheap materials in the form of excess tuna from Heinz's StarKist operations— which goes into more than 15% of Pet Foods' products— and some proprietary manufacturing processes. "Step two," says Johnson, "was a draconian reduction of cost."[1]

Part of the corporate strategy involves positioning. Is the product positioned as the market leader, thereby commanding a premium price? Which competitors are you most directly linked with? Sometimes the price/value positioning can be affected by the selection of competitive comparisons. When Woolite (a detergent for fine washables) first entered the market, it positioned itself as an alternative to dry cleaning, rather than a substitute for less-expensive soaps. It was consequently perceived as a better "bargain." Similarly, when the Chrysler Towne & Country introduced its new-model minivan in 1995, it positioned the various features against luxury vehicles, again modifying the perceived competitive price. Take an active role in helping your customers determine the reference value they use in determining whether your product's price is acceptable.

Profile Customer Segments and Assess Value

The second step is estimating the price elasticity of the target market(s). Although some research-based techniques exist for estimating price sensitivity, conducting this type of research is at best difficult. As a starting point, begin with a managerial assessment, asking the following questions:

· How strong is the product positioning, its differentiation in the customers' eyes? Is the differentiation based on an important, relevant characteristic? (The stronger the differentiation and the more important it is perceived by the customer, the less sensitive to price the customer is likely to be.)
· Is there a lot of competition? Are customers aware of the competition? Can customers find substitute ways of fulfilling the same need without buying any product? (The fewer options the customer has for providing the same benefit(s) a product provides, the less sensitive to price the customer is likely to be.)
· What was the impact on sales when price increases/decreases occurred in the past? Consider both internal and competitive price changes. (If prices were raised in the past without a significant loss to the competition, the customer is likely to be less sensitive to price.)
· Is the product part of a larger purchase? (The smaller the product purchase is as a percentage of a larger purchase, the less sensitive to price the customer is likely to be.)
· Is the product a capital expenditure or an expense item? (The less expensive the absolute price of the product, the less sensitive to price the customer is likely to be, unless a small unit-volume item is bought in such large quantity that it results in a major expenditure.)

After completing the managerial assessment, research might be necessary to gather more specifics. Some of the information that would be beneficial includes:

· What are the highest and lowest prices that fall within the customer's relevant range?
· What does price mean to the customer?
· Is the absolute or comparative price more important?
· Are customers considering shipping and operating costs as part of the price?

Part of this analysis should include a search for new products and markets where price is less important, as was the case when Becton Dickinson launched its InterLink needle (see Business Brief 5.1).

Remember that a market can be multilevel. If the product is sold *to* as well as *through* intermediaries such as distributors, dealers, and retailers, the price charged has to consider them as well. First, set the price so that their margins will be large enough to motivate them to do what they need to do. Second, consider how the margins they add affect the price that end-users ultimately pay. Third, corporate and pricing positions must be consistent with the image of the channel member. When you evaluate the costs (step 4), look for opportunities to fine-tune the discount structure for the channel.

Part of the job of a product manager is to *manage the expectations of her customers*. First of all, it's important to not artificially raise expectations (through advertising or sales promises) to a level that cannot consistently be attained. When true performance falls short of expected performance, customers perceive a lower level of value (and feel the price is too high). Second, you can help customers set realistic expectations by thoroughly explaining contract terms, providing benchmark data on standard product performance, or demonstrating the impact on their bottom line given price-performance data.

Determine Competitive Price Position

The next step in pricing requires a look at the competition. First, how do the prices compare with the major competitors? What benefits do the products provide that have perceived value to the customers? It is useful here to try to put a monetary value or cost on the differences between the product and its competitors. Much of the information will be subjective, but it still forces a more careful evaluation of the cost–benefit analysis. Start with the competitor's price, and then add and subtract internal estimates (Table 5.3).

A typical challenge faced by product managers is how to respond to an aggressive price competitor. Before defensively cutting prices to protect market share, product managers

Business Brief 5.1   Using innovation to reduce price competition.

As always, one way to exit a price war is to innovate. Take Becton Dickinson's hypodermic needles. The company produced over a billion each year, at a paltry dime apiece, worth over $100 million in sales. During one particularly painful period in the late 1980s, a Japanese competitor began selling its wares for 7 cents a unit. In other words, you would not want to be stuck in the needle business. Then, Becton Dickinson got together with Baxter International, which had developed InterLink, a needleless needle.

The point to remember is that the needles doctors stick in your arm account for about 50% of the market. The other half are used to hook up intravenous lines to other IVs, which is where the Baxter-Becton team made its mark. InterLink looked like a regular syringe except the needle is replaced by a hard piece of tapered plastic tubing that ends in a blunt tip. Baxter created a new type of plastic-and-rubber seal that could be punctured and then would reseal around such a plastic spike. Baxter asked Becton to produce the spike.

Hospitals gladly paid more for InterLink because the pointless needles lowered the risk of accidental needle sticks. [In 1993], health care workers reported about one million sticks, costing hospitals upward of $400 per incident in lost time and paperwork, excluding any legal or long-term health costs. "That's the attraction," says Gary Cohen, a marketing VP with Becton Dickinson. "Even though InterLink needles cost about 25 cents, hospitals save money."

The innovation trend has also moved into consumer products, where companies have been struggling to win price increases. Procter & Gamble has decided to jazz up humdrum brands by adopting Gillette's well-known razor-and-replacement-blade strategy, and by incorporating mechanical or electric features. The $14 Swiffer® mop (with its $5.75 replacement pads) has been a profitable new product, generating both initial sales and follow-on sales. Tide StainBrush® (a battery-powered brush), Mr. Clean AutoDry® (a water-pressured car-cleaning system), and other gadget-related items accounted for about 8% of P&G's $54 billion in 2004 sales.

Source: Andrew E. Serwer, "How to Escape a Price War," *Fortune* (June 13, 1994): 90. Robert Berner and William Symonds, "Welcome to Procter & Gadget," *BusinessWeek* (February 7, 2005): 76.

Table 5.3   Estimating Monetary Value of Competitive Differences

Competitor's price		$5,000
Value of added benefits		
Monetary savings		
Longer life	$500	
Lower failure rate	250	
Labor savings	1,000	
Total savings	1,750	
Monetary costs		
Switch-over costs	−500	
Economic value to the customer		1,250
(The $1,250 is a best estimate of the true "worth" of differences between the product and the competition. It should be added to the competitor's price to arrive at the economic or financial value to the customer.)		
Incentive to switch	750	500
(The $750 is the amount subtracted from the economic value to make the product more attractive and provide an incentive to switch.)		
Your price		$5,500

should look at the potential long-term strategic consequences of such a move. As George Cressman and Thomas Nagle point out in their *Business Horizons* article, today's price concession could impact your future market situation:

- A customer who wins a price concession due to a competitive offer learns that encouraging competitive offers is a profitable activity. In the future, the customer will solicit and occasionally accept competitive offers simply to win more leverage over the preferred vendor.
- Competitors losing deals because of higher prices may choose to push prices even lower.
- Many customers not initially interested in the competitor's offer eventually learn that other customers who were less loyal got better deals. They resolve to stop "getting taken" and become more aggressive negotiators.[2]

Although product managers can't always evade price cuts, they should avoid a quick fix. Evaluate the decision within the context of the overall product-line strategy. Is this a significant sale, because the customer or market is too important to lose? Will losing *this* business cause you to lose *other* business? Is this product and market important enough to the competition that it will trigger a price war? Can you protect the business without resorting to price cuts? A 1% change in price (up or down) has a more exaggerated impact on the bottom line than does a 1% change in volume or costs, as indicated in Table 5.4.

Gauge Relevant Costs

As mentioned earlier in the chapter, evaluating the costs related to the pricing decision often is more difficult than it seems. Companies use different approaches for allocating costs, so the variable and fixed costs can become blurred. Nevertheless, definitions of these common pricing terms are relevant.

Table 5.4   Comparative One Percent Changes

	Original	1% Price Increase ($202)	1% Volume Increase (5,050 Units)	1% Cut in CGS ($108.90)	1% Cut in Fixed Costs ($346,500)
Sales (5,000 @ $200)	$1,000,000	$1,010,000	$1,010, 000	$1,000,000	$1,000,000
CGS (5,000 @ $110)	550,000	550,000	555,500	544,500	555,000
Gross margin	450,000	460,000	454,500	455,500	450,000
Operating costs	350,000	350,0000	350,000	350,000	346,500
Net pretax income	$100,000	$110,000	$104,500	$105,500	$103,500
Percent change in income		10%	4.5%	5.5%	3.5%

Variable costs are those that vary (in total) with production of the product or service. This could include direct materials and labor. For a given production level, these are constant per unit and provide the floor for pricing decisions. Fixed costs do not vary with production or sales; they exist whether the product is even produced. Fixed costs can be allocated according to square feet of production space or percentage of a product's contribution to total revenue, split equally among product managers, or a variety of other approaches can be used to allocate them. In the long run, *all* costs must be covered, and the long-term pricing of products should consider all costs. However, in the short run, any price obtained that exceeds variable costs can at least contribute to fixed overhead and (potentially) to profit.

Variable costs often will be equal to the cost of goods sold and be the only incremental costs relevant to a pricing decision. Exceptions arise when fixed costs are incurred for a bid situation, for example, that are incremental to that decision. In that case, the incremental fixed costs must be added to the variable costs to determine the floor for pricing decisions.

This information should be reflected in a contribution report form of an income statement. A simplified income statement is shown in Figure 5.3.

Fixed costs can include the fixed costs directly attributable to a product line, as well as other allocated costs. The fixed costs directly attributable to a product line are the operating expenses for that product. Subtracting these from the contri-

	Sales
Less	Variable costs
	Contribution margin
Less	Fixed operating expenses
	Net operating income
Less	Other expenses
	Net income

Figure 5.3 Simple contribution income statement.

bution margin yields the operating income that a product manager provides. Other allocated costs are subtracted from this figure to arrive at net income.

The following break-even formula can be used as a starting point for evaluating a price. The standard break-even formula shows the number of units that must be sold at a given price to cover all costs. The formula is:

$$\text{Break-even units} = \frac{\text{Fixed costs}}{(\text{Price} - \text{Variable cost per unit})}$$

Therefore, if relevant fixed costs are $42,000, the product has a price of $10,000, and the variable cost per unit is $4,000, it would be necessary to generate sales of seven units to break even. By experimenting with different price levels, and matching that with expected demand, the product manager can begin the pricing analysis. In addition, a target return (profit) can be included in the numerator (along with fixed costs) to assess the unit sales necessary to contribute a specified profit. For example, if a required profit of $12,000 were added to the fixed costs in the numerator, it would be necessary to generate sales of nine units to break even.

Building on this example, suppose a product manager for consulting services handling 10 projects for $10,000 each has direct costs of $4,000 per project and overhead costs of $42,000. Each project contributes $6,000—the difference between the price and the variable costs—to overhead and profits. The operating profit would be $18,000, as shown in the first column of Table 5.5.

But, if facing competitive pressure, the product manager drops the price to $9,000 per project, each project would contribute only $5,000 to overhead and profit. Assuming no other changes, the new revenue would be $90,000, and the new bottom-line profit would be $8,000. The 10% drop in price (from $10,000 to $9,000) would result in a 55% drop (from $18,000 to $8,000) in operating profit (see the second column in Table 5.5).

To keep its profit at $18,000, the firm would need to land two more jobs. Because we assumed that operating expenses—

Table 5.5   Price/Profit Comparison

	(1)	(2)	(3)
Revenue			
(10 @ $10,000)	$100,000		
(10 @ $9,000)		$90,000	
(12 @ $9,000)			$108,000
Cost of Sales			
(10 @ $4,000)	$40,000	40,000	
(12 @ $4,000)			$48,000
Contribution Margin	60,000	50,000	60,000
Operating Expenses	42,000	42,000	42,000
Net Operating Income	$18,000	$8,000	$18,000

fixed costs—don't change with an increase in unit sales, the objective is to provide a contribution margin of at least $60,000. Hence, the firm would need to handle 12 projects rather than 10 ($60,000 divided by the new per-project contribution of $5,000), as shown in the third column of Figure 5.4. The two additional jobs represent a 20% increase in sales to compensate for the 10% drop in price.

By adapting the break-even formula, it is possible to quickly look at the impact of a price change. The modified formula is shown in Figure 5.4. CM stands for contribution margin (the difference between price and variable cost, or $10,000 − $4,000 = $6,000, in this example). The %CM refers to the contribution margin per unit, expressed as a percentage of the price ($6,000 ÷ $10,000). The result is the percentage change in unit sales necessary to contribute the same profit return as now.

$$\% \text{ break-even sales change} = \frac{-(\% \text{ price change})}{(\%CM + \% \text{ price change})}$$

$$\% \text{ break-even sales change} = \frac{-(-.10)}{.60 + (-.10)} = \frac{.10}{.50} = .20$$

Figure 5.4   Modified break-even formula for a price change.

This formula can be used in an electronic spreadsheet (e.g., Excel) to see the impact of price changes. Putting relevant contribution margins in the columns, potential price changes in the rows, and the formula in the cells yields a spreadsheet similar to that shown in Table 5.6.

What would have been the necessary change if the variable costs were lower (e.g., $3,500), so that the contribution margin was 65%, with everything else equal? In this case, it would

Table 5.6 Spreadsheet Example of Break-Even Analysis of Price Changes

Price Change	Contribution Margin								
(%)	0.65	0.60	0.55	0.50	0.45	0.40	0.35	0.30	0.25
0.10	−0.13	−0.14	−0.15	−0.17	−0.18	−0.20	−0.22	−0.25	−0.29
0.09	−0.12	−0.13	−0.14	−0.15	−0.17	−0.18	−0.20	−0.23	−0.26
0.08	−0.11	−0.12	−0.13	−0.14	−0.15	−0.17	−0.19	−0.21	−0.24
0.07	−0.10	−0.10	−0.11	−0.12	−0.13	−0.15	−0.17	−0.19	−0.22
0.06	−0.08	−0.09	−0.10	−0.11	−0.12	−0.13	−0.15	−0.17	−0.20
0.05	−0.07	−0.08	−0.08	−0.09	−0.10	−0.11	−0.13	−0.14	−0.17
0.04	−0.06	−0.06	−0.07	−0.07	−0.08	−0.09	−0.10	−0.12	−0.14
0.03	−0.04	−0.05	−0.05	−0.06	−0.06	−0.07	−0.08	−0.09	−0.11
0.02	−0.03	−0.03	−0.04	−0.04	−0.04	−0.05	−0.05	−0.06	−0.07
0.01	−0.02	−0.02	−0.02	−0.02	−0.02	−0.02	−0.03	−0.03	−0.04
−0.01	0.02	0.02	0.02	0.02	0.02	0.03	0.03	0.03	0.04
−0.02	0.03	0.03	0.04	0.04	0.05	0.05	0.06	0.07	0.09
−0.03	0.05	0.05	0.06	0.06	0.07	0.08	0.09	0.11	0.14
−0.04	0.07	0.07	0.08	0.09	0.10	0.11	0.13	0.15	0.19
−0.05	0.08	0.09	0.10	0.11	0.13	0.14	0.17	0.20	0.25
−0.06	0.10	0.11	0.12	0.14	0.15	0.18	0.21	0.25	0.32
−0.07	0.12	0.13	0.15	0.16	0.18	0.21	0.25	0.30	0.39
−0.08	0.14	0.15	0.17	0.19	0.22	0.25	0.30	0.36	0.47
−0.09	0.16	0.18	0.20	0.22	0.25	0.29	0.35	0.43	0.56
−0.10	0.18	0.20	0.22	0.25	0.29	0.33	0.40	0.50	0.67

have been necessary to increase sales by only 18% to break even. What if variable costs were significantly higher (e.g., $7,000), so that the contribution margin was only 30%? Again, with everything else the same, what sales change would be necessary to break even? Now the answer is 50%, or five additional projects. Price increases also can be evaluated by using Table 5.6. However, if a price increase is necessary, it can be useful to time the increase with a product change or additional service that adds value.

So, in looking at price changes, it is necessary to understand what impact those changes have on required volume to break even, and then ask a few questions:

· How much leverage do competitors have? If their variable costs on this product are lower, they would be able to withstand a price cut longer.
· How likely is it that they would want to cut price and sustain it?
· Also, how sensitive are customers to price changes?
· Is it possible to sell the required volume change?

Remember that the information in the spreadsheet doesn't give you "the answer." It simply provides one data point to help you make a better decision.

Stay within Legal Guidelines

The Sherman Anti-Trust and the Robinson-Patman Acts are the two pieces of legislation most relevant to pricing decisions. The Sherman Act (along with amendments of the Clayton Act) prohibits practices that reduce competition or inhibit trade. Collusion or price fixing is one such practice. Companies may not legally collude with competitors to set prices (horizontal price fixing), and they may not require channel members to charge certain prices (vertical price fixing).

The Robinson-Patman Act prohibits certain forms of price discrimination. In general, it is illegal to sell "products of like grade and quality" at different prices to competing resellers if the result is to restrain trade or put one reseller at a competitive disadvantage to another.

Establish and Implement Prices

The sixth step in pricing demonstrates the bottom-line impact of the prices and price changes—typically in the form of a profit and loss (P&L) or income statement. Some companies that use a cost-plus-markup approach want to see the impact of price changes on a per-unit basis. This is appropriate when a relatively low number of high-ticket sales occur. However, for most products, the impact of a markup can be deceiving if forecasted sales are not taken into account. If several products are in the line or multiple price combinations exist for different market segments, it is useful for planning purposes to present all this information in an impact table, perhaps using a spreadsheet format (Figure 5.5).

	Product 1			Product 2			Product 3			Total
	Price A	Price B	Price C	Price A	Price B	Price C	Price A	Price B	Price C	
Sales units										
Revenue										
Cost of goods sold										
Gross margin										
Total gross margin										
Operating expenses										
Operating income										
Other expenses										
Net income										

Note: The "Total" column provides the bases for the income statement in the annual product plan.

Figure 5.5   Price change impact table.

For most B2B sales, prices are negotiated, resulting in inconsistent prices. Even if a product manager makes the right strategic decisions, without transaction price management, significant reductions can occur in the bottom-line profit. The list price is carefully determined, but after numerous discounts, incentives, and allowances, the realized price of the transaction (sometimes referred to as the pocket price) can be quite different. Companies that control this "pocket price waterfall" can improve overall profitability, as noted in the following example from *McKinsey Quarterly*:

> Many companies can find an additional 1% or more in prices by carefully looking at what part of the list price of a product or service is actually pocketed from each transaction. Right pricing is a more subtle game than setting list prices or even tracking invoice prices. Significant amounts of money can leak away from list or base prices as customers receive discounts, incentives, promotions, and other giveaways to seal contracts and maintain volumes.
>
> The experience of a global lighting supplier shows how the pocket price—what remains after all discounts and other incentives have been tallied—is usually much lower than the list or invoice price…. Every light bulb had a standard list price, but a series of discounts that were itemized on each invoice pushed average invoice prices 32.8% lower than the standard list prices.[3]

Convey Value through Marketing and Sales Programs

The last step in pricing is to incorporate pricing into the marketing plan. As mentioned earlier, how you position your price against the competition and the tactics you use to manage customer expectations should be built into the marketing plan. It is also important to think about what makes your product different from and better than the competition. Then find ways to make these differences visible, beneficial, and believable. When a mattress company wanted to visibly demonstrate how its inner coil springs operated independently from one another, it set up bowling pins and dropped a bowling ball on the bed. Since the ball was able to bounce without causing the pins to fall, it demonstrated the benefit of the coil springs. When car companies or tire companies want to focus on the benefits of their safety, they frequently use a baby to represent the importance of the safety feature. When companies want to convince customers of a particular fact, they will use third-party testimonials or government documentation to make it believable.

Do not forget that several internal customers (e.g., customer service, sales, other product managers) must be informed of the approved changes. Also, some pricing strategies might require additional promotional material, changes in packaging, or other things that could affect the marketing plan. If a price change is being tested in a certain region or for a certain period of time, be prepared to track the results to use in making future decisions.

Finally, keep track of the pricing tactics used by other firms both inside and outside of your industry. Sometimes, novel approaches can be adapted to unique needs. Here are a few examples to start an idea file:

· *No-haggle pricing* is offering a set price in an industry known for "negotiation." This was used by Saturn in the 1990s in the automotive industry.
· *Always the low price* is charging a constant low price rather than using frequent promotions. This is used at the retail level by Wal-Mart and at the manufacturer level by Procter & Gamble.
· *Step pricing* is a discount policy in which prices are reduced for set quantities in a step-wise fashion: for example, one price for 1–100 units, a reduced price for 101–300 units, a still-lower price for 301+ units, and so forth.
· *Price point pricing* is setting price points across a product line to denote quality differences. Many consumer products are priced this way, using a "good-better-best" approach in terms of quality. Structure the prices so that customers are most likely to buy the highest-profit product in the line. Sometimes, it is preferable to introduce a lower-priced variation than to reduce the price of a core product (see Business Brief 5.2).

Business Brief 5.2   Product line pricing.

Zebra Technologies Corp., a Vernon Hills (Illinois) maker of barcode printers, had developed a reputation among customers as a manufacturer of high-quality, top-of-the-line printers. But the company also saw a lot of sales potential in the low-end portion of the marketplace. A low-priced, low-frills printer was a cinch to make. But offering such a model posed two risks: It might tarnish Zebra's image of quality with its customers, and, worse, it might cannibalize the existing product line.

The solution? Zebra came up with a no-frills version with a plastic housing that pleased its clients. But it didn't give away the store: It made sure that the stripped-down $1,495 printer couldn't be upgraded to ensure that it wouldn't compete with its high-end $1,995 model, which was faster and could print on different kinds of materials. The result: The new Stripes printer helped Zebra's sales climb 47%, and margins on the new printer matched those from Zebra's original line.

Apple has taken a similar approach with its move downstream. In an effort to bring out products for the low end of its two core markets, Apple announced the Mac Mini and the iPod Shuffle. The Mac Mini is a stripped-down version of the Mac, and is the least expensive computer Apple has ever released. The lower priced product is an effort to convince users of Windows-based products to switch to the Mac. The lower price, along with Microsoft's current vulnerability to computer viruses, could tempt some customers to reconsider their computer-buying behavior.

The iPod Shuffle is a simple, inexpensive version of Apple's standard iPod with less functionality and a lower song-storing capacity (estimated at 120 songs versus 5,000 songs). It targets a more price-sensitive, younger market, who may be tempted to move up to a pricier iPod after getting hooked on buying music from Apple's iTunes Music Store.

Both the iPod and Mac business showed brisk growth after the launch of the new products. The company reported a sixfold increase in second-quarter 2005 profits, as revenue rose 70%. Some analysts believe there will be a resurgence in Apple's PC business as a result of a halo effect from the iPod.

Source: David Greising, "Quality: How to Make it Pay," *BusinessWeek* (August 8, 1994): 58. Nick Wingfield, "Apple Scores with Cheaper Lines," *Wall Street Journal* (April 14, 2005): A3. Peter Burrows and Andrew Park, "Apple's Bold Swim Downstream," *Business Week* (January 24, 2005): 33–35. Nick Wingfield, "Apple Tries a New Tack: Lower Prices," *Wall Street Journal* (January 12, 2005: D1–D5.

- *Peak-time pricing* is charging a higher price for peak-period usage and a lower price for nonpeak times. Phone companies, utilities, and movie theaters routinely use this approach.
- *Bundled pricing* is creating a "package" of features or products and selling the bundle for one price. Car companies use this approach with their option packages.
- *Unbundled pricing* is taking packages apart and selling components individually. Many products in the mature phase of the product life cycle use this approach, allowing customers to select and pay for specific features only. Unfortunately, customers frequently attempt to start with the low price of a main component and negotiate the inclusion of free features, thus reducing the effectiveness of this technique.
- *Trial pricing* is charging a low price for new products or new customers to encourage their trial of a product.
- *Quantity discount pricing* is a technique that involves several variations. Companies can charge a reduced price for a given quantity per order, cumulative quantities over a fiscal year, or some combination of these options.
- *Cross-connected pricing* is allowing a discount on one product/service when purchasing another. It is commonly used among airlines, car rental firms, and hotels.
- *Leasing* is paying a time-based fee (e.g., weekly or monthly) for the right to use a product. It is used increasingly in the automotive industry as an alternative to purchasing the vehicle.

Checklist: Financial and Pricing Performance

- Be sure to understand and analyze the cost drivers (e.g., expediting) behind your products and customers as part of the pricing process.
- Use contribution reporting to get better information for decision making. Understand the contributions by both product and customer.
- Gain a comfort level with income (profit and loss, or P&L) statements, as well as with balance sheets.
- Clarify the return or hurdle rate required for new-product development.

- Forget everything you know about how pricing is done in your business. The best new ideas you can get are from outside your industry.
- Avoid raising or lowering prices simply in response to competition or internal costs. Assess how your customers might respond to the change and determine whether this reaction justifies the change.
- Consider a no-frills product variation as an alternative to price cutting when faced with competitive pressure.
- Time your price increases with added value.
- Understand the contribution margins of all products in your line, and the impact that has on pricing decisions.
- Conduct a managerial assessment of how sensitive your target market is.
- Innovate and look for new product-market segments where price sensitivity is lower (and your product will be able to obtain a higher price).
- Anticipate competitive reactions before making price changes.

Interview with Eric Mitchell, President of the Professional Pricing Society

Eric Mitchell's business background includes 14 years of extensive pricing management at Xerox Corporation and Ford Motor Company. He also is the author of seven workbooks on pricing.

Q: *In a nutshell, could you describe the Professional Pricing Society?*

A: The Professional Pricing Society is an association that supports price decision makers and price management personnel from a wide variety of industries in over 50 countries. Pricing, marketing, and general management executives from Fortune 1000 and mid-sized firms are typical members of the Pricing Society.

Q: *Pricing is a skill that product managers always want to hone. What have you observed as the biggest mistakes product managers make in pricing?*

A: Mistake #1 without a doubt is product managers who price their new products with rose-colored glasses. As a result, you see overpricing of new products due to the absence of realistic feedback and outside price and price-positioning research. The product manager insists that the launch price reflect all the value-add "goodies" that he and the team of product designers have invented. The thought of pricing their new "baby" anywhere near or—heaven forbid, below—existing offerings or competition is forbidden.

Mistake #2 on the "product manager pricing faults" list is ignoring feedback from the customer marketplace and even from the internal sales force, when it is reported that their product has become more commodity-like and its price should be cut. Again, the symptoms are similar to mistake #1. Some products, exiting their initial growth stages, naturally should have their prices cut or should make room for more discounting.

Mistake #3: Product managers know their list or suggested pricing well, but don't know or follow the street price. After the list is set, it seems that pricing disappears off the product manager's radar. Pretty soon, the suggested list price of $100 ends up gathering the firm only $47 in actual revenue (i.e., the pocket price). Only sales and accounting know what happened, and the poor product manager never learned the waterfall.

Q: *Do you think B2B product managers face different pricing challenges than B2C product managers?*

A: Yes, very much so. The true B2C professional needs to study and comprehend the unique characteristics of the retail channels before pricing. They now must have the skills to price products through both traditional and electronic channels and be able to reconcile differences when customers complain that they have seen different prices. They must understand value from both a trade and end-user perspective.

B2B product managers, on the other hand, must be careful about directly adopting consumer product pricing approaches. A frequent lecturer at Pricing Society events, Dick Harmer (President of B2Bpricng.com) says it best.

> Over the last 30 years, the world of B2B marketing has come to suffer increasingly from Consumer Think—the infiltration of ideas from consumer marketing into the realm of B2B. As this has happened, many people have lost sight of the fact

that business value (financial contribution to a business customer's bottom line) is something quite different from consumer value (the satisfaction of consumption needs, wants,
whims, dreams, and other "feel good" desires). They have for-
gotten that the economics of value *creation* are quite different from the economics of value *consumption*, and that the
two often call for quite different marketing and pricing
strategies.

Q: *What changes in pricing philosophies, strategies, or concepts do
you expect over the next 5 years?*

A: Wow, so much change. Well, two things in particular come to
mind. First is the advent of elaborate pricing software tools. Starting
in the late 1990s, a bunch of venture capital–funded enterprises
started developing pricing software that would bolt onto or mesh with
infrastructure transaction software like SAP and Oracle. As of today
(early 2005), the pricing software industry has survived the dot.com
bubble of 2001–2002 but has not yet risen to the level of excitement
that a field like CRM software achieved. So, the depth of this industry and the usefulness of its tools are still being decided.

The second trend is the explosive growth of pricing departments.
After the cost-cutting frenzies of the late 1990s, a trend emerging
now from C-level offices and boardrooms is dedicated staffs and personnel to manage the top line better. We have seen an explosion in
pricing departments and pricing professionals since 2000. Most of
this growth is attributed to CEOs and high level executives in large
firms asking that someone maximize revenue growth—and this certainly starts with being smarter about pricing and instituting better
processes and strategy, so that firms don't leave money on the table
when they set and manage prices.

Q: *What is the best advice you ever received?*

A: Make sure your pricing actions match what your management
wants you to do. One time, as a product manager, I cut prices nation-
wide on a copier in all the educational markets. I had great success
in keeping a mature product alive. Sales soared. However, this was
180 degrees opposite of what management wanted. They were about
to introduce a higher-priced, new-technology copier, and wanted me
to *raise* prices to reduce the price gap between the new product at
launch and the mature one. I made the price gap *large* and caused all

kinds of cannibalization problems. I kept my job, but my VP made it clear—don't be a "Lone Ranger" product manager, acting in isolation and forgetting the company's big picture. Great advice.

Q: *What advice can you give product managers about pricing?*

A: If your firm has a pricing department, involve the pricing manager in your process—whether it is pricing a new service or managing pricing of product extensions and ancillary products and services. If there is no department, then pricing usually falls on the shoulders of either the marketing department or the product manager. In either case, do research on all the strategies and tactics in your industry when it comes to pricing practices. Stay in touch with the field and pricing trends in both price level for products and their pricing structures; watch how discounting is managed and learn what the pricing waterfall is for your products and services.

Learn when to add price changes to the marketing equation and when not to. There are several levers to product management that are substitutes for pricing actions—starting with brand management, customer segmentation, channel management, and of course, advertising. They all interplay, as product managers know. But sometimes we all forget and go straight to price corrections, when other levers may be more profitable.

For more information on the Professional Pricing Society refer, to http://www.pricingsociety.com/.

Notes

1. Andrew Serwer, "How to Escape a Price War," *Fortune* (13 June 1994): 88.
2. George E. Cressman, Jr., and Thomas T. Nagle, "How to Manage an Aggressive Competitor," *Business Horizons* (March–April 2002): 23.
3. Michael V. Marn, Eric V. Roegner, and Craig C. Zawada, "The Power of Pricing," *McKinsey Quarterly* (2003, Issue 1): 27.

Part Two

Product Planning and Implementation

After completing the strategic foundation covered in Part One, it's time to move on to more specific product portfolio planning and the implementation of a number of product strategies. The portfolio goals and the process of innovating through new products will be the subject of Chapters 6 through 8. Chapter 6 deals with the "fuzzy front end" of product strategy and ideation. Chapter 7 moves from ideation to the preparation of a business case for further product definition and development. Chapter 8 emphasizes the importance of a solid launch strategy for new product success.

The final two chapters rounding out this section deal with strategies for existing products, including revitalization, maintenance, and liquidation. Given the importance of marketing programs in implementing these strategies, Chapter 10 overviews the marketing planning process.

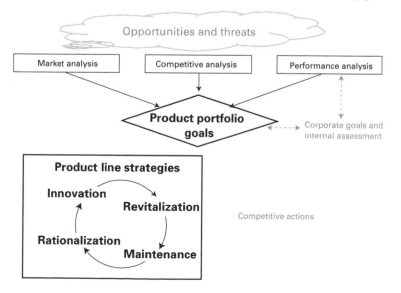

Chapter Six

Strategic Growth through New Products

As mentioned in Chapter 1, strategic product planning requires an understanding of corporate and divisional strategic goals. Most long-term visions have some implicit (or explicit) statement of the future "picture" of the company and its product offerings. The product manager has to understand the role her product(s) play in this vision. It is not enough to know the percentage of profits expected from a new-product line, although that is important information. The product manager must also know what new markets, new technologies, and new directions should be incorporated into the long-term product plan.

Strategic Product Thinking

Strategic product thinking is a precursor to new-product development, because it forces product managers to envision a future that does not yet exist—to lead the market and create products before customers ask for them. This requires a certain level of risk and creativity. Product managers must ask themselves: How will the customers of tomorrow be different from the customers of today? What products/services will these customers expect? What existing capabilities can we expect to use in the future, and what new abilities will we need to develop?

The emphasis is not on projecting the present into the future. Rather, the emphasis is on trying to understand how the future will be different from the present and the impact that will have on present planning.

Fostering a Customer Mind-Set

Fostering a customer mind-set requires the product manager to step back and redefine the business in terms of customer functions. It may also require redefining what it means to satisfy the customer. When David Whitwam became CEO of Whirlpool, his vision was to transform the company into a customer-focused organization and to shift thinking from product to customer, as indicated in the following excerpt from an interview in *Harvard Business Review*:

> The starting point isn't the existing product; it's the function consumers buy products to accomplish. When you return to first principles, the design issues dramatically change. The microwave couldn't have been invented by someone who assumed he or she was in the business of designing a range. Such a design breakthrough required seeing that the opportunity is "easier, quicker food preparation," not "a better range."
>
> Take the "fabric-care business," which we used to call the "washing-machine business." We're now studying consumer behavior, from the time people take off their dirty clothes at night until they've been cleaned and ironed and hung in the closet. What are we looking for? The worst part of the process is not the washing and drying. The hard part is when you take your clothes out of the dryer and you have to do something with them—iron, fold, hang them up. Whoever comes up with a product to make this part of the process easier, simpler, or quicker is going to create an incredible market.[1]

Targeting Current, Tangential, and New Markets

Products can have varying levels of risk, and it is usually wise to have a portfolio of new products to balance the risk–return equation. New products with the lowest risk are line extensions—slight modifications ("New and improved!" versions) of an existing product. Larger or smaller package sizes, stronger or weaker flavors, and lighter or heavier components are all examples of line extensions. Most of these modifications are intended to increase usage among or provide more options for current customers. Sometimes the same (or a slightly different) product can be repositioned to attain usage among tangential markets. The classic example of this is baking soda, which was repositioned for numerous applications beyond baking. Bayer pain reliever extended to five models to increase usage among tangential markets such as people with arthritis or heart-attack victims. Finally, taking the existing product to a new market can be potentially profitable, but it must be marketed correctly. For example, the Bendix Brake Division of Allied Signal wanted to increase its brake sales in the do-it-yourself (DIY) market. It discovered that its packaging didn't connote high quality, so it redesigned its packaging to incorporate a strong color blue as part of the repositioning strategy. In one year, its sales moved from less than 1% of market share to more than 20%.

Products that are more than line extensions are also new, and they can be marketed to the same customer segments, tangential segments, or totally new markets. Of these three alternatives, the least risky is reaching the existing customer base through franchise extensions. A *franchise extension* (also referred to as a *brand extension*) refers to taking what the product (or brand) connotes and applying it in a different product category. For example, Arm & Hammer baking soda extended its brand franchise to detergent, toothpaste, and similar products for which the concept of "clean and fresh" was appropriate. Castle & Cooke found that its Dole brand connoted more than pineapple, and it used the brand name to launch Dole Fruit & Juice bars. These types of extensions can have definite benefits, but they require some strategic thinking and planning.

Flanker brands are used when a company wants to enter a slightly different market segment (e.g., the "cost-conscious segment"), but does not want to dilute its current image. Flanker brands allow a company to retain its current position with existing customers, while still expanding into different segments. Marriott has used flanker brands to extend its position. Fairfield Inn is a low-price, low-frills product of the Marriott chain (see Business Brief 6.1).

Business Brief 6.1   The power of line extensions.

Most products will die if they are not reinvented as the marketplace changes. Since consumers now cook less (reducing the amount of aluminum foil and plastic wrap used), Reynolds and Glad Wrap introduced line extensions to revive their products. Reynolds discovered that one of the biggest complaints customers had about aluminum foil was that it stuck to food. This research led to Reynolds Release™, the first variation of the product since 1947, and it caused an increase in usage. Clorox found that its Glad™ plastic wrap did not provide the leakproof seal that consumers wanted, and soon thereafter launched Press 'n Seal™.

Extending a franchise offers a number of benefits that *new-to-the-world* new-product development does not. The major one is that extension capitalizes on the company's most important assets—its brand names. Thus, the company moves into a new category from a position of strength. A further benefit is that the investment outlays typically necessary to establish a new brand—a significant expense— are minimal. However, line extensions must offer new value to customers. Companies that are successful at line extensions tend to regularly rotate the brand assignments of their product managers to prevent them from getting stuck in ruts. This reduces the likelihood of proliferating virtually identical products.

A consumer is exposed to hundreds of brand names every day. Being a well-known brand is not sufficient to be a good brand extension. Few consumers want Jell-O® shoelaces or Tide® frozen entrees. A brand can be successfully extended to a new category when it has both fit and leverage:

- Fit is when the consumer accepts the new product as logical and would expect it from the brand.
- Leverage is when the consumer, by simply knowing the brand, can think of important ways that they perceive the new brand extension would be better than competing products in the category.

Since a brand's meaning can change over time as brand extensions are introduced, management must develop a brand plan—what extensions are introduced short term and what others become possible long term. Note the changing possibilities Ocean Spray faced as they

Business Brief 6.1   continued

moved from cranberries to cranberry juice, to being a full-line bottled juice supplier. One must develop a long-term scenario to avoid diluting important elements of the brand and to improve the odds of pursuing more remote areas where the brand could have leverage.

Source: Adapted from Edward M. Tauber, "Brand Leverage: Strategy for Growth in a Cost-Control World," *Journal of Advertising Research* (August/September 1988): 28; and Eileen Roche, "Product Development: Why Line Extensions Often Backfire," *Harvard Business Review* (March/April 1999): 19–21. Micheline Maynard, "Wrapping a Familiar Name Around a New Product," *New York Times* (May 22, 2004): C1.

The riskiest approach is to create a new product for a new market, especially if the product is not just new to the company but also new to the world. Unless the new market can be reached through existing distribution channels, and/or the product can build on core competencies, this is a questionable endeavor. The company must carefully assess whether the risk is worth the effort, whether it will be possible to develop and protect a competitive edge in the future, and even whether the idea is best left for the competition.

Create a Product Portfolio Plan

The net result of a product manager's strategic product thinking should be a long-term strategy or portfolio for the product line. Rarely will a product manager develop this strategic plan in isolation, or without input from others in the organization. Rather, it will be a multiperspective effort—especially if technology roadmapping or new organizational capabilities are part of the process.

The portfolio plan should specify the mix of new and existing products. A product portfolio—similar to a stock portfolio—is a group of investments. This group of investments should increase long-term profitability by balancing risk. Since forecasting sales and profitability is at best an inexact science, product managers strive to have both high risk (assuming high return) and low risk products. DuPont, for example, determined that it was diverting too many resources—two-thirds of its R&D budget—to making improvements on existing products, rather than investing in new ones. By 2003, the split was 50-50, with a goal of spending about 65% of the R&D budget on new products.[2]

The plan should define the new product objectives, such as *penetrate a new market, alter an image,* or *provide a complete customer solution to some problem.* An effort should be made to reduce risk by balancing short versus longer-term horizons, and line extensions versus products with greater degrees of "newness." It's also advisable to stagger the new product pipeline, so that a slow stream of new products is introduced, rather than a log-jam of several at launch at the same time, followed by a vacuum.

New-Product Development Basics

New-product development (NPD) involves many functions within a company, not just the product manager. But because product managers are frequently charged with the ultimate success of a new product, it is important to discuss their involvement in the process. Although new-product development goes beyond the fiscal-year planning horizon of the marketing plan for a product line, certain portions must be addressed each year. For some years, researching and submitting product proposals will be the extent of new-product efforts. At other times during the development project, milestones should be written into the annual plan. And, finally, as commercialization draws near, launch documentation must be developed and integrated into the annual plan.

Understanding Past Successes and Failures

To improve the potential for new product success, it helps to calculate your company's "hit rate" in new products and determine the reasons for it. Compare successful product launches with unsuccessful ones. What were the common elements of successful development efforts that were different from unsuccessful development efforts? Was there a difference in R&D

investment and shared communication? The number of ideas generated? The sequence of steps in the development process? The understanding of the market? The application of core competencies? All these can be significant factors and must be part of the strategic thinking process. The Medical Products Group of Hewlett-Packard, for example, uncovered 14 critical internal processes that differentiated successful and unsuccessful products.

> When executives at Hewlett-Packard's Medical Products Group studied 10 of their new-product failures along with 10 of their successes, they were surprised to identify a total of 14 essential tasks that determined which products worked and which didn't. The steps covered a wide range of corporate skills. Among them: figuring out which new products play to a company's core strengths, understanding how a new product should be sold, and getting an early fix on a project's costs.[3]

R&D and manufacturing personnel are important contributors to successful strategic product planning. Product managers should determine with manufacturing how wide a product line can be without putting a strain on efficiency. This includes understanding how future products can be developed from a common platform. When Whirlpool (the appliance company) went global in the 1980s, they spent over half a year looking at appliance markets around the world, and believed that consumer needs were similar enough to justify a common platform. That allowed them to significantly reduce costs and bring innovations out faster—moved them from a $3.5 billion company to a $13 billion company in 2005.[4] Prevent product proliferation by deciding which products can be dropped when new ones are introduced. If products are not to be dropped, the product manager must lobby for increased R&D and/or operations support to attain the strategic product goals.

Previewing the Process

Product innovation and speed of development are becoming increasingly important in our global economy. Although the role of the product manager in new-product development will vary by company, the product manager at minimum should take care in understanding and articulating the market potential and in participating on the product development team. Figure 6.1 and Table 6.1 identify the steps in the development process, along with the potential role of the product manager. The flow chart in Figure 6.1 is "typically average," although in practice there will be variations. It's worth noting that there may be additional steps for innovations and a compression of steps for line extensions. Platform and technology products may require further modifications. That's why product managers should adapt the process to meet the unique needs of their companies and situations.

Note that after a product strategy is spelled out, the first step of a specific new-product development project is idea generation. Ideas are fleshed out into a proposal and presented to top management (or a new-product review committee comprised of key executives of all the functional areas) for screening. For major product ideas and concepts that pass screening,

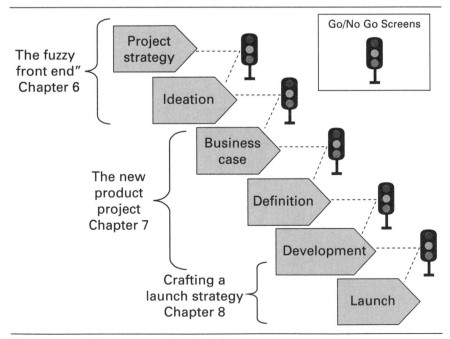

Figure 6.1   The new-product development process.

Table 6.1   Product Manager "Deliverables" in the NPD Process

Stage	Description	Product Manager Outputs
Product strategy	Vision of future products	Product innovation charter specifying portfolio goals and target product concepts
Ideation	Generation of a steady stream of potential product ideas	Initial idea proposals to be screened along pre-established criteria (Project teams might be established at this point, if their input is necessary for the business case)
Business case	A structured economic proposal for an investment in a new product project	A clearer description of the concept and opportunity, including forecasts, risk assessment, and financial projections. May involve developing and comparatively testing different concepts.
Definition	Establishment of clear functional specifications, and possibly prototypes	Team agreement on the requirements for the product, beta test results, and commitment to manufacture. Product managers begin launch strategy and documentation
Development	Product manufacturing	Finalization of launch materials
Launch	General availability or introduction of the product to the sales force	PR, training, advertising, and other activities to create customer awareness and sales
Project/process evaluation	Comparison of results to initial objectives	Corrective actions as necessary for the product
	NPD process evaluation	Suggested improvements for future projects

management assigns representatives from relevant functional areas to a multifunctional project team for this particular new-product endeavor. The team members select a leader (who might or might not be the product manager) to organize and monitor the project, guiding it through the critical path schedule developed by the team. All members do as many tasks as possible in parallel to shorten the product development cycle. For example, product managers can conduct focus groups on concept evaluation at the same time that engineering is conducting technical feasibility studies.

The dotted lines going to the stop lights prior to moving on the subsequent stages indicate that concepts that test poorly should be considered for elimination as early as possible, rather than investing more resources in their development. The stop lights represent what are commonly referred to as "stage-gates." The term Stage-Gate[5] is a registered trademark coined by Robert Cooper to refer to the continued assessment of a product concept as it moves through the new product process. These stages of evaluation points *incrementalize* the decision process to further reduce risk.

During the business case phase, product managers refine the ideas into more concrete product concepts. During the definition phase, the team attempts to freeze a product's desired benefits (or preliminary specifications) by collecting marketing research information, conducting quality function deployment (QFD), and/or developing engineering drawings. If this is an innovative product (as opposed to a line extension), a prototype may need to be developed and beta tested.

The prototype development, testing, and evaluation starts with the creation of a working model or preliminary version of the product. This model then is put through use tests, either inside the company's facility or by customers. *Alpha tests* refer to having the product used by employees or a department in the company. For example, a food item might be tested in the firm's cafeteria before testing outside the company. *Beta tests* refer to having a select group of customers using the product under actual usage conditions. This phase could uncover potential defects that necessitate product elimination or redesign, or it may proceed to prelaunch scale-up and production planning.

Before moving into development, the team should obtain approval from the new-product review committee for any capital expenditures required to build the prototype. It's worth noting that, although prototype development is presented after concept testing and development in this chapter, the reverse order also is possible. There are circumstances in which customers cannot assess a concept in the abstract, such as when evaluating the taste of a new food product. In these situations, a prototype is required early in the process.

The prelaunch time is the period of final preparation for commercialization. Product managers pull together details for the marketing plan, and engineering and production complete final product drawings and tool debugging. During the launch phase, the product is taken to the market, possibly through a planned roll-out. After launch, the new-product project is evaluated with a goal to either take immediate corrective action or to improve the process for the future. Each of these stages is described in this and the next two chapters from the perspective of a typical product manager.

Developing Product Ideas

The number of ideas generated can affect successful product commercialization by increasing the likelihood of uncovering the best product concepts. Although many argue that no shortage of ideas exists per se, it can also be argued that many good ideas never surface because the available ideas are accepted as "good enough." Product managers are frequently under pressure to generate new products quickly. Because they also juggle existing products at the same time, they do not allow themselves the luxury of thoroughly examining all alternatives. They resort to line extensions or "me-too" products, because thinking is muddied by the present. That is why the strategic gestation of ideas and having a portfolio plan can be a useful prelude to product development.

Several sources exist for strategic product ideas. An important source is customers and potential customers. Unfortunately, too many companies don't use a disciplined approach to obtain futuristic ideas. For business-to-business products, a useful research approach is a systematic customer visit program. A customer visit program is a structured approach to data collection through which specific customers are targeted for their expected contributions to an issue being studied, company personnel are recruited to participate in the program due to their importance to the decision being made, and written objectives are established for the data collection. Customers who are future-thinkers, who are industry leaders, or who have unique applications for the product are asked to participate in the program. These *lead users* often provide more innovative ideas than the more "representative" customers.[6] A small group of people from R&D, operations, and marketing are briefed on the goal of the project, and arrangements are made to call on the selected customers. The resulting insights from the customer visit program are then synthesized into potential long-term product ideas. Trade shows are another vehicle for reaching customers. Conducting a focus group at a trade show can be a lower-cost alternative for obtaining new product ideas.

Brainstorming sessions focused on a particular goal also can be a valuable tool for product development. During the session, participants are encouraged to think in terms of metaphors and analogies. The application of analogies was used successfully when Canon was attempting to develop a drum for its minicopiers.

> Canon designers realized that 90% of all maintenance problems are related to the photosensitive copier drum.
> Therefore, they wanted to make it disposable, but at acceptable price and quality levels. Coincidentally, the team ordered out for beer, triggering a discussion on whether the process for making an aluminum beer can could be applied to a copier drum. This led the team to a process technology that could manufacture aluminum drums at an appropriate cost.[7]

Product managers also must be aware of the company's core competencies and be willing to work with other functional areas and other product managers to leverage these skills into future products and markets (see Business Brief 6.2).

Business Brief 6.2   Innovating innovation.

How does innovation happen? For many product managers, competing demands on their attention cause short-term needs to be more pressing than long-term possibilities. Or alternatively, they explore so many opportunities that they don't focus enough on any one. That's why a product portfolio plan or a product innovation charter, which actually sets boundaries, paradoxically encourages innovation.

Nokia Group, for example, focuses its innovation efforts by "studying user needs, emerging technologies, and the changing business environment within the mobility and communications space." By limiting new ideas to these customer-need categories, extraneous pursuits are minimized.

Similarly, Air Liquide shifted focus from product innovation to what they termed *demand innovation*—meeting existing demand in a new way. As a supplier of industrial gases to the pulp and paper industry, the firm's income dropped as the product became a commodity in the 1990s. After unsuccessfully investing R&D resources into an ozone-friendly alternative to bleach for paper and pulp, they discovered a need for gas-management services. These services, which accounted for 7% of their revenue in 1991, grew to 30% by 2004.

GE Healthcare encourages an active involvement of lead users—who are referred to as *luminaries*. Most are well-published doctors and research scientists from leading medical institutions. GE brings them together for regular "medical advisory board sessions" to assess the evolution of GE technology.

P&G encourages innovation through cross-pollination from one product to another rather than inventing from scratch. Tide StainBrush™, an electric device for removing stains from clothing, uses the same basic mechanism as the Crest Spinbrush Pro™ toothpaste. They also encourage thinking in terms of generating more solutions to customer needs, rather than in terms of extending products. P&G gained a greater "share of mouth" with its Spinbrush™ and Whitestrips™, while Colgate was focused on toothpaste.

These best practices at P&G became popularized as "Open Innovation"—as in the book by the same name by Henry Chesbrough. Some of the philosophies of this concept include:

- It is essential to work with smart people both within and outside your company.
- Commercial and technical innovations should be integrated more seamlessly.
- A better business model is superior to getting to the market first.

(continued on next page)

Business Brief 6.2   continued

- Share and benefit from intellectual property.
- Make the best use of internal and external ideas, and you will win.

Source: Adapted from Liisa Välikangas and Michael Gibbert, "Boundary-Setting Strategies for Escaping Innovation Traps," *MIT Sloan Management Review* (Spring 2005): 58–65. John Teresko, "P&G's Secret: Innovating Innovation,"

Industry Week (December 2004): 26–32. Anonymous, "Business: The Rise of the Creative Consumer: The Future of Innovation," *The Economist* (March 12, 2005): 75. Nanette Byrnes, Robert Berner, Wendy Zellner, and William C. Symonds, "Branding: Five New Lessons," *BusinessWeek* (February 14, 2005): 26–28. Anonymous, "Special Report: Don't Laugh at Gilded Butterflies," *The Economist* (April 24, 2004: 81.

Although ideas can come from a variety of sources, both internal and external, the product manager should actively be looking for new-product concepts (Figure 6.2). Do not believe that too many ideas already are under consideration. It is not just the number of ideas, but also their quality that is important. The product manager is best suited to determine whether a flanker product is necessary to offset a competitive entry, or if a group of customers has adapted a product to a unique application that can be extended to other market segments. Subscribe to technological clipping services (either published or online) to monitor new developments and capabilities. Make customer visits to uncover different ways of thinking about the product category. Attend technology-sharing meetings (either within the company or through trade associations). Keep communication open with sales staff to identify opportunities. Monitor shifts in market size or composition that could suggest changing needs.

If no repository exists for product ideas in the company, create a database of ideas related to the product. Even ideas that didn't pass screening now may turn into winners in the future. Skim the database on a regular basis (perhaps quarterly or semiannually) to determine whether any ideas should be dusted off and re-examined.

The ideas should be subjected to a preliminary screen to determine if more effort is justified. Screening criteria might include the following:[8]

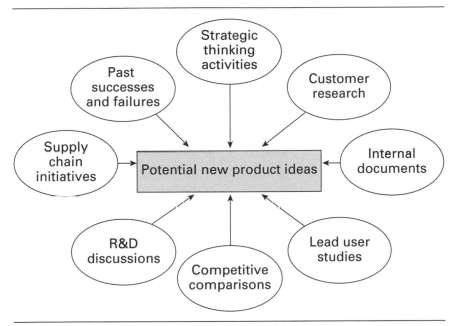

Figure 6.2   Sources of new product ideas.

· Fit within existing product mix
· Patentability
· Risk of competitive entry
· Ability to sell through existing distribution
· Compatibility with strategic plan
· Acceptable payback period
· Growth potential
· Cost of tooling and machinery
· Compatibility with core technologies

The criteria for a specific company could include all or none of these factors. However, the act of listing them forces the issues to the surface and provides a forum for the discussion of product concepts. The criteria should be developed separate from, and in advance of, screening particular ideas.

Many different approaches can be used for this screening process. Some companies simply indicate "must have" criteria for new products to be considered. Others list several criteria that can be evaluated on a yes-no basis. Still others use criteria with weights and ratings, as shown in Figure 6.3. In this example, the most important screening criterion was "compatibility with strategic plan" as designed by the weight of 0.20. The committee rated this particular idea 0.7 for "compatibility with strategic plan," yielding a rating of 0.20 × 0.70 = 0.01 (rounded from 0.014). Each row is calculated this way, then added together to arrive at the weighted rating. Note that the product idea being evaluated obtained a weighted score of 0.44. If several other ideas being evaluated simultaneously obtained scores of 0.56, 0.62, and 0.70, the relative priorities would become clear. The real value of these priorities is the ability to decide how to best allocate developmental resources.

A mathematical rating device, such as that shown in Figure 6.3, does not necessarily quantify results, because the evaluations are still subjective. However, a screening checklist provides the opportunity for individual members to evaluate new-product ideas according to consistent parameters prior to meeting together as a group. It also fosters discussion within the new-product development review committee and focuses the conversation on aspects considered important to the company.

Whatever type of screening tool is used, it is important that it allows a reasonable balance between being too strict and too loose. A too-strict approach can cause potential winners to be killed. A too-loose approach results in mediocre products being pursued.

After the product idea passes screening, a cross-functional team is established to work on the product. The team usually is comprised of the product manager and counterparts from operations, design, and, in some cases, procurement, a key customer, legal, finance, customer service, and sales. The role of the salesperson will vary by company. Although sales input and up-front support are critical, not all sales staff can identify with the top 10% of potential or targeted customers that represent leading trends. A recent study by AT&T comparing sales staff's judgments with customers' judgments about an innovative new-product concept found that the sales force was "consistently more optimistic and exhibited different preference pat-

Requirements for a Successful New Product	Relative Weight (A)	Rating of Product Line											Rating
		0.0	0.1	0.2	0.3	0.4	0.5	0.6	0.7	0.8	0.9	1.0	
Fit with existing product mix	.15					x							.06
Patentability	.05				x								.02
Low risk of competitive entry	.10								x				.07
Ability to sell through existing channels	.10									x			.08
Compatibility with strategic plan	.20								x				.01
Acceptable payback period	.10										x		.09
Growth potential	.10						x						.05
Low cost of tooling and machinery	.05			x									.01
Compatibility with core technologies	.15				x								.05
Weighted Score													.44

Figure 6.3   Product-screening checklist.

terns."[9] In that case, it may be more beneficial soliciting input from a *variety* of sales staff than in having sales as a core member of the team throughout the process.

The next chapter focuses on taking these (sometimes yet raw) ideas, developing a business case for them, and guiding them into products than can be commercialized.

Checklist: Preparing for Strategic Product Planning

- Challenge yourself to (at least occasionally) lead the market and create products before customers ask for them.
- Strive to build a portfolio of core capabilities, rather than simply a portfolio of products.
- Understand the reasons for your past successes and failures in new-product development.
- Work with engineers to understand and possibly implement a platform strategy for strategic product planning.
- Don't underestimate the need to come up with new-product ideas. It's risky to assume that the new-product ideas you now have are the best you can come up with.
- Talk to other product managers, other divisions, and other units in your company to assess whether some capabilities can be leveraged within your product area.
- If brands are crucial in your industry, create a vision for the future growth and development of the brand identity or brand equity.

Interview with Greg DiCillo, President and Co-founder of Life Cycle Strategies

Greg DiCillo has 25 years of sales and marketing experience and has successfully introduced and implemented life cycle planning processes and product management.

Q: *In a nutshell, could you describe Life Cycle Strategies? How did it get started?*

A: Life Cycle Strategies was formed in 1998. We are a consulting and training firm specializing in product management and planning with a primary focus on B2B companies. We've worked with companies that sell products and services in a variety of industries, from automation and building controls to financial and travel services. The genesis of Life Cycle Strategies was based on our own experiences within companies that were trying to convert product specialists into product-line managers.

Q: *What major changes have you noted in the product management discipline over the past 5 years?*

A: One of the biggest changes I've noted in the product management discipline is the attention that is being given to new-product development, and specifically, new-product development processes.

Q: *What will be the primary challenges for product managers in the next decade?*

A: There are a number of challenges that product managers will face in the next decade. First, product managers have to enhance their credibility within the organization. There is still a pervasive culture in most companies that view the product manager as a "project manager," who lacks the skills and expertise to manage the product line. Second, they will be challenged to be better time managers as they are asked to do more with less, direct resources that are decentralized, and manage products in a truly global marketplace. Third, they are going to be challenged with ever increasing market pressures to commoditize products regardless of the value provided.

Q: *What advice can you give product managers about coping with these challenges?*

A: None of these challenges is simple to overcome. To enhance credibility, product managers need to focus on improving knowledge. The old adage that knowledge is power is true. Most product managers lack credibility because they can't answer even basic questions about markets, customers, and competitors. If product managers really want the responsibility of managing the product line, they have to prove to management that they have the knowledge and facts to support their decisions or recommendations. As for time management, a key factor for product managers is to clearly understand their roles, responsibilities, and metrics. They're going to have to rely on delegation and influence to allow them more time to focus on their responsibilities. At the product level, product managers are going to be required to do better due-diligence in their markets to better understand customer value and the components that make it up in order to avoid having their product offering viewed as a commodity.

For more information on Life Cycle Strategies, refer to http://www.lifecycle.com/index.htm.

Notes

1. Regina Fazio Maruca, "The Right Way to Go Global," *Harvard Business Review* 72 (March/April 1994): 143.
2. Amy Barrett, "DuPont Tries to Unclog a Pipeline," *Business Week* (January 23, 2003): 103–104.
3. Christopher Power, Kathleen Kerwin, Keith Alexander, and Robert D. Hof, "Flops," *BusinessWeek* (August 16, 1993): 79.
4. Janet Guyon, "CEOs on Managing Globally," *Fortune* (July 12, 2004) the 2004 Global 500 special insert.
5. Robert G. Cooper has several books in which he described his Stage-Gate® process. His most recent book, *Product Leadership*, 2nd edition (Cambridge, MA: Basic Books, 2005) provides a discussion of process variations depending on the type of product and other variables.
6. More information on lead user research can be found at http://www.leaduser.com/.
7. "The Knowledge Creating Company," *Harvard Business Review* (November–December 1991): 101.
8. A more complete listing of screening (or business case evaluation) criteria can be found in Philip A. Himmelfarb, *Survival of the Fittest* (Prentice Hall, 1992: 107–111).
9. Peter Strub and Steven Herman, "Can the Sales Force Speak for the Customer?" *Marketing Research* (Fall 1993): 5, no. 5, 32–35.

Chapter Seven

The New
Product Project

Developing and defending a new-product business case can be
an intimidating task for many product managers. This chapter
examines the business case development and the shepherding
of the concept to a commercialized product.

Business Case

When a relevant idea is identified, the product manager is
charged with developing a "business case" that justifies pursuing the opportunity. The business case is a skeleton plan that
provides the financial, competitive, and market justification for
the project. It is essentially an economic proposal for an investment, and it should build from the type of research described
in Section One. It is sometimes helpful to think of a business
case in the context of an entrepreneur compiling a business
plan in an effort to get venture capital.

Depending on the risk and/or financial requirements of a
prospective new product, the product manager may need to
make a formal presentation of the idea to management. In that
case, it's important to identify the "hot buttons" of each person
prior to the meeting and come prepared to address them. Top
management will be interested in the return (expressed by NPV
or IRR) and payback. Sales executives will want to know the
strengths of the product, as compared with the competition.

Operations executives will be concerned about design complexity and manufacturability. Consequently, the product manager must present a clear opportunity assessment, proposed benefits and costs, risk (and measures to contain them) assumptions, alternatives, and an implementation plan. The goal is to provide a rational basis to use in making the decision about whether to invest in the new product concept.

The business case typically will contain most of the following components.[1] While most executives will jump to the financials, product managers must realize that the revenues and cash flows are meaningless without realistic forecasts based on a solid understanding of the market.

1. *Executive Summary:* A brief synopsis of the idea and proposed plan.
2. *Present Situation:* An assessment of the corporate fit and the portfolio fit, along with the reasons this new product is being considered at this particular time.
3. *Product Description:* The specific user benefits and advantages of the product along with how the product fits into the company's total offering, with photos, illustrations, or other techniques to make the concept more tangible. Incorporate scope and boundary definitions, as appropriate.
4. *Market Analysis:* An assessment of current and future market(s) for the product, competitive conditions and positioning, and any regulatory concerns. It may be a good idea to include a best-case and worst-case scenario.
5. *Assumptions and Uncertainties:* What happens if assumptions change? What would a sensitivity analysis do to the numbers?
6. *Product Development Plan:* Any resources or technology required for the proposed product (Who will be the core team?) that can be a key to credibility.
7. *Marketing Plan:* The objectives and strategies for each area of marketing, including pricing, distribution, advertising, sales, and product support.
8. *Financial Analyses:* Projected cash flows and income statements and anticipated funds required. What justification

can you provide for the cash flows? Might graphs generate better understanding than tables of numbers?

9. *Supporting Documents:* Marketing research summaries or any other material that supports the project.
10. *Implementation Plan*

Initial Market Opportunity Identification

Ideas that make it to the business case phase are refined and converted into more realistic product concepts. Here, the product manager is heavily involved in: (1) determining the appropriate features and attributes to maximize customer satisfaction and acceptance, (2) identifying the relevant target price, and (3) revising estimates of sales potential and profitability. It's important that these activities be integrated. Changes in attributes may cause a target price to be unattainable, and the realized price may change the willingness to buy (a key factor in sales volume). A holistic perspective of these factors must be present in defining product features to minimize future change orders. Otherwise, conflict between product managers and project managers is likely to occur.

Start with secondary data. Conduct online searches to get more information on market characteristics, trends, and competition. Look for any purchasable marketing research studies that have been conducted on the market. If relevant, conduct patent searches to ferret out potential future competitors. Talk with industry experts and potential customers to assess attitudes toward the product idea. Getting market input from "typical" customers is appropriate for many line extensions, whereas getting input from lead users is important for innovative products. Both are important for attaining voice of the customer (see Business Brief 7.1).

Table 7.1 shows a hypothetical spreadsheet defining the market opportunity for high definition television (HDTV). The first column lists the market potential by year, as calculated from a variety of key variables. The second column contains the total population, as defined by relevant demographics in census data. The technology realization column lists the probability that technology would be available during that year to enable an

Table 7.1 Example Market Opportunity Forecasting

Time Period T	Market Potential	Population Base	Technology Realization	HDTV Awareness	Program Availability	Intention To Buy	Average $ Price	Analogy Market Growth Penetration	
	(TV households 000)		(Judgmental indices)			(Market survey data)		(Color TV growth)	
Model	Pot =	pop ×	tek ×	awr ×	avl ×	buy	pri	% of pot	pen
Year 1	698	93,000	0.50	0.25	0.50	0.12	2,000	.50	349
Year 2	1,488	93,930	0.55	0.40	0.60	0.12	2,000	.52	774
Year 3	3,287	94,869	0.60	0.55	0.70	0.15	1,800	.48	1,578
Year 4	5,232	95,818	0.70	0.65	0.80	0.15	1,800	.51	2,668
Year 5	10,452	96,776	0.80	0.75	0.90	0.20	1,600	.47	4,912
Year 6	17,281	97,744	0.85	0.80	1.00	0.26	1,400	.48	8,295

Condensed from Robert J. Thomas, *New Product Development: Managing and Forecasting for Strategic Success* (John Wiley, 1993;174).

Business Brief 7.1   Customer input in identifying market opportunities.

Lead users—companies or individuals with more *extreme* or *demanding* needs for a product—are important sources of innovative product ideas. More representative customers provide more input for line extensions, concept development, and life-cycle sales forecasts. But all contribute the "voice of the customer" to new product development projects.

Toshiba America Medical Systems has developed strong relationships with leading U.S. medical institutions to better understand the market opportunity for medical imaging products. They took advantage of a physician advocate and ally at Johns Hopkins to establish a group of thought leaders and leading medical experts. The team sits on Toshiba's advisory board, reviewing beta products and pushing innovation.

Procter & Gamble, on the other hand, is interested in both innovations and improvements to existing products and marketing strategies. In April 2005, they instituted their first annual "Consumer Is Boss" event to solicit new product ideas. One idea from a 7-year-old girl was to have consumers vote for the next flavor of Crest. As a result, there will be a Web-vote to select between lemon, berry, and tropical fruit flavors to extend Crest Whitening Expressions™.

The Iams managers of P&G also learned that some pet owners added treats (table scraps) to their dry dog food to induce older pets to eat it. Follow-up quantitative research revealed that 40% of owners used such methods. So the brand launched Savory™ as a more nutritious alternative to table scraps.

Although multiple approaches can be used, product managers should continually challenge themselves to focus on why people do the things they do—and the relevant competition at those times—and use the information in product development and marketing. Clayton Christensen, author of *The Innovator's Solution*, suggests that the reason many products fail is because managers don't look at markets the way customers experience life. For example, when a fast-food chain wanted to improve their milk-shake sales and profits, they first asked customers whether the shakes should be thicker, chunkier, or have different flavors. They made the changes requested by customers, but nothing happened. They brought in another group of researchers who discovered that most of the customers consumed shakes to make a long, boring commute easier. Since it could take 20 minutes to sip the shake through a thick straw, it relieved the boredom of the trip. The competition

(continued on next page)

Business Brief 7.1 continued

was not just other shakes but also "boredom, bagels, bananas, doughnuts, instant breakfast drinks and, possibly, coffee." The new perspective changed the new product concepts.

Source: John Zimmer, "How to Win a Marquee Account," *Sales and Marketing Management* (February 2004): 72. Jack Neff, "P&G Kisses up to the Boss: Consumers," *Advertising Age* (May 2, 2005): 18. Clayton M. Christensen and Michael E. Raynor, "Creating a Killer Product," *Forbes* (October 13, 2003): 82.

acceptable level of product quality. HDTV awareness was a subjective estimate of the percentage of target customers aware of the product. Program availability referred to the estimated percentage of broadcast time devoted to HDTV programming. The intention-to-purchase at a given price was based on survey data. Given that this spreadsheet was developed when HDTV was an innovation (as opposed to a line extension), it's reasonable to look at the yearly market penetration of an analogous product, in this case, color TV. Multiplying all the variables together yields a product in the first column that is a calculated estimate of market potential by year.

Concept Development and Voice of the Customer

To refine the understanding of the market need, solicit input from key customers who are knowledgeable and cooperative. These customers don't have to be representative, but they do have to be willing to suggest improvements and modifications to the initial concept. Probe for specific modifications that could affect the sales potential of the product. What if certain features were enlarged? Minimized? What if the product was harder? Softer? What if the dimensions were more standardized? More customized? Is color important? How about location? Get as much input from these key informants as possible.

In some cases, this type of qualitative research using a small sample is sufficient to develop the concept. In other cases, a larger sample is required to fully understand needs.

Once the concept is more fully developed, it is important to test it among a large group of customers. This group will be more representative of the target market. No one best approach exists to concept testing, but most are variations of qualitative research and focus-group discussions. Generally, several versions of a concept (possibly including competitors or placebo concepts) or several different product concepts that address the same need (i.e., substitutes) are explored in one concept test. This is because people usually provide better information when comparing alternatives, and the resulting information is more reliable than absolute evaluation. Mock ads, product descriptions on cards, drawings of the concept, and rough prototypes can all be used as part of the research. In some cases, the product's technical documentation and owner's manual is part of this analysis.

Some of the questions to be addressed during the concept test include:

- Does the proposed concept make sense to the customers?
- Is it preferred over what is currently available?
- How much value do the improvements have over existing alternatives available to the customer?
- Is the product consistent with the way customers currently perform the function, or will it require a change in mindset?
- Would they be willing to pay more?
- What are the flaws?
- Are there changes that would make the product viable (or more viable)?
- What is the basic need that this product will satisfy?
- Has the brand name or trademark been included in the concept test?

Intention-to-Buy

The concept tests usually include some indication of intent to buy at some specified price. "Intent to buy" refers to the respondents' indication of the probability that they would buy the product if it existed, usually expressed along a scale (e.g., 1 = "definitely would not buy" to 5 = "definitely would buy"). This is an important component of the concept test, but it should not be projected literally as the actual sales potential. Customers will almost always overestimate their willingness to buy in an artificial setting such as a focus group. Obtaining pricing information is difficult at best. However, determining a target price is critical for establishing a target cost for the product-development process. Although no research method is infallible, a few techniques are worth trying.

One approach is to ask customers to supply a price range: What is the highest price you'd pay, above which you'd feel you were being gouged? What is the lowest price you'd pay, below which you'd question the quality of the product? Another approach is to split the concept test groups into experimental and control groups. Give each group a different price for the same described concept and determine whether differences are present in the willingness to buy at the stated prices. A third strategy is to ask customers what value (in monetary terms) the new product would have over what they are currently using. A final approach is to ask customers what they would be willing to pay for the product and what features they would be willing to give up to attain that price. In each case, an intent-to-buy question should be included.

At this point, the product team should attempt to establish a target price. The target price is necessary to estimate target costs for the developmental process. "Design by price" is an approach used by several companies in industries with rapidly changing technologies, short life cycles, and pressure on pricing.

The target price depends on the value perceived by the market. Determining value will be different for low-unit-value, frequently purchased items (e.g., consumer packaged goods) than for high-priced, infrequently purchased goods (e.g., capital equipment). The purchase of consumer packaged goods has an element of habit and inertia in the decision process. Higher-priced products may have groups or committees involved in the process. The differences in decision making, as well as the different decision makers, must be included in the analysis.

Moving toward Specifications

By this time, the team should be able to list and display all the potential product features in a concept development table similar to Table 7.2. The table shows an example of a bicycle

Table 7.2   Example Concept Development Table

1 Needs	2 Importance	3 Initial Metrics	4 Competitor A	5 Competitor B	6 Revised Metrics
Lightweight		Total mass in kg.			
Can withstand rain and water contamination		Time in spray chamber without water entry			
Safe in a crash		Bending strength of materials			
Easy to install		Average time to assemble			
Works with a variety of attachments		List of attachment and sizes			
Competitively priced		Target cost range			

Adapted from Kent Ulrich and Steven Eppinger, *Product Design and Development* (New York: McGraw-Hill, 1995): 54–65.

frame. The first column lists the needs as identified through customer and lead-user research. Note that the needs are what the customer wants to get out of using the product (the benefits), rather than how it is to be designed. The second column contains the ranking or rating of importance of each identified need. The third column converts the benefits into targets or goals for the designers to use in developing the frame. For example, the desired mass in kilograms provides direction (i.e., a goal) without specifying materials or production techniques. Also, the target cost range is determined by starting with the target price(s) and deducting an acceptable margin. Columns 4 and 5 list the metrics for the major competitive products. By comparing the initial and competitive metrics with the importance ratings supplied by the market, adjustments may need to be made in column 6. The final revised metrics are the output of the concept development and testing phase. Since this point represents a milestone in the new-product development process, the initial review committee should sign off to indicate their acceptance of the metrics, in effect freezing the benefit set (although actual product specifications won't be frozen until after prototype development).

It can be difficult to complete the concept development table for breakthrough products. Customers (whether consumers or industrial buyers) do not have competitive products to use to set their benchmark price. Therefore, the analysis must start with the function being provided by the product. How is that function being done now without the benefit of the new product or service? What benefits and costs are related to changing the way it is done now? Then, both the rational and emotional motives for switching to the new product must be considered and valued.

To estimate a target price, several things must be considered, specifically the possibility of competitive attack, the price sensitivity of the market, and the degree of competitive differentiation. Figure 7.1 shows a tree diagram with the considerations in new-product pricing. For example, if the target

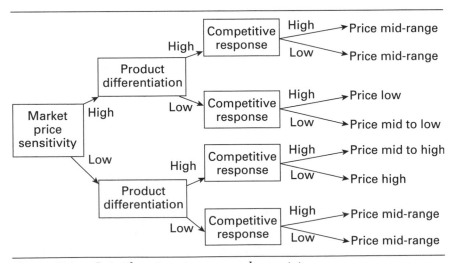

Figure 7.1   Considerations in new product pricing.

customers are not price sensitive, the product is highly differentiated, and competitive response is not expected, it is conceivable to charge a relatively high price. On the other hand, if the price sensitivity is high, product differentiation low, and competition heavy, a low price will be necessary.

The appropriate technical people should be involved in the concept testing to assess the technological feasibility of any suggestions that customers might make. The concepts that appear to have marketing, technical, and financial feasibility are then subjected to a more detailed business analysis.

Projected Financial Analysis

A rough business case may have been prepared prior to the preliminary idea screening, and it will have been refined concurrently with the concept testing. It should be continually evaluated and made more definitive as new information becomes available. At minimum, it should be updated whenever a significant milestone has been reached. The skeleton business plan presented at the beginning of the process can now have some of the gaps filled in. The product description should now be more detailed, with marketing and cost objectives included. The market analysis should have more specifics on potential segments and niches, customer applications and key customer identification, and competitive benchmarks. The product-development plan should include the composition of the project team, product specifications, a critical path chart with key milestones and target dates, and implementation schedules. The marketing plan should specify planned rollouts, short- and long-term resource requirements, identified risk factors, and suggestions for minimizing risk. The financial analyses should be expanded to include more detailed income statement and cash-flow information than was available at the proposal stage. Table 7.3 shows a simplified projected financial analysis for a hypothetical industrial product.

The revenue line is based on the market analysis and resulting forecast. The cost of goods sold is obtained from technical and manufacturing personnel on the product-development team. The accuracy depends not only on their best assessment

Table 7.3   Projected Financial Analysis

	Year 0	Year 1	Year 2	Year 3	Year 4	Year 5
Revenue	0	10,700	13,843	17,689	25,428	29,242
Less cost of goods sold	0	3,583	4,635	5,923	8,515	9,792
Gross margin	0	7,117	9,208	11,766	16,913	19,450
Development costs	−3,150	0	0	0	0	0
Marketing costs	0	7,200	5,814	7,430	10,679	12,281
Allocated overhead	0	1,070	1,384	1,764	2,548	2,924
Gross contribution	−3,150	−1,153	2,010	2,572	3,691	4,245
Supplementary contribution	0	0	0	0	0	0
Net contribution	−3,150	−1,153	2,010	2,572	3,691	4,245
Discounted contribution (15%)	−3,150	−1,003	1,520	1,691	2,111	2,110
Cumulative discounted cash flow	−3,150	−4,153	−2,633	−942	1,169	3,279

of per-unit costs, but also on the precision of the product manager's sales forecasts. The difference between the revenue and cost of goods sold is the gross margin available to cover fixed costs and contribute to profits.

The development costs include any costs already incurred for R&D and concept testing, as well as anticipated costs for prototype development, equipment and materials, labor, product testing, and additional marketing research. If the roll-out requires additional capital expenditures, they should be included here as well.

The marketing costs start at the prelaunch. These include advertising, distribution, sales force coverage, sales promotion, and any miscellaneous selling and communication costs.

Allocated overhead refers to administrative costs allocated to various products. Some companies will assess a lower (or even no) overhead cost to new products until they have established themselves, while other companies believe that all products should provide an equal (or greater) contribution to fixed costs (i.e., a type of "hurdle"). Regardless of the company's attitude toward cost allocation, it is imperative that the estimated *revenue* (either price or number of units) is not artificially inflated simply to cover these costs.

The gross contribution is the amount of revenue remaining after development costs, marketing costs, and overhead costs are subtracted from gross margin. This is the amount of money that the product is expected to contribute to the indirect fixed costs of the firm and taxes and profit.

The supplementary contribution is used when new products have an effect (positive or negative) on existing products. The resulting cash flows should be included on this line and either added to or subtracted from the gross contribution to arrive at the net contribution. In Figure 7.1, gross contribution and net contribution were the same because the new product was not expected to have any impact on existing product sales.

The discounted contribution line shows the net present value of each net contribution figure, discounted at 15% per year. The last line shows the cumulative cash flows over time.

Before progressing to prototype development, it is important to revisit the questions that were used to evaluate the initial project and verify that it is still an attractive endeavor. If the new information gathered results in the project no longer passing the initial screening questions, the new product may need to be modified or cancelled. This can be a critical milestone when another go/no-go decision must be made.

Prototype Development

If the proposed product passes the concept test and evaluation, it moves into R&D and/or engineering to be developed into a physical product. Up until now, it existed only as a verbal description or a rough mock-up. Now, it must be translated into a technologically feasible product. This does not mean that marketing (or product management) is no longer involved. Rather, the product manager's job is to ensure that the core benefits that were the essence of the product concept are not lost during the development process and that progress is being made on the marketing plan, trade-name search, and other factors critical to new-product success. That is why a project team approach is so crucial.

After the prototypes have been developed, they should be put to rigorous functional and customer testing. The functional tests are conducted under both laboratory and field conditions to be sure the products are safe and reliable (i.e., consistently perform as they are designed to perform). Customer tests are conducted to be sure that the design is appropriate. Market testing, in-home testing, and beta testing are all variations of the types of tests to be performed at this stage.

> Some manufacturers have built gigantic mechanical gizmos that can replicate almost any kind of abuse a product encounters. For example, a car takes a trip through Chrysler's huge climate-controlled lab where robotic drivers subject it to scorching heat and ice storms. Gerber recruits future customers of both sexes at birth and, with the help of enthusiastic parents, maintains a test panel of 2,500 toddlers through age 3.
>
> In order to make its PowerBooks even more customer-proof, Apple Computer puts all new models through common indignities. These include drenching them in Pepsi and other sodas, smearing them with mayonnaise, and, to simulate conditions in a car trunk, baking them in ovens at temperatures of 140 degrees or more.[2]

The selection of appropriate beta sites can have an impact on launch success for several reasons. First, the companies or individuals selected should have sufficient knowledge to thoroughly test the product and identify any potential problems or improvements. Second, they should have "reference value" to use as success stories at the time of launch. Third, they should have good relations with the salesperson in the territory, as well as with the company, to be able to withstand the risk of product failure without long-term damage.

Some questions to be answered during this stage are:

· Does the prototype work as intended?
· Does it meet specs?
· Does it satisfy customer needs?

- Are production problems anticipated? Can they be overcome within a reasonable time and cost?
- Has production scheduling been finalized? Is it on schedule?
- Have costs been confirmed?
- Have raw materials been ordered?
- Can minor modifications improve the product or its value without adversely impacting the project?
- Will a need for a significant change necessitate a delay in the project?

If all these questions can be answered positively, the product specifications should be frozen, and the management review committee (i.e., top functional positions) should sign off to indicate their acceptance of the specifications. Then, the project is ready to move to the prelaunch, as discussed in the next chapter.

Checklist: The New Product Project

- Write the business case to serve as a proposal for a new product investment.
- Prepare to present the business case by identifying the *hot buttons* of everyone on the management team *prior* to the meeting.
- Use appropriate customers for input into line extensions versus breakthroughs.
- Estimate price, and use it as part of the concept description when gathering intention-to-buy data.
- Develop your financials based on realistic sales forecasts.
- Test the prototype with knowledgeable and cooperative users who will provide honest input on functionality.
- Know the market and what it needs.
- Select new products that play to a company's core strengths.
- Create a multifunctional project team early in the process.
- Get an early fix on costs and price.
- Get quality and price right the first time, even if it means delaying the launch.

- Build checkpoints into the system to make sure the developing product still meets the initial criteria under which it was approved.
- Do not introduce a new product simply to meet a new-product goal; be sure that it fits the corporate strategy and customer requirements.
- Freeze the product concept (i.e., obtain commitment on what benefits it will provide the customer) after the concept development stage.
- Freeze the product specifications after successful prototype development.
- Conduct alpha, beta, or market tests to gather user input.

Interview with Steven Haines, Founder and President of Sequent Learning Networks

Steven has over 24 years of experience and has worked in the technology, health care, industrial products, and defense electronics industries. Prior to founding Sequent Learning, he served as Senior Director of Product Management at Oracle.

Q: *In a nutshell, could you describe Sequent Learning Networks? How did it get started?*

A: Sequent Learning Networks was started because we recognized a need to reduce the variability with which product management is practiced across industries, across organizations, and even within different lines of business in the same company. Another driver, which became apparent to us during our corporate careers, was the difficulty we found in finding qualified people to put in charge of the product lines for which we were responsible.

Q: *What major changes have you noted in the product management discipline over the past 5 years?*

A: Best-in-class product management puts the product manager at the center of all activities related to the management of products and services. However, after many years of mergers, downsizings, and a variety of other economic influences, the actual practice of product management seems to have been marginalized. Those who had many years of experience found themselves unemployed. In a nutshell, the means for the transfer of knowledge and experience—essential elements for sustaining the discipline of product management—evaporated in many companies. Emphasis was placed on product development or engineering, or brute-force selling. We believe many companies in many industries eroded their ability to observe and sense markets, competitors, and customers. Products were developed without clear value propositions, as pet projects from other functions were pushed into the market.

What we see now is a marked shift in the attention to this critical profession. One of the most outstanding opportunities for companies to consider is that product managers who lead cross-functional business teams, own the P&L for their product, and understand the operational dimensions of their businesses, are building the essential skills and experiences required to become the future business leaders and executives. What better candidates could you possibly want to put into those leadership roles?

Q: *What will be the primary challenges for product managers in the next decade?*

A: Product managers need to really understand what is required to do their jobs. They should demonstrate a strong, entrepreneurial, self-initiating style. They need to have a powerful feel for people, processes, and the tools needed to plan, commercialize, and optimize the performance of their products. (A little charisma never hurt, either!) They need to understand and practice the disciplines of strategy, product planning, and financial planning and analysis. Moreover, they really need to understand the multidimensional characteristics of the industries within which they operate, the competitive influences, and should demonstrate sharp customer orientation in their everyday business lives so that they can continually fine-tune their market segmentation models and watch ever-shifting targets. These insightful skills need to be underscored through the cultivation of critical leadership skills. To summarize, product managers should demonstrate clarity of vision; knowledge about their products and the needs satisfied by those products; the markets within which they operate, as well as others, which may represent new opportunities; their customers (past and current); strategies; metrics; their stakeholders; and the numbers!

Q: *What advice can you give product managers about coping with these challenges?*

A: Take initiative, and manage your products as if they were your own business. Know the basics of business, including the numbers, and recognize that functionally aligned organizations tend to process information in a serial fashion, so you'll really need to know how to break down those barriers and build true cross-functional business teams. If you know what drives customer needs, you'll be in a better position to figure out how to meet those needs—in the most creative, innovative ways possible. Finally, help everyone you can. Share information across the business functions so that everyone knows where you're headed.

For more information about Sequent Learning Networks, refer to http://www.sequentlearning.com/.

Notes

1. A good discussion of the components of a business case, particularly from a financial perspective, can be found in Marty Schmidt, *The Business Case Guide*, 2nd edition (Boston, MA: Solution Matrix, Ltd., 2002).
2. Faye Rice, "Secrets of Product Testing," *Fortune* (November 28, 1994): 88–95.

Chapter Eight

Crafting a Launch Strategy

The deadline is approaching. Stress is rising. A mix of excitement and worry fills the air as the launch date gets closer. Will the product be ready for shipment in time? Have all the ancillary activities been planned for? Will there be any surprises? This is a launch *process*—and the launch is actually a journey rather than the destination. The product manager is the tour guide who ensures that a strong new product doesn't fail due to a poorly executed launch. It's been said that a new product project is like climbing a mountain. The team is enthused and energized as progress is made toward reaching the summit (i.e., the product is developed). But the team still has to trek down the hill (i.e., launch the product successfully). By then, they are tired, hungry, and ready for the trip to be over. It's at this point that the product manager has to generate a new "buzz"—with sales staff, the channel, and with customers.

Although the launch is being planned from the moment the original idea *passes go*, now the action moves forward at a quicker, more deliberate pace. This chapter focuses on the activities of launch preparation (pre-launch), the launch considerations when introducing the product to the sales force and channel, and the follow-through activities after launch to track progress and improve processes.

Pre-Launch

The pre-launch is that period prior to commercialization when the product manager verifies that all preparations have been made for the actual product introduction. If market testing is necessary, it will be conducted at this point to evaluate the validity of the proposed marketing strategy. During this stage, the product manager must identify all stakeholders and determine their information requirements. Customer service must be prepared to handle inquiries and fulfill orders. Technical support personnel may require specialized training. The distribution channel may require advance notice of any unique requirements of the product or service.

Market Testing

Beta testing of the product, as mentioned in chapter 6, is an effort to "debug" a product under real-world conditions. These use tests already should have determined the viability of the *product*, but they might not have addressed the best way to go to market. In that case, a market test or a simulated market test of the launch strategy (not just the product) may be necessary. Test marketing helps assess whether the right price is being charged, whether the appropriate message is being communicated, and whether the proper distribution strategy is being employed. Of course, test marketing is expensive in terms of both money and time—and in terms of alerting competition to your launch strategy. Therefore, it should be undertaken only when the risk of not doing it is great.

For a typical test market, the product manager selects a geographic area that is as representative of the product's target market as possible and markets the product on a limited basis in that region. The key decisions to be made include how many test markets, which ones, and how long the tests should run. Most companies select two or three test markets that provide good representation of their target customers. *Good representation* refers to assuring that critical demographic variables are dispersed in the target area in about the same proportion as they exist in the total market area. The length of the test market will vary depending on the type of product. Some will require 6 to 9 months, and others will need 2 years. The factor to consider is the length of the buying cycle, with the test market being at least as long as two buying cycles.[1]

Identify the "What-If?" Items

Few launches occur without any glitches. So it's useful to go back to the beginning and retrace your steps to look for omissions. Develop a pre-launch checklist (perhaps like that shown in Table 8.1) to help you stay on track. The checklist should identify responsible parties and reaffirm launch readiness.

Start with a reality check on the product itself. It's almost a given that the end product is not exactly the same as the original idea. Determine whether the product still provides the benefits it was designed for. Make sure there is a clear understanding of the target market it is best suited for. If changes have occurred in the market or the competition since inception, verify that competitive superiority still exists.

The packaging is one of the first "contacts" a customer has with your product, so you want to be sure it is appropriate. When the cholesterol-lowering Lipitor was launched in the late 1990s, it was considered one of the most successful pharmaceutical launches ever. And the company credits part of the success to the literature contained within the package.

> Look at the literature in the package insert that compares Lipitor with each of its major competitors in the power to lower cholesterol and triglycerides. There is probably more food for comparative promotion than most products would have in a complete life cycle. That demonstrates the outstanding job performed by our clinical development and marketing teams working in collaboration, even up to the point of launch.[2]

Regulatory approvals are critical to most products in the health care industry, and these can delay a launch if not obtained on time. If a product is being launched globally, separate approvals may be required for individual countries. Verify systems readiness from IT, production, technical support, and

Table 8.1   Launch Readiness Worksheet

	Who?	Due Date	Contingencies
Product reality check			
Does it fulfill the original idea?			
Does it still fit the market?			
Is there competitive superiority?			
Packaging			
Will it facilitate storage, use, transport, and convenience?			
Does it provide customer-friendly information?			
Regulatory approvals and standards			
Have all country, governmental, and industry approvals been obtained?			
Can you demonstrate compliance and efficacy?			
Systems readiness			
Is IT ready for ordering and billing?			
Are preliminary production runs complete?			
Service and tech support			
Is infrastructure in place?			
Warranty programs ready?			
Service programs defined?			
Spare parts, loaners, upgrade tools?			
Logistics			
Process map for physical movement to customer's location			
Marketing decisions			
Pricing policies by market			
Roll-out sequence planned			
Marketing communications on track			
Marketing support			
Sales and customer service training set			
Kick-off events and activities planned			
Collateral material ready			

other operations groups. Be sure that your warranty program is clear, and claims can be handled if necessary.

You also should verify marketing readiness. Pricing policies, including distributor discount programs and internal transfer programs, should be in place. Your roll-out strategy should be finished, with priority markets identified. Your advertising group (whether internal or external) should be ready with the appropriate marketing communications at launch. Sales support—including training, kick-off events, contests, short-term incentives, collateral, and so forth—should be on track.

Launch Preparation Documentation

In addition to the pre-launch checklist, other preparatory documents might be relevant. Four specific components to consider are: (1) market and product profiles, (2) a milestone activities chart, (3) the marketing strategy to support the launch, and (4) an early indicator chart with control plan. All of these guide the launch and early commercialization.

The market and product profiles are critical components of the launch. The market profile should define the focused market of *ideal* customers, using as many segmentation variables from Chapter 2 as are appropriate. Describe both the rational and emotional reasons the customer would be interested in buying this product. Explain the customer's decision and purchase process(es), and possibly the role of influencers. Unfortunately, too many product managers list all markets that might someday buy the product in an attempt to build enthusiasm for its many applications and uses. But claiming that the product solves all the world's problems, and everyone is a potential customer yields rolled eyes and cynicism in the sales force. This shot-gun approach squanders resources and dilutes the sales effort.

The product profile works in concert with the market profile to clarify the customer-based value. It explains what the product is and why it's better than the competition, and then goes on to provide proof of the claims. If different value exists for different markets, it's worth noting that here. Pharmaceutical brand managers realize the importance of establishing clear value by stakeholder, as explained in Business Brief 8.1.

The milestone activities chart lists the desired dates of completion for significant activities such as purchasing equipment for the launch, finalizing package design, obtaining legal clearance, subcontracting specialized labor, and preparing the

Business Brief 8.1 Establishing brand value in early launch.

According to conventional wisdom in the pharmaceutical industry, a new brand has 120 days after launch to create momentum. Therefore, product managers must establish a clear value proposition for all relevant stakeholders during the pre-launch time period. Patients who purchase the product in the pharmacies are looking for relief from some ailment. Managed-care professionals purchasing the product for in-hospital use are concerned with reimbursement issues. Physicians purchasing the product for clinic use want relief from paperwork and clear proof of efficacy. Value and benefits must be expressed in terms relevant to these particular audiences.

Product managers also should identify markets that may be resistant to the new product, and build in appropriate contingency plans.

In the 1990s, Merck promoted its new agent, Proscar (finasteride) as a way to enable primary care physicians to treat benign prostatic hypertrophy (BPH), thereby sparing older men

a painful, invasive surgical procedure known as a trans-urethral prostatectomy (TURP). The problem was that men with BPH were treated by urologists, a large portion of whose incomes came from performing the procedure. They refused to surrender their patients and fought against Proscar, which never fully overcame their resistance.

Similar concepts of segmented brand value can apply to other products as well. Tools aimed at do-it-yourselfers versus professional contractors must address different levels of competency, price sensitivity, and channel—even if the product is essentially the same. Products being launched into different countries must be "glocalized" to meet specific value requirements. And the roles of users, decision makers, payers, channel members, and other influences must be considered as well.

Source: Adapted from Roger Green and J. Martin Jemigan, "Building Brand Value," *Pharmaceutical Executive* (September 2004): 36–45.

owner's manual. Each of these may require several steps and may vary in importance, depending on the project. Their potential impact on product success must be considered in assessing priority. For example, electronic or high-tech consumer products require clarity in technical documentation to be successful. Customers are increasingly seeking simplicity in a complicated world. Unfortunately, as a *BusinessWeek* article stated, "Plain English is a language unknown in most of the manuals that are supposed to help us use electronic products."[3] The format of the milestone activities chart can vary from a simple list of activities and dates to more formal project schedule and control techniques like Gantt and PERT charts.

The marketing component of the launch materials details the branding, packaging, pricing, advertising, and related topics. As with the annual product plan, the new-product marketing plan should start with an objective such as "Convert 25% of current customers to the product upgrade and obtain trial by an additional 25%." The marketing tactics then would be put into place to accomplish this objective. A sample outline for this new-product marketing strategy is shown as Table 8.2. Some companies include all or most of the listed components; others must be more selective. Line extensions might require only an abbreviated outline, whereas breakthrough products will need extensive marketing strategy plans.

As mentioned earlier, a decision then must be made whether to price a product high initially to recover the development costs or to price it low to gain market share faster. Now you have more information than was available early in the process, and you are able to fine-tune the pricing. A number of factors affect this decision. First, how likely is it that competitors will enter the market soon? The ability of competitors to enter the market will be based on the investment required to enter, the ease of entering, and their own strategies. The faster that competition is likely to enter, the more appropriate a penetration (low) price strategy. Second, is a large enough segment of customers willing to pay a high price for the product initially? Third, is the company, product, or service positioned appropriately for the price strategy being considered? Finally, what

Table 8.2   The Supporting New-Product Marketing Plan

A. New-product objectives
   1. Sales volume
   2. Market penetration
B. Background summary
   1. Total industry sales volume and trends
   2. Major competitors and analysis
   3. Market potential and segments
   4. Corporate charter
C. The company's new product/service
   1. Product specifications/description
   2. Brand name, trade name, and/or trademark
   3. Why is your product better?
   4. Main user benefits
   5. Customer profile(s)
   6. Primary selling points
   7. Positioning
   8. Potential barriers
   9. Frequency of purchase/use
D. Entry strategy
   1. Timing: when should the launch be planned?
   2. Roll-out sequence: what are the priority markets?
   3. Publicity
E. Company support/preparation
   1. Internal announcements
   2. Sales force tools
   3. Customer service training
   4. Technical support training
   5. Field seminars
   6. Policy statements
F. Marketing plan
   1. Product marketing objectives
   2. Target markets

   • New or existing customers
   • Demographics; psychographics
   3. Distribution
      • Channels (including Internet)
      • Mark-ups/commissions/other incentives
      • Available selling tools
   4. Pricing
      • Base price and discount schedule
      • Promotional pricing programs
      • Option pricing
      • Product-line pricing
   5. Promotion
      • Sampling
      • Merchandising
      • Customer training
   6. Advertising
      • Product announcements
      • Press releases
      • Trade shows
      • User groups
      • Direct mail
      • Advertising (media and copy strategy)
G. Cost and schedules
   1. Development of sales support
   2. Training costs (including lodging and travel)
   3. Trade shows
   4. Media and advertising costs
   5. Sampling and merchandising costs
   6. Calendar of training schedules
   7. Media calendar
   8. Event schedule

are the payback period, "hurdle rates," and return required by the company?

The final component of the launch documentation (after completing the milestone activities chart and the various event calendars and schedules from the marketing plan) is a calendar of early indicators of potential launch success. Early indicators refer to outcomes, such as the number of inquiries, that can help predict or provide early indicators of the level of launch success. For example, history might indicate that 30 inquiries typically convert to one sale. In that case, tracking the number of inquiries could provide an early indicator of future sales. Other early indicators might include the number of sales calls made on the new product, the percentage of distributors willing to carry it, the awareness level of the market, the number of facings retailers give to the product, and so on. After identifying the early indicators, the next step is to set time-based (e.g., weekly, monthly) goals to achieve each outcome. The early indicator chart, then, lists the outcomes expected by the end of designated time periods (e.g., each month), enabling the product manager to compare actual against expected performance without waiting for final sales data.

With launch documentation prepared, the product is ready to move to the launch phase. It's worth noting that sales training may sometimes be required during the prelaunch phase (perhaps 6 to 9 months prior to the official launch), or it may be part of the launch process. The information on sales training is presented in the next section covering the launch stage.

Timing

Timing—whether relative to the competition or relative to seasonal or industry events—can be a critical component of new-product success. If competitors might be (or are) entering the market, the product manager must decide whether to get there before, with, or after the competition. First entry usually provides an advantage, but if rushing results in a flawed product, the result can be more damaging than good. According to Fernando Suarez and Gianvito Lanzolla in their *Harvard Business Review* article, "first-mover advantage is more than a myth but far less than a sure thing."[4] They argue that the combined effects of market and technological change affect a firm's chances of first-mover advantage. Specifically, gradual evolution in both the technology and market arenas provides the best conditions for lasting impact. On the other hand, abrupt changes in technology (or changes in both technology and markets) will give later entrants weapons to attack an early lead. The assessment of competitive response and market acceptance must be considered in timing and implementation decisions.

Timing an entry *with* competition can neutralize the competitor's potential first-mover advantage as well as possibly increase the potential market faster. Delaying an entry until after competition is in the market might make it possible to capitalize on competitive flaws as well as benefit from any competitive advertising that educates the market. Timing also is important if a product has seasonal or cyclical aspects or if success depends on visibility at a key "new products" trade show.

Decisions regarding timing should consider what impact the new product may have on the rest of the product line. Launching a product before components essential to its usability are available is premature timing. Similarly, launching substitute products must be appropriately timed. If substantial pipeline inventory is in the channel, you may want to postpone the launch until some of the old product has been sold. On the other hand, if a delayed launch risks a vacuum period, during which no inventory exists of either the old or the new product, it can create a period of potential advantage for the competition. In that case, plan a period of overlap, using pricing and/or channel strategy to differentiate the substitutes and minimize cannibalization. Timing can become a significant issue in the pharmaceutical industry when products are going off patent, as explained in Business Brief 8.2.

Geographic Strategy

It also is necessary to make decisions on a geographic strategy. On some occasions, a national or international launch is appropriate, but many new products start with a full roll-out strategy. Prioritize the markets (e.g., regions, industries, or countries) and decide on an entry sequence. For example, it might be desirable to first enter the most attractive markets in terms of size and dollar potential. Or, it might be more desirable to enter markets in which competition is weak, thus pro-

Business Brief 8.2   Product line planning for patent expiration.

With more than $80 million worth of blockbuster drugs approaching patent expiration by 2008, it's not surprising that 71% of pharmaceutical companies are aggressively pursuing life-cycle management tactics. This may include introducing generic versions, flanker brands, encouraging Rx-to-OTC switching, and extending the brand through follow-on product, reformulations, or new delivery systems. A fundamental question is how quickly customers will switch to generics, since that affects the timing of these decisions.

The acceptance of generics is growing. The Federal Trade Commission reports that between 1984 and 2002, the share of generic prescriptions has grown from 19% to 47%, with experts estimating it at over 50% today. According to Jon Hess, a senior analyst at Cutting Edge Information, "With so much riding on the right strategy, companies are really taking a closer look at what others have successfully

been doing in the industry. Right now, of the patent-protection strategies available, line extensions appear to offer companies the greatest potential for lucrative returns."

Bristol Myers Squibb, GlaxoSmithKline, Johnson & Johnson, and Pfizer have all explored or planned to authorize generics or flanker brands within the past couple of years. As an example, before Prilosec went off patent, AstraZeneca was able to successfully transfer 40% of the users to its new acid reducer, Nexium. While not all companies face the type of impact affecting pharmaceutical companies when their products go off patent, they can learn from the thought processes used for life-cycle management.

Source: Jon Hess, "Line Extensions: Most Common Patent-Protection Strategy," *PR Newswire* (March 2, 2005): 1; and Edward Tuttle, Andrew Parece, Anne Hector, "Your Patent Is About to Expire: What Now?" *Pharmaceutical Executive* (November 2004): 88+.

viding an ability to gain experience, exposure, and market position. The selection of roll-out markets also can be based on different product applications, pipeline inventory in the markets, ability to gain distributor or retailer support, company reputation in the market, or a host of other factors.

Although the roll-out might appear similar to test marketing, it differs in a couple of important ways. First, in a test market, the product manager targets regions that are representative of the final launch. This is not the case with a roll-out: Here, the markets are selected based on their ability to provide an early cash flow or to gain commitment from an influential market needed for the continued roll-out. Second, the test market is a final test *before* the commercialization decision is made. The roll-out occurs *after* the commercialization decision is made.[5]

Launch

The next step of the new-product development process—launch—results in the introduction of the product into the market. Here, the product manager's job is to educate, motivate, and keep the momentum going. Implementation will require putting the timing and geographic strategies into action. It will require training and providing incentives for the sales force and the channel. And it will require executing the communications plan previously engineered.

Sales Training

Whenever possible, identify clients and prospects by name. The more detail that can be provided here for the sales force, the greater the chances of encouraging them to sell the new product. Work closely with the sales force to provide them with information that will help them sell. Prepare "how to sell it" booklets that discuss customers (not target markets), applications (not features), and useful questions to ask on a sales call. Make sure that customer service stays in the loop, with sufficient communication through internal newsletters, informal and formal meetings, and various announcements.

The introductory marketing strategy details introductory pricing, base price, and option pricing; press releases and product announcements; direct mail and e-mail blasts to select customers; shipping policies and procedures; channel and end-user communications; and training for the sales force and/or customers. The sales training in particular should help sales staff *sell* the product rather than simply *pitch* the product (Figures 8.1 and 8.2).

Figure 8.1 Avoid the "pitch-the-product" launch.

The sales training that is part of the product launch should educate and motivate the sales staff to sell your product. In other words, why should the sales staff believe the product will perform as claimed? What motivation exists for them to sell it? For a modification of an existing product, the best proof is past sales success. For completely new products, a bit more persuasion is necessary. Results from test marketing or beta testing, statements from sales managers or other sales staff indicating their success in a roll-out region, sales that you (as product manager) have personally made, or trade shows and lead-generation programs in place can help convince sales staff that the product is worth their time and effort to pursue. In addition, financial and nonfinancial motivators should be considered. Higher commissions, better bonuses, and desirable contests can work under the right circumstances. Nonfinancial motiva-

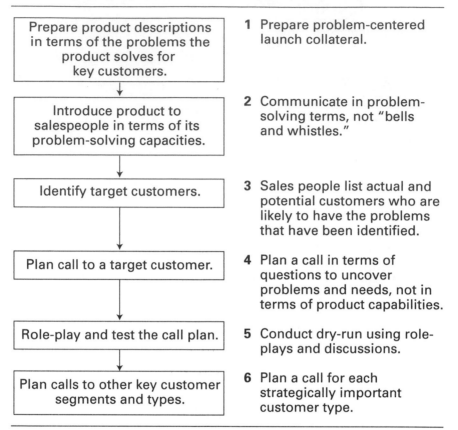

Figure 8.2   Provide need-centered sales training in the product launch.

tors could include customer input that suggests less sales effort is necessary to be successful, the ability to sell the product along with another product with a minimal increase in selling time, or unquestionable proof of competitive superiority.

Sales training also may need to extend to the channel. Distributors, dealers, and other resellers don't have the same vested interest in the new product that internal stakeholders might. Yet, they all play a crucial role in getting the product to target customers. Not only do these resellers need to believe it is a good business decision to make an investment in your new product, they also must be motivated to create the best environment to make the product a success. What training will their sales staff need? Will they need to provide technical training to their support personnel? How much inventory is necessary? Does the new product require minimum shelf space or specific shelf facings to be successful? Will the reseller need help in promoting the product? Some companies find that contests and additional funds are required to establish the "excitement" necessary to give the new product a chance to be successful (see Business Brief 8.3).

Business Brief 8.3   Launching a new product through a dealership network.

Many new products are sold through dealers, distributors, wholesalers, or retailers. These organizations have a significant impact on the launch process. They want new products that can increase revenues and profits from their customers, but sometimes need help in executing the plans. Chrysler, for example, has stepped up its efforts to launch a stream of new products and establish a closer cooperation with dealers. David Cole, Director of the Center for Automotive Research in Ann Arbor, Michigan, recognizes the importance of these relationships. "Chrysler has a lot of new products. The real problem is that everyone else does, too. It's how companies and dealers execute the other things that is going to make the difference between the winners and losers."

Starting in 2003, Chrysler rolled out a more comprehensive program to support new product launches through its 4,400 dealers. These dealers are independently minded entrepreneurs who have spent tens of millions of dollars on their operations and want assurance of the best future cars to invest in. Many dealers had complained that previous training and support materials were insufficient for their needs. The program, therefore, was designed with several components.

- Day-long "ride-and-drive" programs
- Salesperson certification after passing on-line course at dealership
- Competition with several $1,000 prizes
- Internet-based contests, with best scorers posted on an online leader board
- Collateral including pocket guides, laminated sell sheets, static-cling disks
- DVDs and other point-of-sale materials
- Programs to help dealers get customers back for future service

Another example of a launch process is the one that Cadillac used to introduce the Catera in the late 1990s. Even though the product was not as successful as hoped, nevertheless, insights

(continued on next page)

BUSINESS BRIEF 8.3   continued

can be obtained from the launch process. When Cadillac introduced the Catera (an entry-level luxury car), it had to shift from its existing market of older, loyal customers and appeal to a demographic segment unfamiliar to its dealers. To inspire dealerships to get behind this new product, it created Catera College. The college consisted of two-and-a-half days of sessions providing information about the new customer base and the vehicle itself. At the college, dealers drove the car and saw it taken apart piece by piece. For dealers who could not attend, Cadillac rented out theaters across the country. On the big screen, dealers were presented with an up-close look at their customers, as well as the teamwork involved in selling the product. While the training itself was not an incentive to sell the product, it provided the tools necessary to make the incentives (such as a contest) work, and both were tied to Cadillac's Standards for Excellence (SFE) awards.

Dealerships were awarded points for success in such categories as technician training, salesperson training, and customer service. Every month, each dealership receives its standing in the contest. The grand prize is a trip to an exotic locale with a twist. Just sending

winners to the beach to drink cocktails and watch the sun set is not part of Cadillac's game plan. The company has made intensive business seminars a major focus of the trip. [In 1997] when the Catera was being launched, the grand prize was a trip to Germany to see the Catera built.

SFE winners appreciate the dual purpose of the trip. "There are meetings in the morning to discuss ways to better your dealership. The goal is to get you to look at your store and find ways to improve it," says Ed Nimnicht, president and CEO of Nimnicht Cadillac in Jacksonville, Florida. "Then you get some leisure time to enjoy winning the contest."

Part of the product launch incorporated tests for dealers. They earned points for answering questions properly, and they had to demonstrate a minimum knowledge level to get into the program. In addition, selling the Catera was a requirement for dealers trying to win Cadillac's "Master Dealer Status."

Source: Adapted from Dale Buss, "Wheeling and Dealing," *Sales and Marketing Management* (February 2004): 36–41. Kenneth Hein, "Preparing for the Launch," *Incentive* (April 1997): 45–49.

Marketing Communications

The message and media strategy for a new product launch will follow many of the general issues for marketing communications as discussed in the next chapter, but some of the issues most critical to a new product launch strategy are mentioned here. When possible, public relations and publicity should be the first step in the new product communications strategy and should *precede* the launch date. The more differentiated and unique the product, the more valuable is the public relations effort. *Public relations* refers to the activities and events a company stages to attain media visibility. These can include, but are not limited to, open houses, tours, speeches, and sponsorships. The information presented in the media about these events, as well as the publishing of articles and press releases, is *publicity*.

Public relations and publicity should be the first communications tool used for products that offer *unique benefits* to customers. (In other words, this will generally be most effective for products that are more than minimally different line extensions or cost reduction efforts.) When Lipitor (an anticholesterol drug developed by Warner Lambert) was in the final stages of testing by the Food and Drug Administration (FDA), it teamed with the American Heart Association in a national cholesterol education program. Through this public relations effort, the company positioned itself as being concerned about cholesterol, thereby providing a solid position for the emergence of Lipitor.

Similarly, when Cutter launched the first insect repellent in the United Stated using picaridin instead of DEET, it had a limited budget and relied heavily on public relations. To gain support for picaridin, it worked with experts such as local health officials, the federal Centers for Disease Control and Prevention (CDC), and the World Health Organization (WHO). These associations gave credibility to the ingredient, and by association, to the product. The firm launched a non-branded Web site touting picaridin's benefits. Managers also attended a West Nile virus conference and encouraged the

CDC and WHO to include picaridin in their recommended products.[6]

A product manager can incorporate other components into a new-product public relations campaign:

- Develop press kits to be used at trade shows and other events. At minimum, these kits should contain beta test results (if available); white papers detailing the importance of the new product; corporate history, positioning, and background information; and copies of press releases.
- Draft articles for select publications explaining how their readers will benefit from this new product. To interest publishers in these types of articles, the product must be truly novel, and the article must provide information value to the reader beyond a sales pitch.
- Again, if the product is truly innovative, it may be possible to provide a demonstration as part of an educational session at a trade show.
- Issue press releases to appropriate media.

After public relations opportunities are exhausted, it's time to begin advertising in earnest. Although the public relations activities often precede the launch date, most of the advertising and other promotional activities coincide with launch. To be sure that happens, the planning must be completed prior to launch.

To begin the promotional communications, go back to your "best-prospect" profile, and determine the most critical benefit to emphasize. Lead the communications with *this* benefit for *this* particular market. Be sure to address the following in the communication:

- What will your product (service) do for the prospect? How will it do that?
- Why is it better than the competition?
- What proof do you have to make your claims credible?
- What can the prospects do if they are not satisfied with the purchase?

Note that the first question identifies the benefit, the second question provides the features that supply the benefit, and the third question demonstrates the advantages. This contains the same components as the typical Features, Advantages, Benefits (FAB) approach to sales training, but reorganizes them so that benefits are the most important thing presented to the prospect. The product manager is responsible for translating the positioning strategy mentioned earlier into a communications message for the customers, and for keeping the message relevant and current. Be sure to capture testimonials from any beta sites that may be useful in the launch. Then, the product manager determines how best to convey the message: through trade shows, the sales force and/or channels, print media, direct mail, electronic transmission, or other means. Targeted advertising in trade journals to coincide with the launch of the product at a trade show can be effective. Try to get your message in front of prospects multiple times through the creative use of potential media.

Direct-sales people will need various types of communications materials including internal (confidential) company information, sales tools they can use on calls, and marketing collateral they can give to customers. The internal documentation contains the product's sales objectives and positioning, along with competitive comparisons and, very likely, proprietary data. (This information may be placed on the corporate intranet as well as being distributed in print format.) The sales tools should be focused on helping the sales staff complete the sales call; therefore, the emphasis should be on *how to sell*. The collateral pieces should be written from the customer's perspective, following the FAB approach. (If the customer is a distributor, the material should focus on how the distributor will benefit from the product. If the customer is an end-user, the material should focus on end-user benefits.) Even when the customer is an end-user, different types of benefits may be relevant depending on the individual's level. Top managers, for example, are interested in how the new product will impact their bottom lines, whereas technical people may be more interested in data sheets. Too often, product managers provide only product features and benefits (relevant to technical people) and don't provide supporting material for sales staff to use with higher-level managers.

Indirect sales channels will have some differences. The company information will be focused more on the "partnership" or "relationship" between the manufacturer and the distributor and will not contain the confidential information. For high-margin products, videos and electronic self-testing modules may be beneficial—but only if the channel perceives a true value in the time commitment. The sales tools will very likely be shorter, with less detail. The collateral pieces should focus on end-user benefits. The percentage of the budget devoted to communications material for direct versus indirect channels will depend on the channel prioritization that is part of the launch strategy.

Post-Launch Evaluation

After (or during) the launch stage, some type of project appraisal should be completed. The main objectives of this stage are to improve future product development efforts and to move the product from a new-product status to being an ongoing product requiring long-term maintenance. Occasionally, it may be necessary to relaunch a product that is not meeting expectations. The relaunch should be considered as early as possible, and hopefully will have been uncovered by the early indicators (as discussed in the prelaunch section). If the product is still an acceptable product, changes to the marketing strategy may need to be made to make it a success. A contingency or control plan should be part of the launch materials. An example of a control plan is shown in Table 8.3.

In addition to evaluating the new product, it also is useful to evaluate the new-product development process. The best way to make improvements for the future is to compare and contrast successful and unsuccessful projects. By documenting your insights, you can increase the probability of success for other new products.

Table 8.3 Sample Control Plan

Potential Problem	Tracking	Contingency Plan
1. Sales staff fail to contact general-purpose market at a prescribed rate.	Track weekly call reports. The plan calls for at least 10 general-purpose calls per week per rep.	If activity falls below this level for 3 weeks running, a remedial program of 1-day district sales meetings will be held.
2. Sales staff may fail to understand how the new feature of the product relates to product usage in the general-purpose market.	Tracking will be done by having sales manager call one rep each day. Entire sales force will be covered in 2 months.	Clarification will be given to individual reps on the spot, but if first 10 calls suggest a widespread problem, special teleconference calls will be arranged to repeat the story to the whole sales force.
3. Potential customers are not making trial purchases of the product.	Track by instituting a series of 10 follow-up telephone calls a week to prospects who have received sales presentations. There must be 25% agreement on product's main feature and trial orders from 30% of those prospects who agree on the feature.	Remedial plan provides for special follow-up telephone sales calls to all prospects by reps offering a 50% discount on all first-time purchases.
4. Buyers make trial purchase but do not place quantity reorders.	Track another series of telephone survey calls, this time to those who placed an initial order. Sales forecast based on 50% of trial buyers reordering at least 10 more units within 6 months.	No remedial plan for now. If customer does not rebuy, some problem exists in product use. Since product is clearly better, we must know the nature of the misuse. Field calls on key accounts will be used to determine that problem, and appropriate action will follow.

(continued on next page)

Table 8.3 continued

Potential Problem	Tracking	Contingency Plan
5. Chief competitor may have the same new feature (for which we have no patent) ready to go and markets it.	This situation is essentially untrackable. Inquiry among our suppliers and media will help us learn more quickly.	Remedial plan is to pull out all stops on promotion for 60 days. A make-or-break program. Full-field selling on new item only, plus a 50% first-order discount and two special mailings. The other trackings listed above will be monitored even more closely.

Source: C. Merle Crawford, *New Products Management*, 4th edition (Irwin, 1994, 317).

Checklist: Crafting a Launch Strategy

- Conduct a *reality* check in early pre-launch to ensure launch readiness.
- Focus, focus, focus. Develop a market profile based on *ideal* customers.
- Include milestone activities and early warning indicators, along with relevant dates, in the launch control plan.
- Design a roll-out strategy to incrementally reach the best markets for the new product.
- Prepare sales training in conjunction with sales management to help people actually *sell* the new product, rather than simply provide presentations about it.
- Brainstorm kick-off events and incentives to generate excitement for the launch.
- Include customer service, support, and the channel in your training plans.
- Capture as much publicity up-front as possible.
- Be creative in your marketing communications efforts for the launch.
- Identify and track *early indicators* as soon after launch as possible, and have a control plan in place.
- Evaluate the success of both the *product* and the *process* of development.

Interview with Steve Johnson, Vice President of Pragmatic Marketing

Steve Johnson is an expert in technology product management, and has launched 22 product offerings in his various marketing roles.

Q: *You spent 18 years marketing high-tech products and launched 22 products. Tell me a bit about your most successful launch.*

A: My most successful launch was the result of customer knowledge, combined with developer innovation, plus a lot of teamwork. At a development meeting, the team described an idea that they had been kicking around, and I immediately saw how it could solve customer problems. I had been touring customer sites and really understood the challenges they were facing. I gave development the go-ahead, and then went back to some of our customers to test the idea and understand the value of its implementation.

I had initially planned to charge $12,000 for the product because the technology wasn't particularly advanced. Once I had profiled the product in the context of the customers' environments, I saw that the solution would save them much more than originally expected, and I decided to charge $72,000. Our developers were quite concerned that we were ripping off the customers! And they were shocked when the customers paid without complaint. That was when the developers really started valuing market knowledge.

We started with a well-understood customer problem and addressed it with our developers' creativity. But that was only half of the challenge. Once we had a product, we still had to launch.

This was the first product I launched for which we had developed the positioning before we developed the collateral. What a difference that makes! Marketing communications used the positioning to build product literature. I worked with a select group of sales engineers to develop a solutions-oriented demo. I put together a sales toolkit with a profile of the buyers and a sales-process document detailing where the collateral and sales tools should be used. When the product was ready to be launched, I had everything necessary for success. On launch day, I trained the sales force on the new product and the sales tools. The first time they heard about the product, they had everything they needed to generate revenue immediately.

We surpassed expectations by selling our annual forecast in the first 100 days, with minimal awareness and lead generation. We had a product that solved problems and a sales force that understood the product—what more could a product need?

For every success, there are failures. In my experience, engineering-driven projects rarely meet revenue expectations. Everyone in high-tech knows about these: The product team comes up with an idea sitting around the cafeteria, and they start working on it immediately with no market input. In most cases, the only market validation is to ask a sales person if he can sell it. ("Of course I can! I can sell anything.") So the launch becomes a process of telling people what we've built, rather than how it will solve their problems. I call this "perfuming the pig." No amount of marketing can get people to buy something they don't need or want. No amount of perfume can overcome the stench of a pig product.

One case in particular was a situation that many product managers might recognize. A development team conceived of a product, but no amount of research could uncover a need for the product. So I canceled the project—or thought I did. As it turned out, the development team secretly completed the project anyway, put together a demo disk and a one-page brochure, and used one of the tech support people to call into the customer base to generate leads. After 3 months, they came to the same conclusion: It was a "great idea" that people didn't care about; it was a product seeking a problem where none existed.

In another case, I was hired to launch a product that was preparing to enter beta. They had acquired the technology and thought it would be a slam-dunk into the market. I started with a quick assessment: Does the product leverage the company's distinctive competence? What market problems does it solve? Has any research been done? What technology is being used, and what do the developers think of it? What is the competitive landscape? In short order, I determined that the product wasn't a good fit for the company or the market, and I recommended termination of the project. I've got to say, it was hard to cancel a product I was hired to manage; I wasn't completely sure that the company would still have a place for me if they agreed to kill it. But the senior executives saw the logic of my conclusions and gave me another product to manage. Success, for me at least, comes from intimate knowledge of the problems in the market, rather than only product knowledge.

Q: *In a nutshell, can you describe Pragmatic Marketing?*

A: Pragmatic Marketing, Inc.® offers training programs specifically designed for dealing with all aspects of technology product marketing. In today's high-tech marketplace, people are often selected to fill product management positions based on their applicable sales or technical background rather than classic marketing expertise. The theory that it is easier to teach them marketing than to teach them the complexities of our technology seems to make common sense. Pragmatic Marketing's training courses emphasize business-oriented definition of market problems, resulting in reduced risk and faster product delivery and adoption.

Q: *After having been with Pragmatic Marketing since 1996, you must have observed many changes in the field of product management. Can you discuss a few?*

A: The change in technology available to product managers is truly incredible. It's sometimes hard to believe how limited we were in the mid-90s: no Web, no mobile phones, no e-mail beyond the company walls. Today, there is so much available online: You can Google stats on the industry; you can get a wiki definition of any concept you don't understand; industry information comes into your e-mail from myriad sources; you can blog to your customers; you can get press releases, executive bios, and product information from your competitors' Web sites. So much is available from your desktop.

But what hasn't changed is the need for product managers to spend time in the field. Product management has always been inclined to become office-bound with business planning, development meetings, and sales inquiries. But these are the administrivia of product management. Credibility for product management has always come from market facts and personal customer experience.

The biggest change I've seen in the last few years is a re-orientation to business focus. Companies are relying on product managers to be the senior executive team's eyes and ears at the product level. Yet, there is a tendency for product managers to become *product* experts and thus, the best source of product information for sales people. Before you know it, product managers are acting as "demo boys" or "demo girls" and are spending 90% of their time supporting the sales force. Supporting the sales effort is important, yes, but for this, companies must have technical sales resources in the field—a resource typically called Sales Engineer. For the best company-wide results, product managers should never help a *sales person*; instead, they should help *entire sales channels*.

The product managers who are valued by senior management are the ones who know the *business* of the product in addition to the *technology* of the product. The best product managers spend time with customers (and the potential customers in untapped markets), instead of with sales people on sales calls to current product evaluators. These are the product managers who know what *ought to be* on the price sheet rather than the details of the products already on the price sheet.

According to research we did in 2003, with SoftwareMinds, companies that value product management enjoy half the time to market than those who do not. Why? Because the feature set is determined by what the customers need, rather than what is technically possible. These companies treat products as a business and not a hobby.

Q: *What will be the primary challenges for product managers in the next decade?*

A: For product managers, the eternal challenge is focus. Technology companies have always struggled with this. They either build to the needs of a single customer or else build a "one size fits all" product for everyone. We can't become a dominant player with either approach.

Developers need to focus on market problems instead of features. Many developers add features "since I was already in the code"—they seem to believe that more features translate to more sales. Yet, usability research continues to show that customers want fewer features, not more. That's why Apple has one button on their mouse; that's why TiVo remotes don't have an option to change to the second audio program; that's why Interlink makes a four-button presenter's remote to replace the one with 35 buttons provided with most data projectors. The trick is to understand the customer and the problem, so you'll know what features are required and which are merely distractions.

Sales people need focus on market segments instead of every company in their territory. Our products are not designed for every-one—or shouldn't be—but sales people want to force-fit the products into every account. That's why so many sales people need to sell *futures*. When the existing product isn't designed for a customer's problems, the product roadmap is used to convince the customer that the product will do so one day. Successful companies focus on products that meet the specific needs of a well-understood market.

Product management is the voice in the company advocating the creation of a complete product that addresses a specific problem of a specific persona in a specific market.

Q: *What advice can you give product managers about coping with these challenges?*

A: Show execs, developers, and sales people that it's both easier and more profitable to sell products that address a well-understood market problem. Recognize that credibility comes from knowing the market, not from surfing the Web. Use market facts and not your personal opinion to make your case. Visit a customer or potential customer every week.

Finally, pick one day a week to be productive. It takes 20 minutes to begin thinking, yet the typical workplace gets an interruption every 3 minutes; you simply cannot do knowledge work in an office. So I recommend blocking off every Thursday on your calendar. On that one day, work from home or from the local library doing all the things that require thought. I call it "International Product Management

Day"—the one day every week when product managers everywhere are getting some real work done.

Q: *What is the best advice you ever received?*

A: "Love what you do, and you'll never work a day in your life."

I've certainly seen many who worked a job only for the money—hating every minute of it. Instead, I have always tried to work with products and companies that excite me. I can't imagine being a product manager for a product that bored me. I've been careful to hire people who knew the domain, rather than those who say "a good manager can manage anything."

For more information on Pragmatic Marketing refer to: http://www.pragmaticmarketing.com/.

Notes

1. C. Merle Crawford, *New Products Management*, 4th ed. (Burr Ridge, IL: Richard D. Irwin, 1994:351).
2. Wayne Koberstein, "Master Launchers," *Pharmaceutical Executive* (May 1998): 45.
3. Bruce Nussbaum and Robert Neff, "I Can't Work This Thing!" *BusinessWeek* (April 19, 1991): 60.
4. Fernando Suarez and Gianvito Lanzolla, "The Half-Truth of First-Mover Advantage," *Harvard Business Review* (April 2005): 121–127.
5. C. Merle Crawford, *New Products Management*, 4th ed. (Burr Ridge, IL: Richard D. Irwin, 1994: 351–353).
6. Mary Jo Feldstein, "How Do You Take a New Product, Create a Need for It and Sell It?" *St. Louis Post-Dispatch* (April 19, 2005): D1.

Chapter Nine

Managing Existing and Mature Products

Most product managers manage both new and existing products. Chapters 6 through 8 covered the responsibilities for new products. Now the focus shifts to existing products. When dealing with existing products, product managers are expected to do one or more of the following:

· Maintain the sales of "core" and secondary products.
· Revitalize the sales of products that should be strong, but have begun to falter.
· Rationalize failing products.

This chapter focuses on the definitions and strategies related to these three approaches. The next chapter describes the marketing activities required for implementation.

Fitting Products into the Portfolio

As mentioned in Chapter 6, a product manager reduces risk by having a portfolio of new and old products. Existing products must be evaluated on an ongoing basis to determine ways to increase revenue, reduce costs, or eliminate obsolete products.

189

Periodically, compare the existing portfolio with competitive product lines or families. List all your products relative to the product offerings of your major competitors and look for gaps. Do they have products you don't have (or vice versa)? Do the differences represent a potential advantage (or disadvantage)? Does the analysis suggest the need for new products?

Perform similar analyses relative to customer needs. Think about how the customer uses your products or services. Do any complementary products or services exist that could augment your offering and make it more valuable to customers? Could these become part of your portfolio? If you haven't thought about your products in the context of customer needs, stop right now and review Chapter 2.

Categorize Products

Product managers, particularly those responsible for large numbers of products, often find it useful to classify products into categories to simplify or streamline decision-making. A number of common approaches can be taken. One is the basic Pareto (80/20) rule: If a significant percentage of sales or profits comes from a few products, give those important products constant attention, with the rest receiving periodic attention. The Boston Consulting Group popularized a matrix whereby products are evaluated and then identified as cash cows, stars, question marks, and dogs. Another approach is to define the products according their position on the product life cycle: introduction, growth, maturity, and decline. A variation of these two approaches categorizes products according to the generic product management strategy: maintain, revitalize, or rationalize.

A *maintenance product* generates a good income stream, but might not justify significant marketing expenditures. It may be a secondary product that doesn't face much competitive pressure, or it may be a core product that has strong brand equity. In either case, the product manager will look for ways to protect market share and prevent losses to the competition. It is typically possible to do so with minimal outlays.

Products requiring *revitalization* can be at any stage of the product life cycle, but are not performing at a level objectively determined as possible. These products require specific demand activities—to gain increased usage or market penetration—as described in the next chapter.

Finally, products that are either clearly not competitive in the product category or at the end of their life cycle are candidates for elimination (or *rationalization*). These products are identified by a lack of ability to achieve goals, a noted decline in sales, or the development of a superior product that redefined functionality. Products in this category can pose unique challenges when a key customer "clings" to the product despite its unprofitable status to your firm.

Institute a Database on Existing Products (Product Fact Book)

The product manager's first job related to evaluating the product portfolio is to ensure that product-related information is in a form conducive to analysis and decision making. This is the product fact book, where all relevant information is in a central location. The information in the fact book can be held in a three-ring binder, a manual filing system, or an electronic database.

There is no one right way to set up a database; it depends on the needs of the product manager. Typically, files will be kept on customer profiles and changes, the perceived importance of various product features, the major competitors and their strengths and weaknesses, the sales or profit contribution history of the product or product line, and technological or macroeconomic trends that could impact product sales in the future.

The information in the database must be updated periodically through marketing research, input from the customer service department, input from the sales force, Internet searching, and/or published information from trade publications. As noted in Business Brief 9.1, the product fact book provides the data necessary for ongoing decisions, as well as for much of the background analysis for annual marketing plans and product launches.

Business Brief 9.1   Colgate-Palmolive's bundle book.

Colgate-Palmolive has adapted the idea of a product fact book into what it calls a bundle book— a three-ring binder containing everything the company knows about a product or category— and uses it to create global brands. The bundle book is distributed to Colgate subsidiaries to provide consistency and uniformity in rolling out brands to different regions.

According to Sharen Kindel in "Selling by the Book" (*Sales & Marketing Management*), Colgate's bundle books provide descriptive plans for a product roll-out:

> Bundle books contain such information as: a product overview, a definition of the marketing opportunity, the product's uniqueness, a vision statement, the product family, a digest of consumer research, packaging, graphics, and pricing strategy. Also included are the advertising plan, support materials, a professional relations program, information pertaining to advertising claim substantiation, and even specific advertising executions. The book will answer questions regarding such technical issues as the formula, additives, fragrance, color, and stability, and provide a list of key contacts to check information or answer questions. Says

John Steele [head of global business development], "We send the subsidiaries the kind of advertising we want. They're tested ads that are already working in some markets." Detailed country profiles provide specifics on the roll-out plan and how the brand has performed to date. Information on competitive brands and their advertising support is also included.

The bundle books can be 150 to 200 pages in length, and in some situations, can exceed one volume. When Colgate launched its Colgate Total™ toothpaste in 1993, the launch was preceded by 18 months of research, resulting in a two-volume book. One volume contained the results of test marketing in six countries, carefully selected to provide a representative range of countries facing different marketing opportunities and constraints. The second volume covered public relations and advertising claim substantiation. Advertising, packaging, pricing, and positioning were consistent among all subsidiaries. Using the bundle book, Colgate's subsidiaries were able to launch Total™ in 66 countries within 2 years, the fastest global launch in Colgate's history.

The material in Colgate's bundle book provides the essence of the background analysis for product marketing planning as well as

Business Brief 9.1 continued

details about the action program. Although Colgate emphasizes its use for global new-product roll-outs, the basic concepts are appropriate for annual planning and domestic strategies as well.

The *business assessment* coincides with the general culture of the company and its impact on the plan. In Colgate's case, the books were in line with the centralized marketing philosophy of the company. Colgate prefers to give direction to its subsidiaries, whereas one of its major competitors, Unilever, allows its subsidiaries more freedom in the use of specific marketing tactics.

The *market analysis* focuses on selecting the appropriate customers for allocation of resources. For Colgate, the bundle books provide a consistent way of looking at the market—even small, fragmented markets. They provide input on the demographic and psychographic profiles of consumers most likely to use the products. This helps subsidiaries uncover new segments that are highly profitable or are underserved by the competition.

The *competitive strategy* depends on Colgate's relative position within a category. Since toothpaste is a core product for Colgate, the launch of Total™ required global speed to preempt competitors from bringing out a competing product and limiting its effectiveness. In the bleach category, a different approach was necessary. Colgate had just recently entered this business through acquisitions. Therefore, the competitive portion of the bundle book contained new information to educate employees. The competitive portion should identify the competitors' general strategies, product differentiation, future moves, and consumer perceptions.

The *performance history*, since Colgate's bundle books focus on new products, contains test market results. Colgate tested Total™ in Australia, Columbia, Greece, the Philippines, Portugal, and the United Kingdom. The information gathered on sampling, the use of television, and other variables were incorporated into the bundle book. For these books to be used for annual marketing planning, it would be necessary to compare planned versus actual sales figures, along with the related analysis of why they occurred.

Trends also played a role in Colgate's strategy. In the past, when few global brands existed and international technology was limited, little need existed for a standardized approach to megabrands. Now, with instantaneous global communication available through the Internet providing a common brand strategy, using a bundle book becomes valuable.

Source: Adapted from Sharen Kindel, "Selling by the Book," *Sales & Marketing Management* (October 1994): 101–107.

Evaluate Product Performance

The beginning point for a product performance evaluation is the audit conducted as part of your regular planning processes. This should have triggered problems and opportunities related to features, potential new-product entries, or quality issues that should be addressed in the product plan for the upcoming fiscal year. Aspects to evaluate about product performance include sales or profits by customer segment, channel of distribution, or geographic region; the complementary value of the product to others in the line; seasonal fluctuations in demand; the awareness and preference level for the product; rate of repeat purchases (retention); and the planned-to-actual performance.

Product managers should avoid thinking about existing products as mature, but should rather treat them as "core brands." Think about the brands as if they were being acquired from another company; envision the possibilities. Study customers to find out not only their buyer behavior, but also what causes that behavior.[1]

Product managers frequently use *competitive matrices* to study their products. A competitive matrix is a visual display of one product versus the competition along two axes. Each axis is a continuum of an attribute, such as ease of use, comfort, price, and so forth. The selection of attributes should be based on what is important to customers.

A competitive matrix (sometimes called a *perceptual map*) focuses attention on the relative competitive positioning a product has along significant factors (Figure 9.1). Start by determining what is most important to a customer when making a buying decision. Ask customers to list and rank attributes in terms of priority and to assess how significant those attributes truly are in terms of affecting their purchase decisions.

Then select the top two or four attributes to utilize for the relative positioning of significant competitors along each attribute. For example, assume that Product A is compared with competing products X, Y, and Z along two important purchase criteria: leadership in the market and ease of use. Note that A is perceived as a leader to a greater degree than the com-

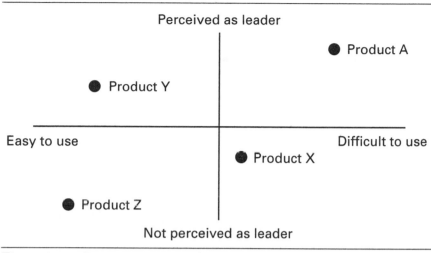

Figure 9.1   Competitive matrix (perceptual map).

petition; this could be used as part of its positioning strategy. However, it is also perceived as more difficult to use than any of the competitors. This could suggest a strategy of providing clearer instructions or redesigning the product to make it easier to use.

Another approach to this, when several factors are deemed equally important, is to list all factors as continua (as bipolar adjectives along a scale, like light to heavy) and ask customers to rate each product along each factor. The average or mean responses for each competitive product can be joined by a line to indicate a "profile" of each. In Figure 9.2, three products are being evaluated against one another. Product A is perceived as slightly superior in terms of product consistency, Product B is easiest to use, and Product C has better delivery.

Both the competitive matrix and profile approaches just described compare a product against its competitors along established factors. The typical objective is to improve attributes that are competitively weak. What is generally missing is the internal cost of the specific factors. Sometimes a product can be made more profitable by reducing the cost of unimportant attributes. If this also results in a price reduction, the result can be more value to the customer. Therefore, it is useful to add cost information to the perceived importance and

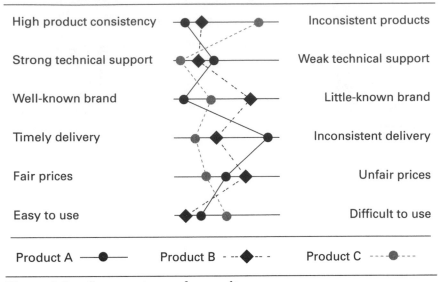

Figure 9.2   Comparative product scaling.

competitive performance of each attribute, as shown in Worksheet 9.1.

Note that the first column of Worksheet 9.1 is for the features and attributes of the product. These must be converted to benefits in the second column. The average importance of each benefit to the market must be determined (through marketing research) or estimated (from informal customer input) and listed in the third column. The next column indicates how well the product supplies the benefit relative to the competition. The final column indicates whether the cost of the related features is a significant proportion of the overall cost of the product.

Look for red flags in the table. The provision of benefits that are highly important to the market should be from features that are at least equal to or better than the competition's in terms of performance. If that is not the case, the product manager should improve on those features. If features provide benefits that are not important to the customer, the relative cost should be low. Otherwise, the feature should be eliminated or provided at as low a cost as possible.

This type of analysis should precede quality-improvement and cost-reduction programs. By working with teams from other

Worksheet 9.1   Costs and benefits of features relative to market importance.

Features/ Attributes	Benefits	Importance to Market	Competitive Importance	Relative Cost

parts of the company, the product manager can use value analysis, quality function deployment, or other techniques to increase customer satisfaction without a commensurate increase in costs, or maintain customer satisfaction while lowering costs.

Evaluate the Product Line

In evaluating a product *line* (as opposed to an individual product), the product manager can use the same steps discussed earlier, particularly when the line is comprised of fast-moving consumer goods (FMCG). First, data must be maintained on each item in the line. Second, relative product performance must be evaluated. This includes an examination of customer behavior for the entire line. Try to determine whether customers can substitute a filler product if the core product is out of stock or whether they are apt to buy a competing product. Third, increase value to the product line by either adding products that enhance the competitive positioning and increase brand equity or deleting products that are not important to the target market and simply increase costs. Finally, increase market penetration by generating more usage through a carefully planned marketing communications strategy.

Regularly evaluate the product line to look for gaps to be filled or products to be eliminated. A starting point may be to compare your product line to competing product lines to highlight potential gaps or to uncover potentially unnecessary products (Table 9.1). Note that, in the example shown in Table 9.1, yours is the only product line in the competitive set not carrying brackets. This could make installation more difficult, causing a potential competitive disadvantage.

It is generally useful to develop tools to rank products. Choose the variables of most importance in evaluating the line and determine the best way to categorize the existing products. If your company does not have a product-review committee, recommend that one be established. The committee should be comprised of representatives from marketing, manufacturing, and finance. The committee should develop a company-appropriate system for identifying weak products. The system should specify how frequently to meet (e.g., quarterly, annually), what criteria to examine (number of quarters of sales decline, market changes, gross margin, etc.), and procedures for product elimination. Whatever recommendations are made should be included in the annual plan, with rationale and a statement of the impact on the overall marketing program. Careful product

Table 9.1   Product Line Comparison

	Competitor A's product line	Competitor B's product line	Your product line
Fail-safe resistors	x		x
Nonpolarized chip		x	
Voltage regulator	x	x	x
Flat chip resistor	x	x	x
Brackets	x	x	
27-inch yoke	x		x

line management and analysis—as discussed in Business Brief 9.2—is an important predecessor to establishing maintenance, revitalization, and rationalization strategies.

Maintenance Strategies

Maintenance strategies are primarily defensive or self-sustaining in nature, attempting to prevent loss to the competition or

---

Business Brief 9.2   The many aspects of product-line management.

Product-line management involves conceiving and developing new products, but also extending existing product lines and building brand equity. Different companies emphasize different parts of these product-line management activities, and a given product manager will emphasize different aspects, depending on specific needs at the time.

Developing New Products

In developing new products, product managers use a variety of techniques to reduce risk and increase chances of success. First, product managers (particularly in highly technical fields) have learned to begin next-generation products immediately after the launch of prior-generation products. Intel started this approach in 1990. Second, developing simultaneous products based on a corporate strategy leverages the success of both products by adding momentum. Intel demonstrated this as well with its ProShare family of products. Third, generating several

products from a common platform spreads out development costs and allows products to be brought to market more quickly and at a lower price. Hewlett-Packard benefited from this knowledge in the introduction of its color DeskJet printer. Finally, establishing barriers to entry for the competition affords at least a temporary competitive edge. Here again, Hewlett-Packard discovered this in its work in inkjet printers.

Hewlett-Packard's Inkjet Printers

In an effort to maintain its dominance in printers, Hewlett-Packard has beaten Japanese competitors by using their own tactics. Over a decade ago, Japanese companies had taken away the lead in hand-held calculators, a market H-P had pioneered. The success was due to a mass-market strategy with low-priced, well-designed products. This time, H-P took that approach with inkjet printers, as Stephen Kreider Yoder explains in "How

(continued on next page)

Business Brief 9.2   continued

H-P Used Tactics of the Japanese to Beat Them at Their Game" in The *Wall Street Journal*:

> H-P engineers adopted two Japanese tactics: They filed a blizzard of patents to protect their design and frustrate rivals, and embarked on a process of continual improvement to solve the inkjet's problems. They developed print heads that could spit 300 dots an inch and made inks that would stay liquid in the cartridge but dry instantly on plain paper. One engineer tested all types of paper: bonded, construction, toilet, and, for good measure, tested sandpaper, tortillas, and socks.

Hewlett-Packard established a solid foothold in the black-and-white inkjet printer market using these techniques. However, it faced another challenge in 1990. At this time, H-P engineers were working on a color printer, intent on bringing out a full-featured, mechanical marvel. Marketing suggested they build on the platform they had already established, since they felt this approach, though less sophisticated, would satisfy the needs of the customers:

> There was a near mutiny among the engineers until a product manager named Judy Thorpe forced them to do telephone polls of cus-

tomers. It turned out people were eager for the product the engineers considered a "kludge." H-P learned that "you can tweak your not-so-latest thing and get the latest thing," Ms. Thorpe says. By sticking to the existing platform, H-P was able to get the jump on competitors in the now-booming color-printer market.

One other thing: H-P's "blizzard of patents" set up a barrier to entry for competition. Competing engineers lost valuable time negotiating H-P's maze of 50 patents covering how ink travels through the head. By the time Canon became a serious competitor, H-P had sold millions of printers and had practiced continual improvement in manufacturing. Later, when Canon introduced a color inkjet in 1993, H-P was able to cut the price of its version before Canon even reached the market. As a result, Hewlett-Packard "owns" 55% of the world market for inkjets. And, like Intel, H-P is leveraging its knowledge of inkjets in other areas, such as fax machines.

Extending Existing Product Lines: Successes and Failures

Sometimes, products are not completely new, but are rather product-line extensions. As a product manager plans for line extensions, a careful balance must be sought between variety

Business Brief 9.2   continued

and redundancy. Fast-moving consumer goods are perhaps particularly vulnerable to this trap. In an effort to respond to competitive entries, to reach smaller market segments, to bolster short-term gain, or to gain more shelf space, many product managers offer too many variations of core products.

Numerous examples of extending product lines abound. When Nabisco introduced its line of Fat-Free Fruit Bars in 1993, the cookie category was growing at a modest 2% per year. Nevertheless, this line of offerings resulted in Nabisco's sales increasing three times as fast as the overall market. Similarly, when 7UP introduced Cherry 7UP in 1987, the new product variant was successful, and the sales of the core product also went up.

Unfortunately, line extensions have their pitfalls. Introducing a product variation under the same name as a core brand could have the potential of weakening brand equity. Line extensions can generally be easily matched by competitors. A number of hidden costs can arise due to increased production complexity, more errors in forecasting, and the loss of consumers due to potential out-of-stock situations.

As an example, John Quelch and David Kenny, in the *Harvard Business Review* ("Extend Profits, Not Product Lines") discuss the plight of a U.S. snack foods company they refer to as

Snackco. Over time, Snackco's product line had grown, but its overall sales remained flat. In evaluating the situation, the company studied the effectiveness of core products, niche products, seasonal and holiday products, and filler products. The percent of the line as well as the percent of the sales volume accounted for by each type of product are shown in the following table.

Snackco's Product-Line Analysis

	Percent of Line	Percent of Sales Volume
Core products	20%	70%
Niche products	10	10
Seasonal and holiday products	5	10
Filler products	65	10

By looking at this analysis, it was clear that changes had to be made. Note that the core products generally followed the Pareto principle: 20% of the products accounted for 70% (instead of Pareto's 80%) of the volume. These were also the key products responsible for building company and brand reputation. Consequently, Snackco managers changed manufacturing and delivery schedules to assure that core products were always in stock.

(continued on next page)

Business Brief 9.2   continued

The niche products were holding their own, contributing 10% of the product line and 10% of the volume. These products were studied to determine in which market areas they had sufficient volume to continue, and in which markets they should be dropped.

Seasonal and holiday items provided 10% of the sales volume, even though they represented only 5% of the product line. These items were maintained with additional store displays provided for active selling periods.

Finally, filler products were evaluated. Even though the per-unit contribution was greater for them than for some other products, it wasn't enough to offset the fact that, with 65% of the product line, they were contributing only 10% of the sales volume. These products were carefully evaluated in terms of true costs and competitive need. The company decided to cut the number of filler products. The greatest cuts were in competitive areas where the company decided to use the shelf space to build share in core products. In leadership markets, the cuts were more selective, with a goal of blocking shelf space from the competition.

Note the steps that Snackco took to perform this analysis. First, the sales, profit, and contribution history of each item in the product line was collected and analyzed, along with data on customers and competitors. Part of this was based on internal records. But to be able to fully evaluate product performance, external research also was required. Random store checks indicated that the most popular items were out of stock up to 50% of the time, and that up to 40% of customers bought either a competitive product or nothing. The remaining customers purchased one of the filler products. The company also used consumer tracking panels to gain data on both household purchases and usage frequency.

After examining this information, Snackco managers were challenged to add value to existing products and to the product line, particularly for retail channel members. As Quelch and Kenny point out, they had to be able to prove that retailers would benefit from the product-line plan being proposed:

Snackco's managers believed that the new strategy was on target, but they also knew that without the support of the sales force any efforts to implement the plan would fail. So, backed by Snackco's president, one of the sales regions undertook a 4-month test to determine the impact of refocusing core products versus continuing line extensions. Not only did market share increase during the test, but sales-force compensation also increased, because of the

Business Brief 9.2   continued

faster turnover of the more popular items in the line, which were given additional shelf space at the expense of the slower-moving items.

To boost market penetration, usage rate and the number of users had to be increased. Some of this was accomplished by scheduling manufacturing and delivery to assure that core products were always in stock, as well as providing additional store displays for the seasonal products. However, some advertising changes were also necessary:

Snackco shifted from an umbrella advertising approach for the whole line to a strategy that focused on its flagship products. Advertisements for these products emphasized the Snackco brand and thereby promoted the brand's line extensions. Over the past 2 years, Snackco has made significant gains in market share and volume, which in turn have generated even higher margins.

Adapted from: John Quelch and David Kenny, "Extend Profits, Not Product Lines," *Harvard Business Review* (September–October 1994): 153–160; Stephen Kreider Yoder, "How H-P Used Tactics of the Japanese to Beat Them at Their Game," *Wall Street Journal* (September 8, 1994): 1+.

prolong a revenue stream. They could be applied to core products, fillers, or ancillary products. Maintenance strategies should require minimal oversight, thus freeing up time for product managers—and possibly resources—to devote to revitalizing other products. When a product manager handles numerous products, different ones may be in maintenance mode during any given year. The marketing of these products should be an appendix or footnote in the marketing plan, rather than detailed out in the action plan. Common examples of maintenance strategies are: (1) stay the course; (2) reduce the scope; and (3) defend the perimeter. In any case, it's important to watch profitability trends carefully to determine when it might be necessary to shift to a revitalization or rationalization strategy.

Stay the Course

Some products exist perennially under the radar, supported by diehard customers. They don't require much push, due to limited competition—and can therefore be relegated to a footnote in your annual marketing plan. Also, if you have limited capacity for manufacturing a certain product, you may wish to maintain sales by doing what you have always done. Local breweries, for example, retain their uniqueness by keeping the production of their beer limited. As the President of New Glarus Brewery (in New Glarus, Wisconsin) stated when demand surged for their product, "Eventually we're just going to throw in the towel and say this is all the beer we can make, and I think we're getting close."[2]

Reduce the Scope

Sometimes a product that might otherwise have been eliminated can be maintained by scaling back and focusing on a smaller niche market. This was the case with the Fisher Space Pen, better known at the "astronaut pen." The growing economy in the 1990s provided the perfect environment for little indulgences, such as a $50 pen that writes under extreme conditions—especially after it was featured on a Jerry Seinfeld episode. Unfortunately, the downturn in the economy in the early 2000s abruptly impacted demand for the product. The only way to maintain sales for the product was to focus on the truly core users—the "extreme professionals" in "extreme jobs." (Police officers could use them to write vital signs on latex gloves at accident scenes.) Therefore, the marketing for the product shifted to advertising in trade magazines for nurses, police, and paramedics.[3]

Defend the Perimeter

One risk of taking your eye off a core product is that competitors can begin to "nibble around the edges"—a phenomenon also referred to as "ankle biting." Therefore, some efforts will need to be made to protect against competitive threats by retaining visibility in front of the customer, while still squeezing every dollar out of your marketing expenditures. While a disproportionate amount of funds may be invested to launch a product, a smaller amount could be spent on reminder sales promotions once "loyalists" have been established in the customer base. For many

medical products, a study by AC Nielsen HCI found that reinforcement media—such as prescription pads, reference publications, and patient records forms—are effective vehicles for
delivering reinforcement product messages. The study found
three advantages to these nontraditional tools:

- Point-of-purchase vehicles (Rx pads, patient record forms,
  reference publications, etc.) reach the physician at the pre-
  scribing moment.
- They reach physicians when they aren't "expecting" to be
  exposed to a message.
- Brand recognition is reinforced even though the sales rep is
  not present.[4]

Revitalization Strategies

The bulk of a product manager's efforts with regard to existing
products will be spent on revitalization efforts. Revitalization
efforts can be grouped into three major categories. The first
adds new value by either augmenting the product with more
features and/or services or reducing costs. The second approach
uses repositioning, including brand refocusing and break-away
positioning. The third approach extends the base through new
users, new uses, increased usage, and line extensions.

Add New Value

It is important to continually rethink and redefine the product
creatively to look for opportunities hidden behind the day-to-
day grind (Figure 9.3). What would happen if some features
were magnified? For example, magnifying the screen on a television created a new market for home theater. Similarly, reducing the screen created sports TVs.

What if a new feature replaced an old one? For example,
Sony created the Walkman by replacing speakers with a head-
set. Can two existing products be combined to provide one with
more value to the customer? The minivan combined the advantages of a station wagon with those of a van. Sometimes, two

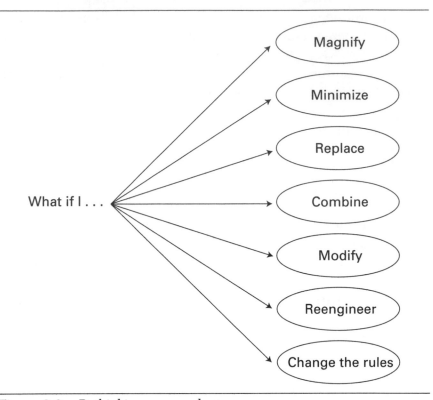

Figure 9.3   Rethinking your product.

product managers can bundle their products together to create more value than selling either one separately to the customer.

Can certain elements be modified? This could include both product features and ancillary services. Sometimes industries become so embroiled in "that's the way we've always done it" thinking that modifications to sales approaches, contract terms, or other things are overlooked.

Can the development process be re-engineered to reduce the overall cost of producing the product or service? Can the traditional approach be changed: For example, can direct mail or the Internet be used as an alternative to the traditional method of distributing the product?

After identifying features that deserve detailed examination, the next job of the product manager is to benchmark these features against the "best-in-class." Start by finding out from sales staff, customers, and industry writings what company or product is recognized as best for the aspect under study. Then strive to uncover why it is perceived as best. For example, when Ford redesigned the 1992 Taurus, it benchmarked more than 200 features against seven competitors. Door handles were benchmarked against the Chevy Lumina, headlamps against the Accord, and remote radio controls against the Pontiac Grand Prix.[5]

However, benchmarking should not be limited to the competition, and it does not have to be limited to product features. By improving the processes used to deliver a product or service, it is possible to provide more value for the customer. Mellon Bank in Pittsburgh, for example, undertook a benchmarking project to improve its credit card billing practices. By benchmarking seven other companies, including an airline, they learned about techniques and software technologies to improve the process. After adopting several improvements, they cut outstanding complaints by half and were able to resolve problems in an average of 25 days instead of the 45 days it took previously.[6]

Reposition

Creating a new competitive posture can give new life to some products, as discussed in Chapter 4. For example, Pampers' brand manager took a major step, in 2004, to feature a man as a primary care giver, contributing to the diaper's share growth from 49% to 59%. Red Bull extended its reach by targeting older consumers with a strategy centered on golf.[7]

Break-away positioning refers to a more radical departure from the status quo. For example, rather than adding more features to a product, strip it to its baseline state. Then decide how you can augment it for specific customers.[8] For example, with the explosion of wireless capabilities being built into products and services, a mini revolution of anti-technology demand is occurring. Some coffee shops, for example, are bucking the trend and have sections outfitted with jammers to prevent cell phones from ringing and laptop computers from working.[9]

Extend the Base

Another tactic the product manager could use is to boost sales volume by increasing the number of users or the usage rate per user. The number of users can be increased by winning competitors' customers, entering new market segments, or converting nonusers into users. Volume also can be increased by finding new applications for the product or by encouraging more frequent usage.

To increase the number of users, a product manager must collect three types of information: (1) why competitors' customers buy from the competition; (2) what, if anything, could convince nonusers to become users of the product; and (3) what market segments are attractive and accessible. Information for the first two items on the list can be obtained partly through sales input in the way of lost order reports. However, this is at best an incomplete picture, because not all customers are contacted by the sales force. Therefore, if this is critical data, some additional research is necessary. Focus groups and one-on-one interviews can uncover new insights into why customers choose alternative products or choose none at all.

To identify what segments are attractive and accessible requires a combination of information and intuition. Start by profiling existing customer segments that have shown higher than average increases in sales. Determine whether these increases are unique to the product's customers or whether noncustomers with similar profiles also have exhibited a need for the product. Then assess whether the total segment (customers and noncustomers) is growing or declining in sheer size. Also, look for segments that have suddenly appeared and have specific needs not being addressed by the competition.

Sometimes, the usage and users can be significantly different from the status quo—especially in the latter phases of the product life cycle. Superior Clay Corporation, for example, was a successful manufacturer of clay sewer pipes. As plastic pipes made most applications of clay sewer pipe obsolete, the company was able to reinvent its product line. By re-evaluating its competencies, it discovered it could transfer its capabilities to fireplace flue liners and decorative chimney pots. By extending its customer base to this new application, Superior Clay became even more successful than it was initially.[10]

Rationalization Strategies

Nearly all product lines could benefit from rationalization, which is the systematic analysis and modification of product lines to better align them with long-term goals. In fact, most firms would become more *profitable* if they eliminated weak brands and products. In 1996, the bulk of Nestle's profits came from around 2.5% of its brand portfolio. Procter & Gamble discovered that 66% of its growth between 1992 and 2002 came from its 10 biggest brands. In 1999, of Unilever's 1,600 brands, more than 90% of its profits came from 400 brands. As Nirmalya Kumar stated in his *Harvard Business Review* article, "the surprising truth is that most brands don't make money."[11]

The starting point, therefore, is to examine your existing products and product lines to look for pruning opportunities. David Anderson has developed the following typical criteria that can be used in the process of review and consolidation.[12]

1. Sales volume: list sales volumes in a bar chart format over time, in Pareto order.
2. Sales revenue: similarly plot sales revenue.
3. Part commonality: plot products by percentage of common parts.
4. Cost of variety: determine and plot variety costs as a multiplier of baseline products.
5. True profitability: at minimum, plot profit contributions without artificial allocations.
6. Polls and surveys: input from various experts.
7. Factory processing: compatibility with manufacturing processes.
8. Functionality: opportunities to consolidate products with similar functionalities.
9. Customer needs: impact on customers if eliminated.

10. Core competencies: based on the firm's clear core competencies.
11. Clean-sheet-of-paper scenario: would you have this product if you were a new competitor?
12. Future potential: does the product overleverage for the future?

After identifying the weak products, a product manager must make decisions and recommendations about what to do with them. Should the price be lowered to stimulate sales and empty the warehouse? Should the price be raised to encourage customers to shift to a substitute product? Should the product be sold or licensed to another company?

Sometimes, the best solution is to kill a product. This is often challenging for product managers who don't want the reputation of "quitters" or "funeral directors." The use of standard criteria, and perhaps a product rationalization review committee (similar to a new product review committee), can streamline the process.

Checklist: Managing Existing and Mature Products

· Before evaluating your products in depth, prioritize them in terms of their profitability and strategic potential. Practice the 80/20 rule.
· Collect and maintain information on your products, your customers, and your competition on an ongoing basis.
· Determine the features or attributes of your product (including supporting services) of highest importance to your customers; then regularly compare these against the best-in-class products and companies.
· Don't limit your analysis to what customers say is important now; challenge yourself to rethink and redefine the product to uncover hidden opportunities for the future.
· Remember that the markets for your products aren't static; look for new ways to increase users and usage.

- In addition to examining individual products, study the total product line or mix you offer your customers. Weed out weak products and add new products to fill in the gaps as appropriate.

Interview with Bob Brentin, President of Product Development and Management Association

Bob Brentin explores and develops new markets for the Dow Corning Corporation in the Advanced Technologies & Ventures Business, and previously had extensive new product experience with Dow Chemical.

Q: *In a nutshell, could you describe the Product Development and Management Association?*

A: The PDMA is a nonprofit professional organization dedicated to serving people with an interest in new products. Whereas many professional associations are vertical organizations specializing in one industry or function, PDMA's membership is horizontal and multifunctional, which is how product development is done. With its diverse membership from accomplished new product companies, academia, and service providers, PDMA represents thought leaders in new product development and management. The mission of PDMA is to improve the skills and effectiveness of people and organizations engaged in developing and managing new products—both manufactured goods and services.

Q: *Given that the job of a "new products" product manager is different from the job of a product marketing manager (for existing products), does the PDMA address the needs of both groups?*

A: PDMA addresses both, with a focus on developing and managing products across the product life cycle. The product marketing manager for current products needs to be thinking about product line rationalization, line extensions, market share, brand, and positioning. The new products product manager assures that the new product addresses a market need, can be produced and sold to provide value to the company and its customers, thereby delivering a sustainable product to grow and manage. In the end, product management integrates the various segments of a business into a strategically focused whole, understanding market needs, maximizing the value of a product, and gaining customer satisfaction while providing long-term value for the company.

Q: *Do you think B2B product managers face product development challenges different from those faced by B2C product managers?*

A: The Comparative Performance Assessment Study conducted by the PDMA Foundation shows that industrial capital goods/materials/services companies and consumer goods/services companies have similar success rates and percents of revenue and profits from new products. There are some differences in product development, notably in understanding customer needs, product life cycle, market segmentation, and channels of distribution. In a general sense, the job is the same—figure out what set of problems some group of people need to have solved, develop a product for which profitably solves those problems, and shepherd the product through your corporate infrastructure and out into the marketplace.

Q: *What changes in product development philosophies, strategies, or concepts have you observed over the last 5 years, and what has been the impact on product managers?*

A: Product managers must deal with rising expectations for better products, developed faster, and delivered at a lower price. The new product development community has responded with advances in techniques to assess customer needs and analyze opportunities, in practices for cross-functional team effectiveness and decision making, and in the management of portfolios and product development processes.

Q: *What will be the primary product development challenges for product managers in the next decade?*

A: Product life cycles continue to shorten while products and markets become more complex. Product managers will need to manage product lines and portfolios across the life cycle. More co-development with partners and suppliers will require increased coordination beyond the corporate structure. Speed is a must—competition is coming from new places, and advantages are temporary—the only lasting competency for an organization is to continuously build and assemble capability chains.

Q: *What advice can you give product managers about coping with these challenges?*

A: Think more broadly, as would a general manager. This means more collaboration and working beyond our functional and corporate silos. Regard change as opportunity for innovation. And join PDMA—to network with others who have faced similar challenges and share in the body of knowledge about product development and management.

Q: *What was the best advice you ever received?*

A: Certainly, the recommendation to check out this group called PDMA! I went to a PDMA conference and found people, in a range of industries, who were dealing with the same new-product development issues I was. This was a group I had to join. The learning, and the networking, have added a lot to my business experience.

Another great piece of advice I received was to join Toastmasters. Beyond working on an obvious lack of presentation skills early in my career, over time, I came to appreciate and learn the importance of listening, evaluation, and critical thinking skills. These skills have been vital in my developing new products and markets. The experience has helped me listen for unmet needs, think through value propositions, and work more effectively in teams.

For more information on the Product Development and Management Association, refer to: http://www.pdma.org/.

Notes

1. James R. Rindall, "Marketing Established Brands," *Journal of Consumer Marketing* (Fall 1991): 5–10.
2. Jason Stein, "What's Brewing?" *Wisconsin State Journal* (May 15, 2005): C10.
3. Paulette Thomas, "Case Study: Narrow Markets Need Cultivation to Thrive," *Wall Street Journal* (November 23, 2004): B8.
4. Steve Varon, "Filling in the Gaps," *Medical Marketing and Media* (June 2004): 52–56.
5. Jeremy Main, "How to Steal the Best Ideas Around," *Fortune* (October 19, 1992): 103.
6. Ibid.
7. Alexandra Jardine, "Next Generation," *Marketing* (November 24, 2004): 31–36.
8. Refer to Youngme Moon, "Break Free from the Product Life Cycle," *Harvard Business Review* (May 2005): 87–94 for a discussion of reverse positioning, breakaway positioning, and stealth positioning concepts.
9. Staci Sturrock, "Time Not on Our Side," *Wisconsin State Journal* (May 15, 2005): I8.

10. Ralph Ruark, "Innovation Matters," *Ceramic Industry* (May 2004): 38–41.
11. Nirmalya Kumar, "Kill a Brand, Keep a Customer," *Harvard Business Review* (December 2003): 86–95.
12. David M. Anderson and B. Joseph Pine II, "Agile Product Development for Mass Customization," *Times Mirror* (1997): 75–83.

Chapter Ten

Creating and Managing Customer Demand Using Marketing Plans

The marketing *plan* is the execution of the strategies you envisioned for your products. But the *process* of planning is a reality check-and-balance. It starts with an examination of data (past and present) as well as future projections, so that your plan is built on fact rather than fad. The planning process should be more than mere form-filling or number crunching. And the plan should provide the basis by which the product manager justifies resource utilization, as well as provides continuity in the event of management or staff turnover. Financials are an important component for gaining approval of the plan.

Marketing planning generally addresses five fundamental questions.

1. Where are you now?
2. Where do you want to go long-term (your strategic product vision and strategies)?
3. What are you going to do this year to come closer to your long-term vision (objectives)?
4. What actions will help you accomplish the objectives (tactics or action plan)?

5. How will you implement, track, and evaluate results (metrics and measurements)?

The process is not necessarily linear; some companies may start with the long-term vision (step 2) and move on to data gathering (step 1) or go back and forth between steps as new information emerges, or as a result of negotiation with senior management. However, all steps are generally covered in some manner.

Where Are You Now?

Earlier in the book, we addressed several of the categories of external information that related to the question, "Where are you now?" Chapter 2 explored customer and market trends, and Chapter 3 looked at competition. (In particular, Worksheet 3.1 should be part of the analysis at this point.) Here we'll add some of the internal data about the performance history of products and marketing activities, as well as a few trend questions that might have been missed, starting with the performance history (Worksheet 10.1).

The performance history looks at how well various products performed over time and relative to plan. It focuses attention on the market share and financial and other numeric or statistical indicators of performance. In addition, answers to product mix questions, like those listed below, provide qualitative data that could highlight problems and opportunities to be addressed in the plan. Here are additional questions to explore as you prepare the marketing plan.

The Products

Your accounting department most likely provides routine data on the sales and profitability of the product(s), but the analysis should go beyond quantitative statistics to include qualitative variables.

Worksheet 10.1   Performance history.

Division: Group: Product Line: Market:

	20__		20__		20__	
	Plan	Actual	Plan	Actual	Plan	Actual
Industry volume (units)						
Your volume						
Percentage of industry volume						
Industry sales ($)						
Your sales						
Percentage of industry sales						
Product sales as percentage of company sales						
Cost of goods sold						
Gross margin						
Gross margin ratio						
Controllable costs						
Promotion						
Field sales costs						
Other marketing costs						
Misc. controllable costs						
Total controllable costs						
Net profit contribution						
Quality index						
New product sales						
Target account sales						
Price index						
Sales per salesperson						
Product/line strengths						
Product/line weaknesses						

- In what stage of the product life cycle are the products? Which are in the beginning phases, which are in growth, which are mature, and which are candidates for elimination? Does this confirm your prior thinking about revitalization, maintenance, and rationalization?
- What does the name of the product imply? Can it be branded?
- Which features or products are distinguishable by the customer?
- For each feature, ask "so what?" to identify the benefits from the customer's point of view.
- Are the products supplied through intermediaries (e.g., dealers)? If so, the analysis of features, benefits, and values should be handled in two steps.
- If a numeric rating were given to product quality (with 1 being low and 7 being high), what would that rating be? Would the rating be the same for all customer segments? For all products?
- What does each item in the product line contribute to sales and profits? To customer satisfaction? Can some of the products be pruned?
- How does the product line rate of return compare with the company's overall rate of return?
- Are the product designs conducive to an efficient manufacturing process?
- What are the engineering costs for product development, product engineering, and manufacturing engineering?
- What are the unit break-even sales volumes for the products?
- Are product guarantees competitive?
- What would happen if the products were more standardized? More customized?
- What is the company's attitude toward private labeling?

Sales Force

Although product managers typically have no authority over the sales staff, an examination of sales force effectiveness can highlight potential opportunities or problems that must be addressed in the product plan(s).

- Is the current sales force structure appropriate for achieving the product objective?
- Are the target customers being reached in the most effective and efficient manner?
- How effective have the product and sales training been?
- What sales tools do the sales staff actually use to sell the product?
- Has the sales force been taught how to help customers visualize the benefits of the product?

Pricing

The right price covers all relevant costs, is positioned appropriately given the competitive value of the products, and takes into account customer perceptions. The product manager should assess whether company policies enable that to happen.

- Have significant amounts of business been lost because of product prices?
- Are errors frequently made in pricing?
- What is the perceived cost of buying the product or service?
- Is the company a price leader or a price follower?
- What is the pricing policy of the company?
- What types of discounts are offered? How does that compare with the competition?

The Promotional Campaigns

Promotional campaigns should be part of an integrated marketing communications effort, with the product manager pushing for a consistent message to customers. Pay attention to new approaches to customer communications, including product placements, e-mail campaigns, test drives, advergaming, and other techniques, as discussed in Business Brief 10.1.

- What is the current image customers have of the product? Is it consistent with the advertising?
- Did prior advertising strategies work? Why or why not?

Business Brief 10.1   The growth of alternative media.

Although the tried-and-true techniques of customer contact will continue to have their place, product managers will be increasingly challenged to bring new marketing activities into their annual plans. The automotive industry, in particular, allocated as much as 10% more of their marketing budgets to alternative media in 2005.

- Chrysler built a half-mile road course at the April 2005 Chicago Auto Show to allow people to test drive its vehicles.
- Toyota partnered with MTV to provide 25,000 cell phone users (in its younger buyer target) with free ring tones of popular songs downloaded from MTV.
- BMW invited its customers to test drive its vehicles during its ninth annual "Ultimate Drive" and donated $1 to the Susan G. Komen Breast Cancer Foundation for every mile driven.
- Volkswagen of America offered a year of free car insurance to customers who bought or leased selected vehicles at Illinois and Wisconsin dealerships in 2004.

Other companies, products, and brands also are experimenting with different marketing and customer-communication approaches. Advergaming is growing in B2B markets, especially for trade shows. The oral health care division of GlaxoSmithKline used a Jeopardy-style game at dentist and dental hygienist trade shows, between 2001 and 2003, to familiarize prospects with its brands. The game attracted "large amounts of people, often several deep into the aisle." Solvay Pharmaceuticals used a car racing advergame as part of a promotion for a testosterone replacement therapy product. In the game, users encountered challenges such as "depression" and "low sex drive" that slowed their cars' speed—and received a boost with the right medical assistance.

Product placements, both actual and virtual, have surged. Cars and packaged goods have appeared as components of video and online games. Suburu Impreza was launched on a Sony Playstation car racing game. Numerous companies are working to get their products placed on movies and television programs.

Other technologies are emerging as marketing communication tools. Company-sponsored blogging provides more personal interaction with customers. Personalized e-mail increases click-through rates. Podcasting allows audio messages to be delivered through the Internet and listened to with an iPod.

Source: Jamie LaReau, "Alternative Marketing Grows Rapidly," *Automotive News* (March 7, 2005): 32B. Catherine Arnold, "Just Press Play," *Marketing News* (May 15, 2004): 1 & 15. An Mack,

Business Brief 10.1   continued

"Pay for Play," *Adweek* (June 28–July 5, 2004): 18–21. Suzanne Vranica and Brian Steinberg, "The Robot Wore Converses," *Wall Street Journal* (September 2, 2004): B1. Michael Fielding, "Four Technologies that B-to-B Marketers Can Leverage Now," *Marketing News* (May 1, 2005): 13–14.

- What nonadvertising promotion has been tried? How well did it work?
- What has been the effectiveness of trade shows?
- Are the product-specific Web pages adequate and up-to-date?

The Distribution Strategy

The sales force and distributors may be the most important face-to-face contacts with customers. The effectiveness of these contacts cannot be left to chance and should be built into the plan.

- What are the channels of distribution? What percentage of the product sales are through each type of intermediary?
- What is the company's relationship with intermediaries (e.g., distributors, agents, retailers, etc.)?
- What are distribution costs as a percentage of sales?
- How does the company's policy for distributor or retailer margins compare with those of the competition?
- What has been the recent history of stock-outs, substitutes, and back-orders?

Support Services

To complete the full cycle of customer value, installation, and repair services may need to be considered in the product's marketing plan.

- Has the value of repair services changed (due to cost increases, repair person efficiency, or any other reason)?

Trend Dynamics

An examination of trends and their dynamics relative to a product's success is the final part of the analysis. External trends have a direct bearing on market potential, although they are sometimes less tangible. In answering the following questions, select major events that are likely to affect the company, the competitors, the product, and markets served by the company.

· What technological changes are likely? How might they impact product sales within the next several years?
· What have been the industry trends in the following areas:
  – Product changes
  – Price levels/policies
  – Distribution changes
  – Power shifts in the channel
  – Mergers/acquisitions/divestitures
· What leading indicators correspond with product sales?
· What are the basic trends and changes in the economy?
· Are there regulatory or political forces that could impact product sales? What are their trends?
· What is the probability of the above trends occurring?
· What impact do these have on the product(s)?

Where Do You Want To Go Long-Term?

Identify the goals and long-term strategies you have determined for your product line. As mentioned in the first chapter, conceptualize your long-term product strategy as a type of future annual report. What will be the product mix, annual sales volume, core customers, and image in the marketplace? Long-term goals are somewhat "fuzzy," but they should provide direction for shorter-term plans.

Think about where you'd like to be in your career 10 years from now, or the house you'd like to own at that time, or the lives you'd like your children to have. All of those are "fuzzy" goals that impact some of your day-to-day decisions. That's similar to the type of thinking you should have for your products.

Compare where you are now with where you *want to go* long-term. Product managers may need to devise separate marketing plans (or separate sections of an overall plan) to address the requirements of different products or product categories (as described in the previous chapter). The gap between where you are and where you want to go will likely require more than 1 year's efforts. Therefore, you must decide what you will do this year to move one step closer from where you are to where you want to be.

What Are You Going To Do This Year?

The third step—defining what you will accomplish this year—actually has several components, including an objective, a target market definition, and a positioning statement. It starts with the identification of problems and opportunities that need to be addressed in the annual plan. Then, it moves to the forecast of sales volume, the marketing objectives that specify the market segments from which the volume will be generated, and the positioning of the product in the customers' minds.

Problems and Opportunities

After examining the market, the competition, the historical performance, and any significant trends, the next step is to synthesize the information to look for problems or opportunities and decide where to go from there. Problems or opportunities are the conclusions drawn from any part of the background analysis. For example, the analysis might uncover new niches that previously had been overlooked, a declining market share that was camouflaged by a growing market segment, or an inconsistent product image. In any case, focus on problems to correct or opportunities to leverage in the product marketing plan. Without this step of drawing conclusions, the data collection process is often perceived as a waste of time and is not made relevant to the marketing plan.

Setting marketing and sales objectives follows the identification of problems and opportunities. Frequently, a product manager is given a financial sales goal, and her job is to design a marketing program to make it happen. In other cases, the product manager must present the sales forecast to management with a justification or rationale. Typically, some combination of the two approaches is used.

Sales Forecasting

The product manager is responsible for forecasting product sales or, at a minimum, understanding the forecasts received. Three categories of forecasting techniques might be used:

· Time series forecasts can be obtained from historical data on past product sales to project into the future for short-term sales figures.
· Compiled forecasts, as the term implies, are compilations of data from qualitative and quantitative research.
· Causal forecasts are derived from relating sales to the factors that cause the sales to happen.

Although a product manager might work with an analyst to obtain these figures, it is important to understand the basic ramifications of the three categories of forecasts.

Time series.   A logical place to start forecasting future sales is to look at historical sales patterns. Time series analyses look at changes in sales over time. Plotting a product's sales over time gives the product manager a picture of the product's sales trends. Trend-fitting, or regression, plots the sales over time and uses a statistical formula to fit a line through the data points and then projects that line into the future. Trend-fitting is relatively simple and fast to do by computer, and it is easy to understand. It can be accurate in the short term if their external factors make the future sales environment significantly different from the past sales environment.

Several averages are time-series based. A moving average forecasts sales using a given number of time periods from the past (e.g., the average of the past 12 months' data). Each data point has the same weight, unless seasonal indexes or other weights are built in. As the average moves into the future, it drops off the oldest data point from the calculations. Exponential smoothing is a form of moving average that provides heavier weights to the most recent data. This is done when it is assumed that recent data are more valuable in predicting future sales than older data.

Box-Jenkins is a more sophisticated version of exponential smoothing. This technique uses a computer to test different time series models for the best fit. For example, the number of data points, as well as the different weights, affect the time-series line, so it is important to track how effective the various techniques were in providing a mathematical line close to the actual line of sales points.

Time-series techniques are appropriate when the sales environment does not change and when the effectiveness of a marketing plan has no impact on sales. Generally, neither of these is true. As a result, marketing research information and/or causal information should be part of the forecasting process.

Compiled forecasts. The marketing research approach used for forecasting can be a combination of compiling secondary and primary data as well as qualitative and quantitative approaches to data collection. Some of the secondary data can be pulled from the product fact book. Worksheet 10.1 provides a template for your information on industry or category sales for a product or line. Look at average market share over time and multiply this average by the projected industry sales for the next fiscal year. The result is an approximate sales forecast based on the industry projection. Adjust this forecast using qualitative information on trends or other elements that could influence product sales.

In terms of primary data collection, both qualitative and quantitative inputs are important. Quantitative input can come from front-line sources. Sales staff provide estimates by account or territory, and regional managers provide estimates by distributor or channel type. An example sales-force customer analysis form is shown in Table 10.1. In the example, the sales staff are asked to estimate sales for each major account for selected products, with their best estimate of the probability of closing the sale during the upcoming quarter. The form can be adapted to include volume rather than dollar revenue, annual rather than quarterly estimates, or other industry-specific variables. The product manager (or analyst) can calculate the expected values by multiplying the sales estimates for each product by the relevant probabilities. In the example, the expected sales of

Table 10.1　Sales Force Customer Analysis Form

Account	Product A		Product B		Product C	
	Sales	Probability	Sales	Probability	Sales	Probability
Vaporware	$1,000	.60	$600	.60	$400	.60
Tunnel Vision	2,000	.50	700	.80	700	.60
Virus-Aid	1,500	.70	900	.75	300	.90
Data-Notes	1,000	.50	600	.85	500	.80

Product A for this particular salesperson would be $3,150 (the sum of the sales times the probability for each account). Customers can also be surveyed directly to assess their probable purchases by product or for the entire line.

Qualitative forecasting techniques also are useful, particularly for new products. Concept testing, in conjunction with intent-to-buy surveys, can be a data point for the new product forecast. Other tools include the *Delphi technique* and trade data. The Delphi technique involves gathering independent forecasts from select experts, sharing the rationale for the forecasts without identifying which expert gave which forecast, and continuing until the forecasts converge. The process takes out the peer pressure that exists with committee or group forecasts, since the inputs are "blind."

Causal or correlation-based forecasts.　Causal techniques attempt to find relationships between sales and other variables. For example, tire sales are related to vehicular sales, and the sales of many household products are related to housing starts. If leading indicators (such as vehicle sales or housing starts) can be used to better understand the sales environment for a product, they should be used in the forecasting process. Sales also can be affected by advertising expenditures, number of sales staff, price changes, or other marketing variables. If a causal relationship between a change in marketing expenditures and a change in sales can be demonstrated, that information can be used not only in forecasting, but also as justification for spending a given amount in the marketing plan.

The forecasted sales figures used in a marketing plan should be based on a variety of inputs. Do not rely exclusively on trend projections, and do not accept upper management's sales forecasts without question. Try to reconcile the unit and dollar amounts based on the background analysis and the anticipated marketing plan/budget.

Setting Objectives

The objectives answer the question, "What are you going to do this year to move a step closer from where you are now to where you want to be?" They also answer the question, "What do you need to do to reach the sales forecast?" Let's say you have categorized your products into maintain, revitalize, and rationalize, as described earlier, with ten, three, and two products, respectively. You decide the ten maintenance products will require *no* changes in marketing, so that leaves five products to focus on. Define what results you want to obtain by year-end for each product (i.e., the objectives), and state it in terms that are SMART:

· **Specific**
· **Measurable**
· **Attainable**
· **Results-oriented**
· **Time-bound**

Specific objectives are quantitative, such as a given percentage increase in market share, unit growth in volume, or a specified number of product trials. *Measurable* refers to the ability to track results. Having a goal of, say, reaching 32% of scientists with artificial limbs is specific, but would be very difficult to measure. Being *attainable* is subjective. Goals, by their very nature require a change in the status quo, but if they are impossible to attain, they are really dreams. The *results-oriented* criterion is perhaps the most important. If the objectives specify the results (rather than the activities) you strive to achieve, they accomplish two things: They provide direction for the plan, and they become a metric against which to compare actual per-

Business Brief 10.2   The importance of customer retention as a marketing objective.

Companies are realizing that customer retention is as, if not more, important than getting new customers. According to *Business Marketing* magazine:

> An October 1994 study by Marketing Metrics showed that of the 165 companies surveyed, respondents, on average, allocate 53% of marketing budgets to retain existing customers and 47% to win new customers. A similar 1991 study showed 46% of marketing budgets went to retention, while 54% went to acquiring new customers.

Cellular One of New York and New Jersey, for example, has part of its marketing department devoted solely to customer retention. Some of the tactics include a 24-hour Customer Care Center and a Corporate Care Center for special corporate accounts. David Straus, Director of customer base marketing, says, "Our job really starts once the customer is in the door."

New York-based Bowne & Co., one of the world's largest financial printers, publishes a customer newsletter as a tool in customer retention. By keeping customers abreast of changes in their industries, Bowne & Co. is better able to differentiate itself from other financial service providers.

Source: Adapted from Kim Cleland, "Firms Want Customers Coming Back for More," *Business Marketing* (January 1995): 4+.

formance. *When* to compare these results metrics against actual performance is bound by the final criterion, *time*.

Objectives can be stated in terms of units or dollars (revenue and/or margin), market share, consumer satisfaction level, and so on. Emphasis should be given to the specific target customers you will focus on, and may include customer acquisition and retention goals. Customer retention, in particular, is a frequently overlooked objective (see Business Brief 10.2).

Typically, the objective starts with a verb (increase, maintain, solidify, etc.) acting on a specific goal (repeat purchases, new trial, sales volume/revenue, etc.) for a stated market (profiled market segment or account) within a specified time period (typically a year). An example objective is as follows:

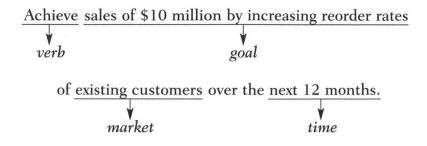

Target Market

What type of customer or group of customers is the most likely to buy the product? Resist the temptation to put every possible prospect into the description. You want to focus on the "ideal" customer—the one who has the greatest need for your product, who perceived value from it, and who is likely to respond to your marketing efforts. Describe the person in hypothetical terms, using both demographic and psychographic variables. The profile not only clarifies who you are trying to reach with your marketing, but also implies who you are not going after. The needs of this target customer drive your product design efforts, your pricing, your channel decisions, and your marketing communications. (If people who are not in your target market want to buy your product, that's fine—as long as it doesn't require a change in the factors just listed.) No product can successfully be all things to all people. Trying to do so results in a diluted product and marketing position.

Sometimes, to be effective in accomplishing the stated objectives, it may be necessary to go beyond the target market of users and identify the influencers who require additional marketing communications. Or, it may be necessary to pursue a secondary target market with a slightly different marketing approach. Note that this is *not* the same thing as having a shotgun approach to the market, but rather focusing on a small number of target efforts. Very likely, a primary target market as well as secondary targets will exist. Those segments that the product manager elects to target determine the marketing strategy as well as the product positioning and communication approaches. For example, Marvin Windows isolated different needs among different segments of window buyers and advanced its position from eighth to third in the industry by stressing the most relevant benefits to each group (see Business Brief 10.3).

The target market decision also will include the marshalling of resources to get the greatest impact for the marketing investment and to accomplish an objective, such as being an industry leader. In the past, industry leadership meant being the biggest and having the most visible brands. Now, with markets fragmenting, leadership can be defined with a niche concept. By focusing a firm's resources on smaller segments, the firm becomes more visible and gains a perception of leadership in that segment.

> The most important insight—the degree to which this whole concept validates the merits of a "niche" or "focus" strategy—seeking to become a large fish in a small pond. A brand of ice cream or beer carried in 500 retail outlets will benefit disproportionately if all those outlets are in Iowa, not spread over the Midwest, and even more if they are in Des Moines. A business-to-business marketer can achieve the same level of visibility and "leadership position" by focusing on one industry. Becoming the leading supplier of inventory software for meatpackers may be not only a feasi-

---

Business Brief 10.3   Segmentation at Marvin Windows.

Marvin, a family-owned and -controlled window manufacturer in Warroad, Minnesota, discovered the value of market segmentation in reaching its customers more effectively. By studying buying processes, it identified builders, dealers, remodelers, and architects as influence groups, and it designed segment-specific advertising messages to reach them. For example, remodelers want windows that fit existing openings and don't require "customizing" the wall to fit a standard window. For this group, Marvin positioned itself as the made-to-order window manufacturer. In reaching building supply dealers, Marvin focused on a lowered need for inventory, thereby increasing dealer profitability. For builders and architects, Marvin emphasized its ability to meet both aesthetic and budgetary constraints.

Source: Adapted from Kate Bertrand, "Divide and Conquer," *Business Marketing* 74 (October 1989): 49–50.

ble objective, but also one that confers all the "snowball" benefits of brand leadership within that industry.[1]

With even the most careful targeting of customers, product managers will not escape competition and will need to develop a well thought-out positioning statement. Whereas the selection of a target market identified *who* you are going after, the selection of a positioning strategy identifies *what perception* these customers should have of your product versus the competition. Different positioning alternatives were described in Chapter 4. Here, it becomes necessary to convert the thinking into a statement that becomes the foundation for several of the subsequent marketing activities. Repositioning is occasionally necessary due to changing conditions, as Hewlett-Packard found when it introduced inkjet printers as alternatives to dot matrix printers (see Business Brief 10.4).

Business Brief 10.4   Hewlett-Packard: Repositioning the DeskJet.

Hewlett-Packard introduced the DeskJet in 1988. Sales came slowly. By 1989, the product wasn't meeting its sales goals, despite absence of strong competition. An analysis determined that the DeskJet was taking business away from H-P's own laser printers, rather than the competition, resulting in a lower profit margin per sale.

After identifying the problem, H-P decided to reposition the DeskJet as a competitor to dot-matrix printers instead of as a lower-cost alternative to laser printers. To attain this objective, H-P started by thoroughly studying Epson, the leader in the industry. The company began to track Epson's market share. It evaluated Epson's marketing practices, profiled its top man-

agers, and surveyed its customers. Engineers tore apart Epson printers to better understand the technology used. H-P discovered that Epson printers were placed in prominent spots in stores, customers perceived the printers as reliable, and the products were designed for easy manufacturability.

Armed with this information, Hewlett-Packard planned the actions that were necessary to reposition the DeskJet. First, the company convinced stores to place DeskJets next to the Epson dot-matrix printers to emphasize the competitive positioning. Second, H-P extended its warranty to 3 years to assure buyers that the DeskJet was reliable.

(continued on next page)

Business Brief 10.4   continued

And finally, the inkjets were redesigned with manufacturability in mind.	Source: Adapted from Stephen Kreider Yoder, "How H-P Used Tactics of the Japanese to Beat Them at Their Game," *Wall Street Journal* (September 8, 1994): 1+.

Positioning Statement

Positioning refers to deciding how a product is to be perceived in the minds of the customer, relative to the competition. Imagine talking to a customer who asks, "Why should I buy from you?" What should your answer be? What makes your product a better buy than competitive products? In this analysis, consider the customer's frame of reference (i.e., the products they would consider likely competitors). Different customers will have different frames of reference that could require a different positioning. Therefore, the positioning statement should identify the relevant market segment, that segment's frame of reference, the product's point of differentiation, and an indication of why a product provides that differentiation (i.e., the internal strength or competitive edge that makes a claim of differentiation credible). A positioning statement might resemble the following:

To <u>small businesses,</u> <u>Desk-Mite</u> is the brand of

relevant market   *brand*
segments

<u>interactive desktop organizer</u> that <u>offers more flexibility</u>

frame of reference   *point of differentiation*

due to its <u>ability to interface with computers,
office machines, and telecommunications equipment.</u>

competitive edge

Start by identifying the attributes that customers are looking for when they buy from the product category, and find out how important each attribute is. Is delivery important? How about minimum tolerances? How important? Next, have customers rate the product in question versus the competition along all the important attributes. Try to isolate attributes for which customers already believe the product is competitively superior and that the company can protect, using its core abilities, knowledge, or other strength. If this cannot be found, the job of the product manager is to determine how to build it into the product.

After thinking about the marketing objectives, rationale, target markets, and positioning statements, you have enough information to complete Worksheet 10.2.

Worksheet 10.2   Marketing objectives and strategies

Division: Group: Product Line: Market:

General marketing objective(s):

Rational for objective(s):

Positioning statement:

To _____ , _____ is the brand of
                (market segment)   (your product name)

_____ that _____
              (frame of reference)   (point of differentiation)

due to _____ .
                                    (competitive edge)

The Marketing Action Plan

Marketing encompasses a multitude of activities involved in getting a product to the right market at the right time and at the right price. Since the product manager is ultimately responsible for this, it is critical that marketing services (e.g., advertising, marketing research) and distribution strategy not be ignored. As emphasized repeatedly in this book, making sure that the right competitive position is established is the starting point for the development of an effective strategy.

How is the product or service different from the competition? This can be a tricky question, particularly for commodity products like mortgages. However, Arbor National Mortgage, a midsize company in Uniondale, New York, has developed a positioning approach that has worked. By repackaging a standard mortgage into a bridal registry, the result was a distinctive identity.

> Arbor takes a standard Fannie Mae mortgage and repackages it into the Arbor Home Bridal Registry. Couples register with Arbor instead of a department store so friends and families can contribute to the newlyweds' first home. "Running the registry is a lot of work, so we aren't as concerned with getting couples to register as we are in getting inquiries about purchasing a first home," says Boyles [Arbor's senior vice president of marketing]. "Only three dozen couples have actually registered, but we've had over 5,000 couples call about the service. Their names are now in our database. We hope to have them as customers someday." Arbor also holds mortgage seminars for real estate brokers, accountants, and consumers. And the company plants a tree for customers who want one, either in their yard or in a public forest.[2]

Product managers shepherd this process through a variety of functional areas and are responsible for communicating the appropriate messages to the target market(s), setting a price consistent with the value provided, and evaluating the distribution activities to ensure superior end-customer satisfaction. The following sections look at the advertising, distribution, and various support components of the marketing function.

Marketing Communications (Marcom) Planning

The marketing communications (marcom) portion of the annual plan addresses the setting of the advertising objectives, media planning, and creative strategy. It is often the largest component of the marketing plan. In some cases, publicity, telesales, and/or sales support will be part of the plan. This is the direction of "integrated marketing," tapping into the potential synergy of all communication vehicles. Product managers are usually more interested in direct-response activities than in purely image or corporate advertising. Even consumer marketers are becoming increasingly involved in database marketing, with the aim of targeting messages more effectively and measuring the response to the investment in advertising.

Setting objectives. The starting point for the advertising sub-plan is the setting of objectives. The statement of objectives should follow the same format as the overall marketing objective. It should include what to communicate to whom and with what results. Should the advertising generate sales, produce leads, or enhance an image? To whom must the message be communicated to make that happen? What will be the result of this communication? $X revenue? Number of leads per prospects reached? A percentage change in awareness? If the product manager runs a mail-order operation with no sales force, it might be appropriate to have an objective of generating $X sales from a defined target market over the next 12 months. Most companies have some combination of sales, lead generation, and/or image reinforcement.

If the product is not sold directly to the end-user, a decision must be made about what part of the budget will be devoted to advertising to the end-customer (a pull strategy) and what part will be devoted to trade advertising (a push strategy). These two groups will require different media and different messages.

After deciding what to communicate to whom and with what results, the next question is how to make it happen. That is the essence of the advertising plan: deciding on the media and creative strategy. Although much of the detail work will be handled by the company's advertising department or through an advertising agency, the product manager must understand the basics to make good evaluative decisions. The media planning will consist of (1) listing potential media, (2) selecting appropriate media vehicles, (3) assessing trade-offs, (4) examining media combinations, and (5) developing a media calendar. The creative strategy converts the positioning and unique selling features into effective customer communications.

Media planning.   Media planning starts with selecting the appropriate media and media vehicles to accomplish the stated objectives. Decide how many to use (to increase reach) and how often to advertise in each (to increase frequency). Then, coordinate resources to get maximum return from the investment in advertising. That means it is sometimes necessary to violate traditional turf boundaries that separate the media (including boundaries between marketing and sales) and focus on the intended results (objectives) of the advertising.

List potential media.   Start by developing a list of all media and promotional methods that could be used to accomplish the objectives. Analyze each according to editorial format, circulation, frequency, and cost. Then prioritize the list according to each medium's ability to contribute to the plan's effectiveness. The larger the potential audience, the more a product manager must consider broad-reach media. The smaller the audience, the more targeted the media must be.

The primary media choices for consumer communications are listed in Table 10.2. It is not a comprehensive list but is simply intended to trigger a few ideas for thinking through the media options. The primary media choices for a business target market include some of the consumer media choices but go beyond as well (Table 10.3).

Select appropriate vehicles.   Second, select the most appropriate media vehicles. A message of quality is best carried in a publication that is a "bible" of the industry, whereas announcements of new industrial products are better placed in new-product digests. For product managers not working through an agency (either internal or external), some preliminary information on the media vehicles can be obtained from Standard Rate & Data Service directories available at those libraries with business collections. From that information, the product manager can estimate the cost per prospect for each media vehicle. After narrowing the list, request media kits from

Table 10.2 Consumer Media Considerations

Category	Some "Best" Uses	Rate/Cost Considerations
Print Newspapers	• Ads that don't require high print quality • Local coverage of all demographic segments • Inserts • Coupons	• Agate line or column inch rates • ROP (run of paper) • Color rates • Insert rates
Magazines	• Demographic selectivity • Color print quality	• Page rates (or fractions of) • Color rates • Bleed rates • Cover rates
Broadcast Radio	• High frequency • Auditory messages • Appeal to specific demographics	• Daypart (e.g., drive time) • ROS (run of station) • Local, spot, network
Television	• Mass coverage • Impact of sight and sound • Short message (except for infomercials)	• Daypart (e.g., prime time) • Specific programs • Local, spot, network
Direct mail	• Direct response • Identified audience • Long message	• List rental • Postage rates
Publicity	• "Newsworthy" events • Credibility	• Personnel/time costs
Miscellaneous Outdoor	• Frequency • Mass local audience	• Poster size • Traffic count
Transit	• Frequency	• Inside/outside/station posters
Point-of-purchase	• Stimulate impulse buying	• Retailer negotiation
Internet	• Interactivity • Two-way communication	• Start-up and maintenance costs

Table 10.3   Business Media Considerations

Category	Some "Best" Uses	Rate/Cost Considerations

Print
Newspapers
	• Frequency
	  (compared to trades)
	• For select markets where
	  newspapers are significant
		• Agate line or column inch
		• ROP (run of paper)
		• Preferred position
		• Color rates (if available)

Trade journals	• Product appeals to specific
	  reader profile
	• Product can benefit from
	  image of journal
		• Page rate (or fraction of)
		• Color rates
		• Preferred position

General
business
publications
	• Need to reach a broad
	  mix of influencers or
	  decision makers
		• Same as above

Consumer
publications
	• No trade reaches your
	  market
	• You can afford the
	  additional impressions
	  even at the expense of
	  wasted coverage
		• Same as above

Directories	• Purchasing agents play a role in the sale	• Ad size
Card decks	• Low-cost products	• Number of inserts
Broadcast Television	• Large target market • Corporate or image advertising	• Selected programs

Radio	• Primary market
	  concentrated in limited
	  geographic areas
	• Frequency
		• Daypart
		• ROS (run of station)
		• Local, spot, network

Direct mail	• Identified audience • Lead generation or direct sale	• List rental • Postage rates
Sales literature/ brochures	• To advance the sales call	• Print charges
Catalog	• Reference material	• Print charges
Trade shows	• Demonstration of product	• Booth charges • Direct and indirect labor
Publicity	• "Newsworthy" events	• Direct and indirect labor
Internet	• Interactivity • Two-way communication	• Start-up maintenance costs

the rest to obtain more specific information on reader profiles, frequency discounts, ability to obtain reduced list rental (both mail and e-mail) with a paid ad, and information about the effectiveness of advertising in the specific publication or broadcast medium.

Assess trade-offs.   Third, assess the trade-offs between the size (cost) of the ad, the impact on prospects, and the number of times it can be placed. The cost of a large ad is more than the cost of a smaller ad. However, because a large ad is seen (noted) by more people, the cost per person noting the ad can provide more efficiency. The assessment also should include placement within the medium. For magazines, ads on the covers, front part of the publication, adjacent to specific editorial content, and/or isolated from other advertisements usually have the most effectiveness. For radio, drive-time spots typically reach more people than ROS (run of schedule). For television, news has the greatest audience size, although specific programs might have a closer match to the target audience. For direct mail, odd-sized and dimensional mailings can have more impact, but they increase the cost, thereby limiting the potential reach and frequency of the mailings. In general, with a given budget, it is usually better to increase frequency at the expense of reach rather than to increase reach at the expense of frequency.

What is the necessary frequency of communication to maximize response? That depends on several things. Messages promoting a unique product or having a unique format require less frequency to be noticed than "commodity" ads. The more advertising messages a person is exposed to at one time (e.g., within one publication), the greater the number of insertions required to break through the clutter. The more complicated the message or the less differentiated, the more likely it is that more than one impression will be required to be effective.

Examine media combinations.   Fourth, examine combinations of media that could increase effectiveness. This is the "synergy" part of integrated marketing (see Table 10.4). For example, timing a telemarketing sales call right after the

Table 10.4   Setting Media Objectives

	Objectives			
	Reach	Frequency	Continuity	Pulsing
Message Needs				
For new or highly complex message, strive for		•		
For dogmatic message, surge at beginning then	•		•	
For reason-why messages, use high frequency at first, then				•
For emotionally oriented messages			•	
When message is so creative or product so newsworthy it forces attention		•		
When message is dull or product indistinguishable, strive for		•		
Customer purchase patterns				
To influence brand choice of regularly purchased products, use		•	•	
As purchase cycle lengthens, use		•		•
To influence erratic purchase cycles, strive for		•		•
To influence customer attitudes toward impulse purchases, use		•	•	
For products requiring great deliberation, alternate	•	•		
To reinforce customer loyalty, concentrate on	•		•	
To influence seasonal purchases, anticipate peak periods with	•	•		
Budget levels				
With a low budget, use				•
With a higher budget, strive for			•	
Competitive activity				
When heavy competitive advertising, concentrate on		•		
When competitive budgets are larger, use				•

Table 10.4   continued

	Reach	Frequency	Continuity	Pulsing
		Objectives		
Marketing objectives				
For new product introductions to mass market	•			
To expand share of market with new uses for product, use	•			
To stimulate direct response from advertising, use		•		•
To create awareness and recognition of corporate status, use	•		•	

Source: Courtland L. Bovee and William F. Arens, *Contemporary Advertising* (Burr Ridge, IL: Richard D. Irwin, 1982: 469).

intended receipt of a direct mail piece can increase the response. Using different media simultaneously can sometimes break through the target market's perceptual barriers. This approach increases frequency, but different media also can increase reach by appealing to different segments of the market or to different influencers or decision makers. Making decisions on reach versus frequency and continuous versus pulsing advertising strategies is part of this analysis. Table 10.4 provides a checklist of considerations for making the decisions.

Develop media calendar.   Finally, after examining the costs and benefits of the various media types and combinations, put the entire media plan into calendar format for the year (Table 10.5). This accomplishes three things. First, it forces the product manager to think in advance. Second, by seeing the combinations of media in one place, the potential impact they have on each other can be improved. Third, the calendar helps focus on integrated marketing communications by incorporating nontraditional communications vehicles (e.g., seminars, newsletters, product placements, video games, sponsored search terms, special CDs or DVDs, and Internet advertising) into the plan.

Table 10.5 Media Calendar

Media	Jan	Feb	Mar	Apr	May	Jun	Jul	Aug	Sep	Oct	Nov	Dec	Summary
Direct mail													
First wave													
Second wave													
Third wave													
Magazine advertising													
Magazine A													
Magazine B													
Magazine C													
Newspaper													
Newspaper A													
Newspaper B													
Newspaper C													
Television													
Radio													
Other media													

Creative strategy. The creative strategy should include the basic message and positioning that should be communicated to the target market. Although an advertising agency might be responsible for the creative design of the advertising, the product manager should at least be able to critique it. As mentioned earlier, the advertising message depends on the positioning statement developed at the start of the planning process. The message should always be consistent with the positioning or unique selling proposition (USP) and include customer benefits that differentiate the product from the competition. Sometimes a company is interested in being positioned as innovative, and it uses patents to "prove" that position. Titleist has used its patented dimpling process to "prove" the quality of its golf balls; Samsonite luggage uses line drawings depicting patents and patents pending for the various product features.[3] In any case, the objective of the advertising is to convince potential customers that your product is different from the competition in an important way, and that this difference is strong enough to motivate them to buy.

For print advertising, the headline should attract prospects to the ad. Sometimes, this can be done by stating the benefit or the promise of a reward. At other times, a provocative question will be more successful. The headline should generally maintain a positive tone and be coordinated with the rest of the ad. The copy should contain a benefit in the lead paragraph and use present-tense, active-voice words. If the copy is long, use subheads to make it easier on the eye. Identify what the prospect is to do as a result of reading the ad. Most business advertising (and a growing amount of consumer advertising) strives for direct response, so the copy should include the 800 number, the Web site URL, or other contact information. The layout should take eye movement into account and have a single dominant element rather than being overly cluttered.

For broadcast advertising, hold the number of elements to a minimum. Words should be conversational and concise. Take advantage of impact if using television commercials. With radio, be sure the company and product name is mentioned often.

For direct mail, set up repeated tests. Test different copy, different package formats, and different mailing lists. If possible, have a control to test against an alternative for each mailing. Personalize the cover letter and talk about the prospect's needs—not about the product. Use a strong offer to encourage people to respond. Do not simply encourage them to contact the company for more information; provide an incentive such as a free booklet, reduced price, or trial offer. If using direct mail (or any direct-response advertising), be sure to have inquiry-fulfillment materials available. Highlight on the envelope that this is the information the prospect requested.

When using an e-mail campaign, testing also is critical. Different subject headers, copy, and formats can have different impacts. As with direct mail, test using experimental and control groups.

Include the sales staff in evaluating direct-response lead generation programs, including e-mail campaigns. Let them see the mail piece before it is mailed to customers and prospects, and ask them for input. Not only will sales staff offer useful suggestions, but they will also be more likely to buy into a program if brought in at the early stages.

Evaluating advertising effectiveness.   Regardless of the medium used, collect as much data as possible on the return generated by each advertisement (return on promotional investment, ROPI). This helps to determine which media are most effective and helps in future budgeting. If advertising is done for long-term image reasons, periodically conduct image surveys to determine whether the investment is being well spent. In any event, try to think creatively about how to reach your customers in a way that helps them make purchase decisions in your favor. Sometimes, the best "advertising" is through nonadvertising approaches, as Red Star Specialty Products showed in Business Brief 10.5.

Sales Promotion

In addition to advertising, product managers might be involved with a variety of other promotional techniques, such as sam-

Business Brief 10.5   Red Star adopts integrated marketing communications program.

In the early 1990s, Red Star Specialty Products discovered that the messages reaching its trade customers were inconsistent. Their market of food technologists didn't know how Red Star products were different from competitors' products. Worse yet, only 10% of those responding to trade ads were "A" leads and 70% were "C" leads.

Since Red Star's $300,000 marketing budget could not be increased, it had to re-evaluate where and how it spent its promotional dollars. First, it scaled back its trade ads and used some of the money for educational materials, such as brochures, newsletters, and seminars. Another educational tool Red Star developed was an interactive software program with a tutorial on flavor enhancers and a guide to using specific products. These helped position Red Star as an advisor to food companies that had slashed their own R&D staff.

The company also developed an improved database to more effectively reach customers and prospects. According to Marketing Manager Tim Roebken, "Before, the most we had done is work with an industry magazine and do a direct mail piece to their list of subscribers. It was still a wasteful, mass-advertising approach. Of the 30,000 subscribers, there may have been 5,000 or 6,000 we wanted to reach."

By examining problems and opportunities and acting on a specific positioning strategy, Red Star was able to increase the effectiveness of its marketing communications without increasing its total budget. The difference is that now two-thirds of the marketing budget is devoted to new vehicles (with only $100,000 spent on advertising), and all are integrated to provide a consistent message to the market.

Source: Adapted from Joe Mullich, "Red Star Crafts a New Marketing Recipe," *Business Marketing* (December 1994): 6+.

---

pling, sales contests, and various other incentive programs. These are referred to as "incentive programs," because they provide inducements to stimulate short-term incremental sales of the product, as opposed to building long-run brand loyalty. Promotions are commonly used to introduce new products, influence the effectiveness of competitors' tactics, or tap into a new market.

Product sampling can be an effective technique for encouraging customers to try a new product. New products that require behavioral change by potential users generally benefit from the ability of customers to try them on a low-cost or no-cost basis. 3M's Post-It Notes, for example, required free sampling for customers to experience using the product. Test drives are a method of sampling in the automotive industry. Rent-with-the-option-to-buy is a form of sampling that reduces cost (and risk) to both parties.

Channel Selection and Support

Unless a product manager's products are distributed differently from all other products in the company, chances are he will not have significant control over the strategic methods of distribution. Most of the activities will be related to working with the existing distributors, dealers, or agents and perhaps expediting shipments as necessary. However, some new products will necessitate changes in the channel of distribution, or market and competitive forces will require changes for existing products. This could also be a critical element of the plan if a product manager is rolling out a product into new regions and/or expanding globally. As a result, distribution strategy should not be ignored as the product manager develops the annual marketing plan.

Whenever a product manager introduces a lower- or higher-priced product, or one that has a different image, it might be necessary to introduce new channels. A potentially successful product can be thwarted by the wrong channel decision, as Huffy found when it introduced its new Cross Sport bike.

> Huffy Corp., for example, the successful $700 million bike maker, did careful research before it launched a new bicycle it dubbed the Cross Sport, a combination of the sturdy mountain bike popular with teenagers and the thin-framed, nimbler racing bike. Huffy conducted two separate series of market focus groups in shopping malls across the country, where randomly selected children and adults viewed the bikes and ranked them. The bikes met with shoppers' approval. So far, so good. In the summer of 1991, Cross Sports were shipped out to mass retailers, such as the Kmart and Toys 'R' Us chains, where Huffy already did most

of its business. That was the mistake. As Richard L. Molen, Huffy president and chief executive, explains, the researchers missed one key piece of information. These special hybrid bikes were aimed at adults and, at $159, were priced 15% higher than other Huffy bikes, and therefore needed individual sales attention by the sort of knowledgeable sales staff who work only in bike specialty shops. Instead, Huffy's Cross Sports were supposed to be sold by the harried general salespeople at mass retailers such as Kmart. Result: "It was a $5 million mistake," says Molen. By 1992, the company had slashed Cross Sport production 7% and recorded an earnings drop of 30 percent.[4]

As markets fragment, different target customers—even for the same product—might seek alternative channels of distribution. Key accounts, for example, might best be served by going direct, whereas other customers can be more efficiently served through distributors. On the other hand, small customers might be handled by telesales, even if outside reps are calling on larger customers in the same territory. Specialized distributors or agents might be more successful with certain segments than existing intermediaries, and that possibility should be periodically explored. Product managers also must evaluate the role of the Web in channel strategy.

Effectively motivating intermediaries can have a positive impact on the bottom line for the products. This starts by keeping a careful record of distributor or rep activity by product and assessing overall capabilities. Product managers should accompany regional or sales managers in routine visits to distributors or reps, and they might be expected to help prepare joint marketing plans. If an advisory council exists, the product manager should review the meeting minutes (at minimum, the sections related to his or her product line) and react accordingly.

Manufacturers' and resellers' goals do not always match. Product managers sometimes tend to view resellers as the destination of their product. Resellers, on the other hand, view the receipt of a product as the beginning of a sales cycle. This can create unnecessary conflict, which can be reduced by a better sharing of information.

Product managers spend a good deal of money and effort to understand end-user needs and how their products fit these needs. Resellers should also be given this information. Providing this education to resellers not only helps them work better, but also enables them to provide valuable feedback to the manufacturer on product performance.

Product Support

Product support can encompass several things: installation, warranty follow-through, product upgrades, repairs, customer training, and so on. The product manager might not be directly involved with these activities, but she should be concerned about whether the policies and procedures are in place for them to happen. Customer satisfaction frequently depends as much on these factors as it does on the product itself. In addition, the product manager might be involved in developing services that optimize profit potential from various segments. We will examine some of the product support issues that a product manager might want to handle operationally or include in the marketing plan.

The cost of installation can be included in the price of the product or be an "optional" or unbundled component. The decision should be made in conjunction with the appropriate personnel (e.g., the service manager). If any significant changes are to be made, they should be mentioned in the marketing plan, with the impact on other marketing activities and on the bottom line.

A warranty or service contract can affect the salability of a product, and it should be examined along with other features. Several questions should be considered:

· What do customers expect?
· Will there be a full or limited warranty?
· Can competitors match the warranty? Will they?
· Should the warranty be handled by the manufacturer, by the dealer, or by an independent organization?
· What are the advantages and disadvantages of service contracts and extended warranties?

As with any other part of the action program, changes to be implemented to the support program during the next fiscal year should be included in the marketing plan along with the impact and rationale.

Marketing Research

After completing the action program portion of the marketing plan, there will likely be information gaps that will require more data before the next planning cycle. This could include formal survey or focus group research, online database searching, and the analysis of internal customer records and databases. If so, it is a good idea to include these activities as action items in the marketing plan to assure that resources and approvals have been attained. When a major project is expected, solicit proposals prior to the development of the action plan so that the time or cost of the project is not underestimated.

Writing the Marketing Plan

The purpose of the annual product marketing plan is to provide top management with a concise marketing and financial summary of objectives and strategies, along with the requirements to achieve the objectives. Enough rationale should be provided to allow them to approve the necessary expenditures without the detail available in a product fact book. Keep the plan as brief as possible, perhaps no more than six or ten pages (excluding charts, exhibits, and appendices that might raise the page count by 10 or 20 pages). Too much detail obscures the main issues involved. Product managers are not paid to make the inevitable happen, so it's not necessary to include the ordinary routines of your job in the plan. Focus on the surprises—the things you will change—and relegate the mundane to an appendix.

On the other hand, do not use the desire for brevity as an excuse for not collecting information. If some information needed to support a recommendation is not available, mention it in the plan (at least as a footnote) to demonstrate that critical data are not being ignored, but that sufficient confidence exists with the other information to justify taking the risk. Include other assumptions you've made that might have an impact on the validity of the plan.

If the product plan is to be presented orally as part of a meeting, be sure to come prepared to answer any questions that might arise. Nothing is more frustrating to top management than to reschedule a meeting or make it longer than necessary because of a product manager's lack of preparation.

The written plan consists of a summary of the product's historical performance, a statement of problems and opportunities, sales forecasts/goals and a summary table of the impact on profit and loss (P & L), marketing objectives for the product or product line, concise strategies for accomplishing the objectives, and a series of financial and other exhibits to permit a quick assessment of the product program and its impact.

Separate strategy documents might need to be prepared for operational use by the product manager. Simply provide a concise summary of each as part of the annual product plan, perhaps in the format of listing the objective(s) for that element of the program and providing a brief overview of the strategy to accomplish that objective. Be careful, however, that the complete plan is coordinated. Do not work on the advertising strategy document, for example, without coordinating it with the other elements of the marketing mix.

Several formats are possible for a written product plan; there is no one best approach. Table 10.6 is only an example. Modify it as appropriate for a given product line, company, and circumstances. The format of objectives and strategies for the various marketing components is quite typical for a written plan, with rationale or justification included.

Product Strategy

Several objectives in the product plan may be necessary to accomplish a stated sales forecast. For example, a product objective could be to attain sales of $X for each of three major

Table 10.6   Marketing Plan Outline

Topic Outline	Description
Product Performance	Two to three paragraphs summarizing the product's performance relative to last year's plan, along with explanations of variances from the plan. Any research conducted on product performance or quality can be included in this section as well.
Background	Highlights from the background analysis, using bullet points as much as possible. It is useful to include the market analysis, competitive analysis, and/or performance history worksheets as attachments or exhibits.
Long-Term Objectives	A statement indicating the long-term direction for your product line and its long-term "fit" within the corporate strategic plan.
Problems/ Opportunities	Problems that might make it difficult to achieve the objectives. List the steps to be taken to minimize the risk. Opportunities that will help in achieving the objectives.
Sales Forecasts/Goals	A statement of the product's forecasted sales for the next fiscal year. If there are several products or product lines to be examined separately, use a tabular format.
Marketing Objectives	Brief statements of objectives for the product or line for the next fiscal year. These can be stated in terms of revenue/profit, new-product trials, retention rates, etc.
Marketing Program	
1. Positioning statement	Use the positioning statement from Worksheet 10.2. Make sure that it lists the unique selling features(s) of the product (i.e., how the product is to be perceived in the customer's mind relative to the competition). The positioning statement should be clear enough to be the "glue" for coordinating the subsequent marketing mix variables.
2. Target market(s)	Several paragraphs with a description of the rationale for the primary and secondary target markets.
3. Product strategy	This section can contain several items, depending on the company and product requirements. There will be one or more objectives, each followed by a brief strategy statement. The format will usually be as follows:
	• Brief product description (such as one contained in a catalog) indicating the competitive differences, along with a table of the sizes and variety of products in the line.

(continued on next page)

Table 10.6   continued

Topic Outline	Description
	• Product objectives, including new uses, repositioning, line extensions/modifications, programs to improve quality, or new-product introductions.
	• Strategy
	• Rationale
	• Capacity utilization, including existing capacity along with manufacturing requirements of the marketing plan.
4. Pricing strategy	A general statement of the pricing strategy used for the product(s). Include any planned changes in price, discounts, warranties, and terms and conditions of sale, along with a table indicating the expected impact on selling and profit performance. The format will be as follows:
	• Brief description
	• Objective
	• Strategy
	• Rationale
	• Impact table
5. Advertising strategy	
a. National advertising	This section will have three components:
	1. The competitive product differentiation to include in the advertising message.
	2. The media plan along with a calendar of expected insertions.
	3. Cost/spending information:
	• Brief description
	• Objective
	• Strategy
	• Rationale
	• Implementation
	• Supporting tables
b. Cooperative advertising	A statement of the goals and general program description of cooperative advertising programs with channel members.

Table 10.6   continued

Topic Outline	Description
c. Trade advertising	If advertising to intermediaries who resell the product, the message and media plan should be summarized in this section.
6. Promotion strategy	There are several types of sales promotions, support materials, trade show plans, and other nonadvertising promotions that may be part of the marketing plan. These may be part of separate plans or strategy documents but should at least be summarized in this section. The format should be consistent with the others: • Objective • Strategy
7. Field sales plan	The field sales plan is almost always a separate planning document. Nevertheless, include any information that directly impacts the product or its marketing plan. For example, any training or incentive programs that are part of the budget or that are recommended in addition to the standard field sales plan should be included here.
8. Distribution strategy	Any recommendations regarding changes to the channel of distribution, including adding or deleting intermediaries, should be included. Also incorporate any programs necessary to motivate channel members or to collect information about the end-user from them. The format is as follows: • Objective • Strategy
9. Product support	Any recommendations regarding the warranty/guarantee for the product, customer service changes, or any other product support issues that affect the achievement of the product objectives. Maintain the format used earlier. • Objective • Strategy
Training Requirements	Any training requirements (e.g., for customers) not included elsewhere in the marketing plan.
Marketing Research	Any planned research for the fiscal year, providing the proposal as an attachment.

(continued on next page)

Table 10.6   continued

Topic Outline	Description
Financial Summary	A pro forma profit and loss statement for the product(s). (See Table 10.7.)
Schedules	An action schedule indicating who does what by when. Allow space for the appropriate individuals to sign and date their agreement to the stated tasks.

products. The supporting strategy would explain what modifications this would require in terms of quality improvements, "bundling," or new uses. The rationale would explain why this is possible, given the background analysis.

Branding and packaging might or might not be a crucial part of the plan, but they should at least be considered. Be sure that the customer need is addressed and explain why a specific product satisfies this need better than the competition does. Also, mention the effect of other products on the product line and/or the effect of the line on the company product mix. If some maintenance products will be self-sustaining during the fiscal year, mention that fact and include the routine activities in an appendix.

New-product plans might be separate because they usually cover a different time period from the annual plan. However, because they impact a product manager's bottom line, they should probably be summarized here. New-product specifications, positioning, budget, and event schedules can be included.

Pricing Strategy

The pricing section should start with a statement of general company policies and how specific product pricing fits within those policies. Any changes in discounts, price packages, warranties, terms and conditions of sale, or any other variables should be listed, along with an explanation of the impact on the profitability of the line and of the "fit" in the overall positioning and product strategy.

Advertising Strategy

The advertising section could be quite long if several types of advertising are used. The national (or regional) advertising directed at the end-customer requires a different message and media than does advertising directed at the trade. Therefore, separate campaigns must be developed. In any case, the product manager must make sure that the media and messages are coordinated to match the positioning statement and overall marketing objectives stated in the annual plan.

Your Internet strategy could be included here as part of an integrated marketing communications campaign, or it could be pulled out into a separate section. The choice depends on the amount of *different* emphasis that will be devoted to it this year.

The media planning part of the strategy should list, in calendar format, the media vehicles used to convey the message. The rationale should explain why this mix of media and insertions would accomplish the reach, frequency, and cost goals of the campaign.

Promotion Strategy

Sales promotion refers to tools, other than advertising, used to stimulate short-term demand. This includes coupons, free samples, contests, premiums, point-of-purchase material, and so on. Customer, trade, and sales force promotions can be included in this section, along with budgets and calendars (similar to the examples mentioned previously).

Sales support materials can be covered in this section or in the field sales section. Also, any trade show strategies, merchandising, or publicity that the company is involved in should be addressed.

Field Sales Plan

The field sales plan is usually beyond a product manager's control, but activities might exist for which product managers are responsible, or activities might exist that must be performed to attain product goals. In those cases, they should be included in this portion of the annual marketing plan.

Distribution Strategy

The distribution strategy section should contain a statement on general policies and the desired penetration or coverage. If any changes are planned, such as adding or deleting intermediaries or creating programs to improve relationships, they should be mentioned here along with the "fit" into the positioning and overall marketing objectives.

Product Support

The product support section should provide a general statement on the policies for warranties and guarantees and repair service, as well as any anticipated changes. As always, this should be coordinated with the rest of the marketing program, so that the positioning and marketing objectives are achieved.

Profit and Loss Statement

The marketing plan is an investment in the product's future equity, and should have a positive impact on the current year's sales. Therefore, a profit and loss statement is either included with the marketing plan, or as a component of a separate product plan. In any event, it's important to monitor the various cost-to-sales ratios both to budget, and over time to highlight red flags that need to be addressed in the future (Table 10.7).

Checklist: Creating and Using Marketing Plans

· Word your annual product marketing objectives so that they indicate what you want to accomplish during the next fiscal year to take advantage of identified opportunities and to overcome potential problems.
· Be sure the objectives are consistent with the long-term vision of the product line and company.
· Identify the group(s) of customers you are going to focus your energies and resources on during the next fiscal year. This becomes your target market(s).

Table 10.7   Profit and Loss Statement

	Previous Year	Percent Sales	Current Year	Percent Sales	Next Year	Percent Sales
Product sales revenue	$		$		$	
Less price adjustments						
Cost of goods	—		—		—	
Gross margin		%		%		%
Controllable marketing expenses						
Advertising						
Trade allowances						
Promotions						
Trade shows						
Sales support						
Training						
Total controllable marketing expenses	—		—		—	
Product manager contribution margin		%		%		%
Other product expenses						
Sales force cost						
Distribution						
Administration						
Miscellaneous	—		—		—	
Total other product expenses						
Total expenses	—	%	—	%	—	%
Product contribution to overhead		%		%		%
Increase/decrease	%		%		%	

· Since many competitors could be going after this same group of customers, use your positioning statement to explain how you want customers to view you as better than the competition and how you can provide evidence of this difference.

· Consider the impact that pricing, advertising, field selling, distribution strategy, and product support have on one another as well as on the success of your product. Write the marketing plan with these impacts in mind.

- Don't limit your marketing budget to advertising the same way you always have. Test new approaches and techniques.
- Be sure your communications reach the right people. It's better to have an average ad with a direct hit than a terrific ad shown to the wrong people.
- Experiment with database marketing to pinpoint the right message for the right customers.
- When creating print ads, strive to have a benefit or a reward in the headline.
- Integrate your marketing communications techniques to increase their effectiveness.
- Consider sales promotions as part of your marketing communications toolbox.
- Don't automatically assume that your current method of distribution is best for your product or that it won't require a change in the near future.
- Match the capabilities of your distributors or retailers with the selling requirements of your product.
- Monitor and control product support as a potential value-added component of your product.

Interview with H. Paul Root, Chairman of the American Marketing Association's Board of Directors

Paul Root's prior experience includes Chief Marketing Officer and President of the Marketing Science Institute (MSI) in Cambridge, MA, Director of the Corporate Marketing Research Division for DuPont, and a tenured marketing faculty member of the Graduate School of Business at the University of Michigan.

Q: *In a nutshell, could you describe the AMA and what resources it might provide for product and brand managers?*

A: The American Marketing Association (AMA) is the oldest—over six decades—and largest—about 38,000 members—association for professionals in marketing. It is a valuable resource for individuals in all areas in marketing and at any stage of their professional career. The membership is on an individual basis and is moderately priced at only $165 per year (as of 2005). Product managers will be particularly interested in the resources available from the many information sources and webinars available from the AMA Web site www.marketingpower.com, as well as the journals and networking opportunities at the conferences and local chapter meetings.

Q: *Marketing is a skill that product managers always want to hone. What have you observed as the biggest mistakes product managers make in marketing?*

A: One of the most challenging tasks is that of understanding what products and services are valued by the customers of today and tomorrow, particularly in the fast changing world of consumer preferences and competition. This has always been a problem, but today there are many new analytical and Web-based tools for improving customer insights.

A more difficult challenge may be in dealing with the pressures for quarterly financial results, often leading to a series of small steps that ultimately damage the long-term value of the brand. To deal with these pressures, it is necessary for brand and product managers to develop "new" competencies.

Q: *What are these new competencies? Do they differ for B2B product managers and B2C product managers? What about service sector product managers or high-tech product managers?*

A: While every situation has unique characteristics, there are more similarities than differences across B2B, B2C, and services. One of the major advantages of being able to participate in a professional association such as the AMA is the networking access across a wide range of industries and market situations.

The similarities and differences can be seen in the need for brand/product managers to be skilled in the new competencies that are needed to create what I call the "ABC's" of owner/shareholder value: To Accelerate cash flows by building Brand equity and creating Customer equity. Regardless of the industry, managers must understand how all marketing expenditures are linked to cash flows over the next several years of the brand. While this has been discussed in many articles in the *Journal of Marketing*, one of the early books that links marketing and financial measures is Peter Doyle's *Value-Based Marketing*. This provides many examples of how short-term financial pressures can destroy the long-term value of a product or brand, and how to develop marketing plans in ways that can be understood and supported by financial analysts.

Both brand equity and customer equity, as that term is now formally defined, are important to the task of accelerating cash flows. However, in most B2C businesses, it is brand equity that is the key goal and metric. For B2B, services, and high-tech firms, it is possible to focus on customer equity due to the information available about individual customers or accounts.

Q: *What changes in marketing philosophies, strategies, or concepts have you observed over the past 5 years?*

A: One important change in the past several years has been the emphasis on the role of marketing in being able to create customer value and connect this to owner/shareholder value. This is in contrast to the "old" thinking that described marketing as only "managing the 4P's." The old thinking has created many problems in both the thinking and practice of marketing.

This new thinking in marketing is now recognized in the AMA's definition of marketing that was revised in 2004 as: "Marketing is an organizational function and a set of processes for creating, communicating, and delivering value to customers and for managing customer relationships in ways that benefit the organization and its stakeholders."

Fortunately, the successful brand and product managers had moved beyond thinking of marketing as just managing the 4P's and had understood the importance of segmentation, targeting, and positioning. However, the new emphasis on understanding how to create value for customers (relative to market and competitive conditions)—and connecting this to owner/shareholder value—is not as well understood nor implemented. This is exemplified by high failure rates of new products and the fact that some firms continue to damage brands.

Q: *What changes in marketing philosophies, strategies, or concepts do you expect over the next 5 years?*

A: The opportunities for marketing professionals, in all areas, have never been brighter than they are today. This is because marketing is the only professional discipline that is now focused on the customer-owner value connection. The biggest change I am hopeful will occur over the next 5 years is that of improving the implementation of this value-connection concept.

Implementation should improve because of the important studies now being done by marketing professionals in academia, business, and consultancies. For example, we now have a much better understanding of how to assess and improve the competencies, capabilities, and culture that are needed to connect customer value to the ABC's that drive financial performance.

Brand or product management is an important competency of a firm, but there is high variability in this competency, as seen in the marketplace and various studies. The differences between successful and struggling firms can be traced, in part, to the competencies of the individuals involved in this interfunctional process. But the culture of a firm seems to make the most significant difference in the variability across firms. Today, the culture, such as a customer-centric culture, a shared understanding of customer values, and so on, can now be measured and improved.

Q: *What advice can you give product managers about improving their marketing competencies?*

A: As explained above, competencies are necessary but not sufficient for improving the product/brand management capability. Thus, understanding how to benchmark the culture within a firm is one of the new competencies needed. It is known, of course, that the old competencies of segmentation, targeting, and positioning via the 4 P's will continue to be important. But understanding the changes in consumer or customer values, given all of the changes in technologies, will become even more important in the years ahead. Thus, my advice is to build these competencies by becoming involved in a professional association such as the AMA.

You can find out more information about the American Marketing Association by referring to: http://www.marketingpower.com/.

Notes

1. Betsy D. Gelb, "Why Rich Brands Get Richer, and What to Do About It," *Business Horizons* (September–October 1992): 46.
2. Andrew Serwer, "How to Escape a Price War," *Fortune* (June 1994): 84.

3. W. David Gibson, "Going Off Patent: Keeping the Wolves from Your Door," *Sales & Marketing Management* (October 1990): 76–82.

4. Christopher Power, "Flops," *BusinessWeek* (16 August 1993): 79.

Part Three

Ongoing Leadership Challenges

Product managers sometimes feel as though they are being pulled in all directions. They have to interact with functions throughout the company. They have to work with global counterparts, competitors, and customers. Organizations introduce and reintroduce the structure of product management in an effort to respond to evolutionary and revolutionary changes. All these factors place ongoing demands on the people and on the organizational structure.

This part examines some of these challenges, starting—in Chapter 11—with the issue of implementing strategies and plans through other people. Chapter 12 focuses on globalization. The final two chapters address the organizational requirements for introducing and managing product managers.

Chapter Eleven

Gaining Status as a Cross-Functional Leader

Planning is just the beginning of a product manager's job. Product management must extend to execution. And for a product manager, that means a significant amount has to be accomplished through people who don't report to you.

For product managers to become change agents or cross-functional leaders, they must understand other functions and establish mutual respect. A product manager, by definition, is a generalist who must rely on numerous functional specialists to get the product or service to the customer. These specialists can be internal or external to the company. The presence of internal support groups (such as advertising and marketing research) means that product managers can be less skilled in these areas and instead focus on managing the product's success. However, the product manager's control over the internal groups may be less than over an external group because she lacks direct authority. A charge-back system can sometimes provide more budget control for the product manager as well as relate costs more effectively to products.

Introducing the Cast of Characters

This chapter discusses some of the typical relationships that a product manager has within an organization. Figure 11.1 shows the results of a recent survey that asked product managers to indicate the extent of contact they have with a variety of areas on a scale from 1 (no contact at all) to 5 (very high level of contact). The groups with which product managers had the greatest level of contact were sales, research and development (R&D), and customers. The mean, or average, responses for each area are shown in the middle column of Figure 11.1.

Depending on the company and situation, the product manager plays various roles in terms of support activities. With regard to field sales, the product manager answers questions from the field, assists on sales calls as needed, provides product information to simplify the sales process, suggests various incentives for new products, and develops literature and other customer pieces to help further the sales effort. With regard to distribution, the product manager might work with distributors or agents, suggest alternative channels, and expedite shipments. Figure 11.2 shows some of the groups with which product managers frequently interact. Those in bold circles generally have the highest interaction. However, all these functions may turn to the product manager as the "answer person," thus requiring the product manager to be diplomatic in time management.

	Mean response	1	2	3	4	5
Sales	4.5					
R&D	4.1					
Customers	4.0					
Production	3.9					
Marketing research	3.7					
Advertising	3.5					
Product service	3.4					
Distribution	3.1					
Finance	3.0					
Ad agencies	2.6					

Figure 11.1   Prodcuct manager contact with selected groups.

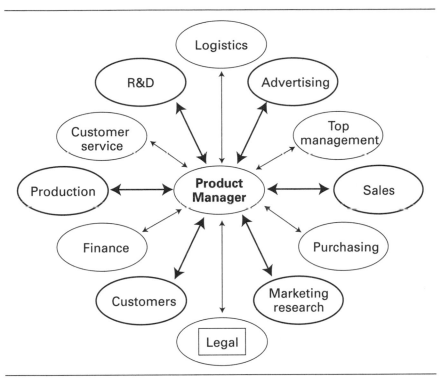

Figure 11.2   Product management: primary role influencers.

Sales

The product manager plays a major role in helping sales staff accomplish the objectives of the company (not to mention the objectives of the sales staff themselves). The nature of the relationship varies according to the culture of the organization and the positioning of product management. A coordinative product manager is likely to be heavily committed to sales support and "putting out fires." The position won't generate a desire on the part of sales to provide market intelligence or push the product. At the other extreme, an authoritarian product manager who expects to provide minimal support to the sales force will get minimal support back from them as well. This type of product manager might attempt to use home-office authority to "force" sales cooperation, and he can severely damage the trust and respect required for a cooperative effort. The most successful product managers fall in the middle of the continuum.

The development of sales forecasts is generally the domain of product managers, but forecasting frequently cannot be completed without the input of the sales force. Sales staff might be requested to estimate sales in their territories in total or by customer and/or product. If the information is broken down by account, it is likely to include an estimate of the probability of attainment. The forecast will be given to the regional or national sales manager, collated, and forwarded to the marketing department. The product manager would work in concert with the marketing analyst to arrive at a realistic forecast for the product line.

Communicating with sales staff.   On an operational level, product managers spend a moderate amount of time on the phone with sales staff and prospects. Sometimes, the calls are requests for price adjustments or special deals that require product management approval or authorization. Other calls will be questions about product attributes. The more itemized the product fact book (see Chapter 9), the more efficient a product manager will be in providing the answers. Even if sales staff have received the information previously, it is often quicker and more efficient for them if the product manager provides the information on the spot.

That does not mean that the product manager should not also provide the sales force with written information. Sales staff should be informed of any product or marketing change that affects their relationships or negotiations with customers before the information reaches their customers!

Many companies require product managers to spend a certain amount of time (e.g., 25% to 30%) making customer contacts, some of which is through calls with sales staff. These sales calls provide an opportunity to learn more about the customer, or on some occasions to help close a sale. However, the specific role the product manager is expected to play must be clarified prior to the call.

Most of the operational activities will not appear on the marketing plan, although they might be part of annual performance objectives (e.g., percentage of time spent in the field). What should be included in the marketing plan are budgets for travel expenses, any special incentive programs (for spurring sales of products that aren't achieving objectives or for introducing new products), or any activities undertaken as part of territory redesign or sales force changes.

Sales training.   Sales force training can cover a variety of issues: sales skills, company data, product knowledge, and market and competitive intelligence. The effectiveness of training can be a significant factor in making a new product launch successful. (See Chapter 8 for more on new product launching.) Although teaching sales skills per se will not typically be part of a product manager's responsibilities, the product training does have to fit within the framework of the selling process.

First, what information will help the sales staff in the function of planning sales calls? They need to know who is most likely to buy the product. Instead of describing the primary and secondary target markets, the product manager should profile the most likely account, suggesting specific customers, if appropriate. If noncustomers need to be cultivated, sales staff need to know the types of uses, applications, and functions appropriate for the product. For example, a company selling flat-panel display screens might direct sales staff to engineers in specific industries that require a monitor with graphics clarity.

Both product managers and sales staff should understand the differences between key accounts, target accounts, and maintenance accounts (as well as, of course, "why bother?" accounts). Key accounts consist of the 20% or so of customers who account for the bulk of gross profitability. Target accounts are those customers who may be the competitors' key accounts, or are significant prospects for a new product or service. Maintenance accounts may include existing small customers and possibly future strategic accounts.[1]

Next, what information from the customers must the sales staff obtain to qualify needs? What does the salesperson need to know about the prospect to determine the appropriateness of the sale? Customer satisfaction results from the best match between product benefits and customer needs. If the sales staff "successfully" sell to the wrong people or for the wrong applications, the revenue will be short-lived. Therefore, the product manager must provide customer-friendly questions that enable sales staff to assess the fit before closing the sale.

Questions should be developed about how prospects perform the function(s) provided by the product, what tolerances are required, what applications they would have for it now and in the future, and so on. The questions should not simply push the prospect toward a sale, but rather indicate whether the prospect has a true need for the product (thereby screening out inappropriate prospects). For example, a college textbook product manager responsible for a line of products to be sold to university professors will need to provide questions that assess teaching philosophy, level of rigor, and content preferences of the faculty, while the product manager selling flat-panel display screens may need to determine whether the screen is used in bright sunlight or office light, whether the primary usage is text or graphics, and whether simple or complex software is involved. Finally, what support and materials will help sales staff be more successful? Product managers should work closely with the sales force to ensure that marketing messages are relevant for the key audiences being called on, as discussed in Business Brief 11.1.

Business Brief 11.1   The importance of marketing-sales collaboration.

Managing the product message being communicated to customers is a challenge in most organizations, including pharmaceutical companies. Product managers invest considerable effort in fine-tuning the key points, hoping to have the sales force deliver a single, carefully defined message. However, significant erosion in the message occurs from product manager to salesperson to physician. Often the messages are not perceived as credible by the sales force, and the product managers as a whole are held in relatively low esteem.

Sometimes, there should be *not* a single message, but rather different perspectives to fit different audiences. A criticism recently aimed at pharmaceutical companies by physicians is that too much marketing-speak is present in the information provided to them.

The physicians surveyed were looking for unbiased, evidence-based, scientific information about products, including head-to-head comparisons, as well as risks and side-effects....

Business Brief 11.1   continued

Physicians are much more likely to ask for information regarding the benefits of the product compared with its rivals in that area and also details on side effects and risks. For others, cost-based information is key, while for yet others, an understanding of the holistic benefits for a patient's overall well-being.

If product managers are going to help sales people develop more value-added relationships with customers, they need to create the right differentiated messages for the right sub-audiences. And they must provide the right collateral and selling tools for the sales force to accomplish this. Collaboration between the two groups is required to accomplish these objectives.

It is crucial that Sales and Marketing work closely together to develop the message. Ideally, compa-

nies should be looking to build a cross-functional team led by the product manager. This not only makes the process more efficient, but ensures that all of the requisite knowledge is included in the material. Such cross-functional collaboration ensures real buy-in from the sales organization.

It is also best practice to factor customer input into the message development process. One of the best ways to do this is to use physician focus groups. These groups can be used to research and test new message options, as well as to help companies gain a deeper understanding of what physicians want to hear.

Source: Alasdair Mackintosh, "Getting the Message Across," *International Journal of Medical Marketing* (April 2004): 102–105.

Operations and R&D

Product managers of both service products and manufactured products depend on operations to create the right product at the right price and deliver it at the right time for customers. Whether operations refers to underwriting, loan management, manufacturing, or logistics, a close working relationship is critical.

New product development.   Perhaps the most visible interaction a product manager will have with operations is during new-product development. The research and development department must assess technical feasibility; manufacturing must evaluate future efficiency and productivity; procurement might need to be involved with make-versus-buy decisions; and overall capacity considerations must be taken into account. The role of the product manager will be to represent the voice of the customer, balancing corporate return on investment (ROI), customer satisfaction, and manufactured cost. Mutually acceptable standards for quality and customer service must be established, so that manufacturing and marketing strategies are complementary rather than conflicting.

Strategic interactions.   The product manager also may be involved in strategy sessions with the operations function, beyond specific new-product projects. During these sessions, the product manager will present marketplace problems or competitive moves that might trigger ideas for new products and highlight a discussion on future capacity needs. This is also the time when product managers learn of technology looking for a market and are encouraged to think of ways to incorporate new technology into existing or planned products in a way that is acceptable to the market. For example, when Ford first developed front-disc brakes, there was concern about how to introduce them into cars, given the inevitable price impact. They decided to introduce them as an upscale option on expensive cars until the price could be driven low enough through mass production to be appropriate for any vehicle:

> The most important lesson was in marketing. Disc brakes were, in principle, not much more expensive to produce than drum brakes; they weren't made of gold. But we were going down the manufacturing learning curve, and were thus comparing costs with a very old design. We had to find a way to get the new brakes paid for without looking dumb.
>
> We solved the problem by choosing an expensive car where the customer would not care quite as much about price, making disc brakes an upscale option for the Lincoln. . . . Once production was automated, the price began to drop. Today, the cost difference between a disc brake and drum brake is minuscule.[2]

The product manager must work continuously with operations to improve and enhance the product line. This requires that a product manager have at least a basic understanding (if in a manufacturing environment) of material scrapped due to worker error, the time it takes to set up a production line, and other operations performance measures. In insurance, product managers may need to understand basic underwriting guidelines. In financial services, product managers may need knowledge of the secondary market for loans and various financial ratios.

Product managers frequently are involved with operations on cost-reduction projects. Because product managers are expected to bring market insights, they must focus on ways of reducing costs that will not compromise the perceived value of a product. Cost reduction should not be fleeting. That is, care must be taken that cost savings are not temporary, with the inevitable result of other costs going up in the future.

Other operations-related activities a product manager might undertake include:

- Leading synergy sessions to ensure that all functions are moving in the same direction.
- Encouraging a discussion of technological advancements that could affect future new products.
- Establishing task forces to conduct value analysis on existing products.
- Monitoring productivity improvements.
- Fostering teamwork to enhance productivity on an ongoing basis.

Customer and Product Support Services

Customer service as a function can exist in marketing, warehousing, sales, or some other department, depending on the organizational structure of the firm. The product manager should both gather information from customer service representatives (CSRs) on product performance and supply information to them to increase customer satisfaction with the product line. Part of the added value for many products is the service level provided by the company. The product manager must ensure that the service standards are established, understood, and attainable by the service staff.

For service standards to be attainable, CSRs require training. Product managers might request support from the company's human resources function, include CSRs in the product training done for the sales force, and/or develop specific training for them. The more important service is as part of the product's competitive differentiation, the more important it is for product managers to take an active role in making sure the training happens.

The handling of warranties, for example, will require clarity among product support staff. If the warranty specifies 30 days, and a complaint is received on day 31, what leeway do the techs have in deciding how to handle it? What leeway should they have?

Finance

Product managers must work with finance to achieve a balance between the way products are costed and the market price desired. Customers don't care what internal cost allocation mechanism a company uses to set a floor for pricing. Their concern is simply whether a product has sufficient value, given the competitive alternatives available. Although all costs must be covered to remain profitable in the long term, contribution pricing in concert with market segmentation or product life-cycle decisions can be valuable. For example, pharmaceutical companies use contribution pricing to determine how long to sell an old product once a new one has been introduced:

> Often, new drugs are introduced that are more effective or
> have fewer side effects than older drugs, but the older drug
> still may be marketed.... Then the price would fall. The
> company would discontinue the product when it no longer
> makes a contribution. It may discontinue sooner if it can
> use existing capacity to produce products with a higher con-
> tribution.[3]

Product managers must also rely on finance to provide line-item information for the budget, pro forma income statement, and product balance sheet. By negotiating what information is critical for decision making, both functions can operate more effectively. The relevance of specific costs varies by situation and depends on the decision to be made. Product managers who can work with finance to ferret out the appropriate costs will be in a better position to make the right decisions.

Marketing Communications

Whether dealing with an internal advertising department or an external ad agency, a product manager needs a general understanding of promotional alternatives to be able to evaluate copy and media recommendations effectively. Typically, product managers will determine what positioning they want for their products, and the communication of that positioning will be left to the functional specialists. Product managers must describe the target market they are trying to reach as precisely as possible, so that the advertising groups can use that information to select the appropriate media and media vehicles.

If several product managers are working for a company, they must consider the relative merits of advertising the company as a whole versus positioning the various products independently of the company. A number of companies are moving to an umbrella approach to branding, in which the company name, reputation, and position are being emphasized as much as or more than the individual brand. The product managers and advertising specialists can discuss the relative merits of each option and come to an agreement prior to investing heavily in advertising.

If a product manager can choose between an in-house and an external agency, which one should be selected? Obviously, several factors must be considered. An external agency can be preferable for the product manager who needs an outside viewpoint, faces internal resource constraints that make it difficult to meet deadlines, or wants to take advantage of an agency's potential for mass media buying. On the other hand, an internal department might be the right decision if the product manager must capitalize on the expertise resulting from knowledge of a very specialized market, has the necessary skill in-house, and wants more control over the total process.[4]

Several questions are involved in agency selection:

· What types of promotion, in addition to advertising, might need to be done? Many companies, particularly in B2B situations, need direct-mail, lead-generation programs, trade show coverage, e-commerce Web sites, or special sales promotion techniques.
· Does the agency understand the target and have the appropriate talent to speak the language? This does not mean that a technical message must be written by a technical person. In fact, a technical slant may be completely wrong in cases where the focus should be on benefits rather than features. However, the copywriter must understand how to translate features into appropriate benefits for the customer.
· Should a large or small agency be hired? Typically, the most effective arrangement is for the client size to match the agency size, and it is better to be the big fish in a small pond than the reverse. However, exceptions may exist, particularly where innovative new products are concerned.
· Will the agency be expected to help with general marketing, Internet marketing, research, and/or strategic planning? If so, this might narrow the pool of potential agencies.

Marketing Research

Although product managers must necessarily have good information on the market and the competition, they are not usually experts in data collection and analysis. That's why much customer research is farmed out to either internal research departments or external research agencies. Product managers can also take advantage of the marketing research supplied by many advertising agencies or even some media publications.

Customers

Customer contact is an expectation for virtually all product managers. Consumer-goods brand managers usually reach customers through focus groups and other research techniques. B2B product managers are more likely to contact customers while on calls with sales staff, although marketing research is growing in importance for that group as well. The critical point in meeting with customers is to be open to both shortfalls in existing products and long-term future needs. As difficult as it is, product managers must visualize innovations that anticipate and satisfy unmet needs

Lights, Camera, Action!

In the corporate theater, product managers are both actor and director, staging a series of events for the benefit of the market—the final customers. Unless something *happens*, all the planning is for naught. Therefore, they must interact directly with all of the functions discussed, as well as with top management. The extent of interaction will vary by company and the experience level of the product manager. Business Brief 11.2 describes product managers in the electronics marketplace.

Business Brief 11.2   Product managers in the electronics marketplace.

The electronics field is known for short product life cycles and fragmented customer segments. Competition and price pressure are intense. Facing these challenges, the product manager must be able to work with and through a variety of individuals.

The product manager's position will, of course, vary by company, as Bill Meserve points out in his *Electronic Business* article, "The Changing Role of Product Management":

At one components division of General Instrument Corp., product managers function mostly as coordinators between engineering product development and marketing, and between marketing and sales. They have direct responsibility for product line advertising and promotion budgets, but only provide marketing input to product development projects, which are initiated and managed by engineering. Hewlett-Packard Co. product managers, in contrast, are frequently the focal point for new product development. They prepare the product development plan, authorize its implementation and monitor its progress.

Regardless of the role given to a product manager by a com-

(continued on next page)

Business Brief 11.2   continued

pany, the product manager must develop management skills to be able to lead teams in product development and product marketing. This involves a number of things. First, the product manager shouldn't be afraid to admit ignorance. Even though most technical product managers do have significant backgrounds in their fields, chances are they don't have the technical skills of the existing engineers on the team. Second, it's important to know when to intervene. Although it's essential that the team members learn to work together, especially in the new product endeavors, the product manager still has ultimate responsibility for the success of the product line.

These skills are built over time. According to Bill Meserve:

Beginning product managers with focused responsibilities need specific knowledge about the company's product and competitive offerings. As job experience and responsibility increase, the focus of skills building shifts to functional areas like financial analysis, promotion, pricing design, new product development, and strategic selling. And when professional responsibilities progress to even higher levels, management skills become central. Product managers learn to build a team, achieve consensus, negotiate agreements, measure performance, and handle personal relationships. Companies such as Allen-Bradley Co., 3M Co., and E.I. du Pont de Nemours & Co. supplement education with direct customer interaction, mentor relationships, and cross-functional training to enhance product management skills.

Source: Adapted from Bill Meserve, "The Changing Role of Product Management," *Electronic Business*, 9 (January 1989): 143–146.

Communicate the Product Vision

Product managers realize that they must get "buy-in" for their strategies, but they often don't know *how* to accomplish that. While the facts and statistics described in Sections One and Two are critical, they must be woven into a story (or scenario) that moves people into action. The most carefully researched insights are greeted with cynicism when the message is lost in PowerPoint slides and dry hyperbole.[5]

Storytelling is one of the most powerful inspirational tools available, and has been used throughout history. Product managers who can paint a vivid picture of the future can transform a colleague's point of view and motivate the desired action. The product vision has to be something people can commit to, not just numbers to pursue.

> Long-renowned for its story-intensive culture, 3M cultivates tales of past successes. Stories about winning innovations help inspire employees to keep new ideas coming. Sales reps are trained to use narratives to explain the advantages of using their products to customers. Recently, 3M leaders began to use stories for strategic planning, having found that this generates more excitement and commitment.[6]

Build a Track Record

An early challenge for product managers is to build—and build *on*—a successful track record. While humility is important, product managers cannot assume that everyone in the organization has knowledge of their expertise. Sometimes, telling a short anecdote about how a recommended approach worked in a prior position in another company not only provides some credibility for the *idea* but also for the *individual*.[7] Position yourself as an expert in that area—but don't stretch your expertise to everything!

The task is a bit more difficult if you are still trying to establish a track record. In that case, it becomes important to work with allies within the organization who can support your product vision and jump-start implementation throughout the company. Select allies who have already gained respect in the firm.

Establish Trust

Trust flourishes in a climate characterized by several components. The first is honesty—no lies and no exaggeration. Do everything in your power to present information in a fair, objective manner. Second, maintain a willingness to share ideas openly. While some people hoard information in an attempt to increase power, it is generally a bad policy in the long run. Third, demonstrate consistent and predictable behavior. While the element of surprise is useful in competitive strategy, it should not be part of organizational behavior. And finally, accept and respect the individual differences and perspectives of the multitude of people you deal with as a product manager.

Keep Learning

Past successes can translate into future failure—and vice versa. Challenge yourself to gain new insights about the market, to embrace an active approach to trend-watching. Interact with people who are different from you. Learn new hobbies. Get involved with futuristic organizations. Read voraciously. Learn to laugh at your mistakes and learn from them rather than being depressed by them. Listen—really listen—to people who have different perspectives, without automatically discounting what they are about to say. However you accomplish it, just keep learning.

Checklist: Gaining Status as a Cross-Functional Leader

- To be most effective as a product manager, focus on being a generalist who can accomplish work through other people and functional departments.
- Position yourself with the sales force so that you're viewed as neither strictly sales support nor corporate dictator.
- Understand how your activities fit into the sales process.
- Be prepared to represent the voice of the customer in meetings with operations and R&D and to demonstrate at least a minimum understanding of operational techniques and standards.
- Don't be afraid to question and critique the work of your internal or external advertising agency.
- Allocate a significant portion of the time you spend with customers gathering information on future product needs and applications.
- Practice the art of storytelling to motivate and inspire people toward product goals.
- Just keep learning!

Interview with Jeff Mikula, Global Manager, Advertising & Branding for GE Healthcare, a Unit of the General Electric Company that Is Headquartered in the United Kingdom

Jeff currently manages the overall global advertising planning and brand strategy for GE Healthcare, and has extensive experience in brand management, strategic marketing, and corporate communications.

Q: *What is the role of brand management at your company?*

A: The brand management teams at GE are responsible for evolving one of the world's most powerful brands, by applying marketing strategies to specific product or segment areas. Our brand managers are focused on increasing the perceived value of our products and services by developing innovative technologies that support the GE brand promise, substantiate our premium value, and effectively position us in the marketplace. Most importantly, brand managers develop long-term product roadmaps to ensure a technology continuum that is reflective of customers needs, drives market share, ties to our corporate vision, and allows us to maintain our leadership in the marketplace.

At a master brand level, brand management is also responsible for corporate identity standard development, brand attribute measurement, positioning strategy formulation, and driving overall brand equity values, as our brand is the most important asset that we have.

Q: *Branding is a skill that product and brand managers always want to hone. What have you observed as the biggest mistakes product managers make in branding?*

A: I think that one of the first mistakes in branding is not maintaining your brand, especially in a shaky economy, when businesses and products are quick to change their identity. You may be tired of your identity, but your customers may have barely been exposed to it. Secondly, I think another mistake is a business' inability to fully commit to branding. Marketing departments shouldn't be the only function driving brand equity. Branding is a discipline that needs to be practiced in all areas of the business, including sales and service. A third big mistake is when marketers don't think analytically, and regard branding as simply a logo or a tagline. Branding needs to incorporate what you, as a product or business, are promising to customers, and how you are differentiating yourself by delivering on that promise.

Q: *Do you think consumer brand managers face challenges different from those faced by B2B product managers?*

A: I think that the discipline and principles are similar; however, brand managers can't lose perspective on what the brand represents, and why customers connect with a particular brand—whether it's a business or consumer. In a traditional business-to-business environment, customers want to buy because they're actively looking for a solution—the decision isn't typically impulsive or transactional. They also tend to be very sophisticated about your industry, your brand, and your offerings as a seller. Consumer brand connections tend to be more personal. Businesses have a more involved sales cycle, and therefore, different expectations in terms of the value of a brand. In both instances, the goal of a brand is to make an emotional connection with the customer and consistently deliver on that brand promise.

Q: *What changes in branding philosophies, strategies, or concepts do you expect over the next 5 years?*

A: I suspect that we'll continue to see brand proliferation over the next 5 years, as customers continue to deal with excessive brand choices, and interact with those brands in new ways. As a result, customers will become more active in their involvement in brands, and we'll begin to see more involvement in seeking products out, versus simply accepting the messaging being pushed on them (e.g. BMW, Burger King). Additionally, with consumer cynicism as high as it is in today's marketplace, the brands of tomorrow will need to be even more authentic and demonstrate an active alignment with customer values. Lastly, I think we'll see a continued trend toward customization of products. Much like the brands they buy, consumers have a desire to differentiate themselves from the mass market. Whether it's a running shoe, a motorcycle, or a medical device designed around the patient experience, tomorrow's brands will be built with consumers in more control over product design and overall experience with brands.

Q: *What is the best advice you ever received?*

A: You do not own your company's brand. In addition, your company's brand is not merely what your marketing department says it is. It's a humbling thought, but a brand is your relationship with your customers—and it's not simple or simply created. It's created in the hearts and minds of your constituencies, and your brand image lives in everything that you do—from products to services to customer relations. When you recognize all of the touch points that a customer may have with you, it becomes apparent that your brand is owned by the customers you serve, and no focus group, survey, or mapping project will change that.

Q: *What advice can you give product managers about branding?*

A: First of all, brand value should be emphasized through quality relationships and products. Product managers also need to understand the aesthetics and rationale behind product design, and how important user experience is in how people feel about your products. In order to evolve your company's brand, you need to be sensitive to shifts in customer perceptions and how to apply those shifts back into the organization. Lastly, brand begins on the inside. A company's brand attributes and values need to be driven by every employee, at every level. Product managers need to continually grow and nurture brands because brands bring coherence, direction, differentiation, and value to businesses. Branding cannot be an afterthought to a business plan—marketing supports the brand, not vice versa.

For more information on GE Healthcare products and services, go to: www.gehealthcare.com.

Notes

1. John Monoky, "Is Your Time Well Spent?" *Industrial Distribution* (February 1, 1997): 83.
2. Don Frey, "Learning the Ropes: My Life as a Product Champion," *Harvard Business Review* (September/October 1991): 54.
3. Robert W. Koehler, "Triple-Threat Strategy," *Management Accounting* (October 1991): 32.
4. Robert S. Blois, "Do You Really Need an Agency,?" *Sales & Marketing Management* (October 1988): 120.
5. Some executives are working with writers, directors, producers, and actors to gain better skills at storytelling. Screenwriting coach Robert McKee discusses this phenomenon in "Storytelling that Moves People," *Harvard Business Review* (June 2003): 51–55.
6. Camille H. James and William C. Minnis, "Organizational Storytelling: It Makes Sense," *Business Horizons* (July–August 2004): 29.

7. Social scientists refer to this as the Principle of Authority, a critical component of persuasion. For more detail, refer to Robert B. Cialdini, "Harnessing the Science of Persuasion," *Harvard Business Review* (October 2001): 72–79.

Chapter Twelve

Preparing for Globalization

A global product manager is not simply one who oversees products sold in other countries. The global product manager is one who thinks and plans with an appreciation of the global competitive arena. Even companies with a low percentage of foreign sales have competitors, suppliers, and customers that extend beyond domestic borders. Global *thinking*—not just sales—is important for these product managers. Regardless of whether a company has multinational locations, these product managers develop long-term product strategies on a global basis. They look for similarities across different world markets, standardizing whenever possible and customizing whenever necessary. This affords opportunities (proactively) for future foreign sales as well as for competitive strategies against global competitors.

Product managers have different responsibilities depending on whether they are based in the country where their business resides (and sell to customers in other countries from the home office), or whether they are located in the country or region where sales take place. The first type is a *domestically based* global (DBG) product manager. The second is a *locationally based* global (LBG) product manager. Domestically based global product managers typically participate in the "upstream" product development efforts. They also may be directly involved in go-to-market activities, or they may work with "downstream" managers in other countries.

Locationally based global product managers can fall along a continuum from downstream (tactical) activities to full-stream (both strategic and tactical). Those involved solely in the tactical activities are given predesigned (and often premanufactured) products to sell in their countries of responsibility, and they are charged with the relevant marketing, sales, and distribution activities. The full-stream product managers create unique offerings for their markets, from design through sale. The locationally based managers may be expatriates who were transferred from another corporate location, or they may be native to the specific region. These product managers must have a thorough understanding of the customer needs in their particular countries. Business Brief 12.1 looks at some of the challenges for product managers in the China market.

DBG product managers typically have strong input into the design of global products. Their product's success depends on their understanding of customer needs and local market requirements. Unfortunately, too many product managers

---

Business Brief 12.1   Being a product manager for the China market.

Shanghai, with its approximately 16 million people, is headquarters to numerous multinational organizations. This area is a fertile ground for many consumer products, for two reasons. First, the millions of expatriates located there desire some familiar products and conveniences. Second, the rising middle class—a phenomenon closely linked to the growth of the multinationals—provides the "early adopter" market required for success. But it is far from the only market in China, and product managers must understand the different segments—both industrial and consumer—that exist there to be most successful.

Industrial companies in different regions of China exhibit different types of buying behavior. In the north, comprised of Heilongjiang, Jilin, Liaoning, and Hebei (which physically includes city-provinces of Beijing and Tianjin), fewer foreign enterprises are present. Because they are less exposed to Western technologies, they are also less exposed to new ideas and less prepared to adopt new products. As a consequence, it is harder to make initial contact. The south contains many overseas Chinese-invested enterprises located in Guangdong and Fujian provinces. Since economic reform originated in this region, its companies are willing to try new

Business Brief 12.1   continued

things. Customers on the east coast (Shanghai municipality and Jiangsu and Zhejiang provinces) mainly operate in the Shanghai style. They have been most influenced by Western culture.

With consumer markets, a dramatic variety exists in terrain, dialect, custom, and cuisine— resulting in potential markets as fragmented and diverse as those in Europe. Demographic and psychographic factors are becoming increasingly important. Teenagers in Shanghai and Xi'an may have similar budgets and aspirations. But differences in beliefs and attitudes will drive Shanghainese to focus more on the emotional benefits of brands, while consumers in Xi'an will tend to focus more on functional benefits.

Whirlpool has also discovered the need to incorporate psychographic segmentation for the sale of their appliances in China. "For example, 19% of Chinese consumers fall into what Whirlpool has categorized as 'pragmatists,' people in lower income brackets who tend to live in more rural areas, who are less educated and older. Key touch points for these consumers are price, cost of ownership, and reliability. Another 20% of the Chinese market consists of the 'aspirational status seekers.' These people are younger, upwardly mobile, and more educated. They are people for whom price isn't the primary issue."

Product variety will be required to match segmented needs. As Austin Lally, P&G's general manager-marketing for beauty care brands in China states, "Winning in China depends on developing a deep understanding of who you are marketing to. If you start designing average products to meet the average Chinese consumer, you usually end up with stuff that isn't sophisticated or differentiated enough to win in Shanghai or Beijing, but you also end up with stuff that doesn't offer enough value for people in smaller cities and towns. What we ended up with is a much broader portfolio than we originally entered China with. Take a brand like Crest. We don't sell one tube of toothpaste in different flavors. We have different tiers of pricing and performance. Those different products we sell are not just cheaper versions of each other; they are designed against different groups of consumers."

Source: Adapted from Don Y. Lee, "Segmentation and Promotional Strategies for Selling CSRB Bearings in China," *The Journal of Business & Industrial Marketing* (2003, Vol. 18, Iss. 2/3): 258–270; George Crocker & Yi-Chung Tay, "What it Takes to Create a Successful Brand," *The China Business Review* (July/Aug 2004): 10–16; Ann Chen and Vijay Vishwanath, "Expanding in China," *Harvard Business Review* (March 2005:) 19–21; Anonymous, "Navigating China's Ever-Changing Marketplace," *Advertising Age* (November 8, 2004): 12. David Drickhamer, "Appliance Envy," *Industry Week* (November 2004): 24–30.

spend limited time visiting customers in these countries and rely too heavily on statistical and secondary data. LBG product managers, primarily those focused on tactical activities, often feel powerless to affect change in product design to reflect the needs of the market they serve. Their challenge is to influence upward, so that the most important and relevant features and benefits are built into their product offerings. Therefore, both should participate in global product strategy.

Where the profit-and-loss (P&L) responsibility lies also influences the role of global product managers.[1] In the late 1990s, P&G adopted a system under which "managers of global business units are responsible for brand management and product development, and managers of regional market development organizations are responsible for sales, trade marketing, media, and multibrand marketing." P&L responsibility resides with the global managers. Unilever has a similar structure, except that "profit-and-loss responsibilities lie with the regional presidents rather than the global category organizations that control marketing, product mixes and strategy."

Transnational Product Strategy

Global strategy for product managers means embedding both domestic and international standards into products and services at the point of design, not as afterthoughts. This implies meeting world standards, while simultaneously acknowledging national differences and local norms. This approach has the obvious advantage of taking into consideration the needs of major markets right at the start, rather than having to retrofit a product developed for one national market.

Product managers start by identifying globally strategic markets and then analyzing the needs of those markets. By searching for commonalities (as well as differences), product managers necessarily think in terms of platform design for global products. Product managers are wise to design the largest possible standardized core, while allowing for necessary customization at the same time. The main goal of the product-development process is not to develop a standard product or product line, but to build adaptability into products and product lines to achieve worldwide appeal.

The idea of a fully standardized global product that is identical all over the world is a near myth. Some of the benefits of global products (or services), however, can be achieved by standardizing the core product or large parts of it, while customizing peripheral or other parts of the product. In passenger automobiles, for example, product standardization comes primarily in the "platform" (the chassis and related parts) and to a lesser extent the engine. The auto industry has been talking about global cars for decades, but implementation has been difficult at best. Honda made progress with its 1998 Accord. By coming up with a platform that can be bent and stretched into markedly different vehicles, Honda saved hundreds of millions of dollars in development costs. By moving the car's gas tank back between the rear tires, Honda engineers discovered they could design a series of special brackets that would allow them to hook the wheels to the car's more flexible inner subframe. Rather than shipping the same car around the globe, only the underlying platform will be used worldwide.

Regardless of the attempt to standardize products or product lines globally, various levels of adaptation are required. Some products need only different language documentation. For example, in the 1990s, when Minolta cameras were shipped from Japan to New Wave Enterprise, a distribution center at the Port of Antwerp in Belgium, they were shipped without support materials. Language-specific documentation (e.g., French, Dutch, and German) was added when the products were shipped across land to other destinations in Europe.

Product strategy can vary across a continuum from (A) a near-universal product (with just labeling and language differences); to (B) a modified product, in which the core is standard, and adaptations are made (such as voltage and color) to reflect local differences; to (C) country-specific products, in which the physical product is tailored to the needs of each country or group of countries. The approach to take depends on several variables. One argument for global brands is based on identifying high-tech and high-touch products.

> *High-tech products* appeal to highly specialized buyers who share a common technical language and symbols. This is the case among computer and Internet users, tennis players, physicians using medical equipment, and musicians—all of whom understand the technical aspects of their particular products. The mere existence of a common "shoptalk" facilitates communication and increases the chance of success as a global brand.
>
> *High-touch products* are more image-oriented than product-feature–oriented, but they respond to universal themes or needs, such as romance, wealth, heroism, play, and the like. Many products, such as fragrance, fashion, jewelry and watches, recreation resorts, and more are sold on these themes…. [W]orldwide brand standardization appear[s] most feasible when products approach either end of the high-tech/high-touch spectrum.[2]

Related research on global brands also suggests new perspectives on how consumers perceive them. A study based on surveys of 1,800 people in 12 nations, published in *Harvard Business Review*, revealed that consumers all over the world associate global brands with three dimensions. The first dimension is a symbol of quality. Consumers believed that since transnational companies must compete more fiercely to develop new products and technologies faster than the competition, they offer more quality and better guarantees. It's interesting to note that this attitude was not directly related to the country of origin, but rather simply to being a global brand. The second dimension is a sense of a global culture. Consumers looked to the brands as "symbols of cultural ideals." The final dimension was social responsibility. The respondents in the study expected global firms to address social problems, to act as "stewards of public health, worker rights, and the environment."[3]

In other situations products could have their life cycles extended by looking for the best fit between market needs and product capabilities. For example, the current U.S. technology for anesthesia ventilators allows plus or minus a few milliliters of oxygen accuracy. However, many hospital operating rooms in developing countries are satisfied with plus or minus 100 milliliters of accuracy, with a commensurately lower price. A major supplier of anesthesia equipment found it could prolong the life of its "unsophisticated" ventilators by offering them in these markets at a much lower price than the "state-of-the-art" equipment.

This approach can apply to consumer products as well. Take basic flour as an example. India consumes about 69 million tons of wheat a year (compared to 26 million tons in the United States), yet almost no whole-wheat flour is sold prepackaged. Selling packaged flour in India is almost revolutionary, since most Indian housewives still buy raw wheat in bulk, clean it by hand, and on a weekly basis carry some to a neighborhood mill, or *chakki*, where it is ground between two stones. Pillsbury found it could increase the sales of basic prepackaged flour (a mature product in the United States) by appealing to this market; it has modified the Pillsbury Doughboy to pitch this "old" product as something new in India.

Procter & Gamble's global marketing strategy is drawing from newly emerging marketing approaches, media, and technologies. A few concepts they are working with include holistic marketing, permission marketing, and experimentation. *Holistic marketing* refers to gaining a thorough knowledge of the consumers at the local level and determining how they prefer to receive information about products. *Permission marketing*, similar to its use in Internet applications, refers to getting contact information (like phone numbers) directly from consumers who indicate a willingness to hear from you. *Experimentation* refers to continually trying different approaches to reaching customers in new markets. Recently, P&G has been using a lot of influencer marketing to get passionate consumers to "seed" the market for product introductions.[4]

With increasing competition able to react quickly when new products are introduced, worldwide planning at the product level provides a number of tangible benefits. First, product managers are better able to develop products with specifications compatible on a global scale. Second, they are able to more effectively and efficiently adapt products to local needs.

And third, they are able to respond more quickly to competitive moves of global companies.

Glocalization

Glocalization refers to the adage, "think globally, act locally." Whether you are selling a unique product in every country or a standard product throughout the world, good product management still requires understanding the local customers. A set of local competitors may also be present, different from those at the global level.

Start with the basics. How homogeneous is the country or region of interest? Segment the market into reasonable clusters of potential customers, and decide which one or which ones you will actively target. This could form the foundation of a product-line strategy for that area. Do the characteristics of any of the segments transcend national borders? Sometimes younger generations are more like their global counterparts than they are like older generations within their own country. If that is the case, they may be more open to a standardized global product.

Determine the *non-negotiable* expectations of the local customers. Cultural mores and lifestyles may dictate changes, even when other factors suggest a global product strategy may suffice. Volkswagen is learning this lesson in the United States.

> Ever since the introduction of the original Beetle, VW has treated the U.S. as an automotive backwater. It used the country as a dumping ground for excess production and made little effort to understand American driving habits. A classic example: cup holders, which for years VW ignored.[5]

When dealing with developing countries, price may be a bigger issue than multinationals have historically accepted. This can pose a challenge—especially for locationally based product managers who are expected to sell a relatively high-priced product that was designed in another country—and can't hit the local price point expectations. These product managers have to seek out thought leaders and innovators who may be willing to buy the product in the short-term, and persuade corporate managers of the need to close the cost gap with local companies to be effective in those particular regions in the long term.

Distributing to Other Countries

Product managers must work with the sales function to determine the best method of distribution into the new market. Most firms initially enter other countries through either indirect or direct exporting. *Indirect* exporting refers to selling through a domestically based intermediary (e.g., agent or distributor). The major benefits of this approach lie in the ease of administration. Even companies with little or no experience in exporting can rely on the expertise of the channel partner without developing substantial multinational cultural skills. With *direct* exporting, the manufacturer deals directly with foreign intermediaries in the distribution of its products. While this approach requires a greater degree of cultural expertise, it also provides the product manager with more market knowledge and potentially greater control.

In addition to determining whether the best location for the intermediary is domestic or foreign, it is useful to examine the differences between agent, distributor, and other intermediaries. Agents, brokers, manufacturer's reps, and export management companies (EMCs) generally *do not* take title to the products they represent. Distributors, dealers, jobbers, wholesalers, and merchants generally *do* take title. Other partners may either have varied contractual relations with the manufacturer or provide specific differential functions. When *licensing* is used as an entry strategy, the manufacturer assigns the right to a patent or trademark to a foreign company. An advantage of this approach is that some governments may prefer it, allowing easier entry. The disadvantage is the manufacturer's dependence on the licensee. *Franchising* is a form of licensing agreement whereby the manufacturer grants to the foreign company the rights to do business in a prescribed manner. This has similar advantages and disadvantages to licensing, but since the franchise agreement is more comprehensive than a licensing agreement, the manufacturer has somewhat more control. Under *contract manufacturing*, a company arranges to have its products manufactured by a foreign firm under a contractual basis. The manufacturing may involve assembly or fully integrated production, depending on the needs of the firm.

In his *Harvard Business Review* article, David Arnold states that the selection of international business partners is especially critical, because of distance and the cultures of the buying parties.[6] He elaborates on seven key points in selecting and working with international distributors and trading partners:

1. "Select distributors. Don't let them select you." The key point is to choose markets first and *then* select distributors and agents.
2. "Look for distributors capable of developing markets, rather than those with a few obvious customer contacts." Select partners who are willing to invest and grow the markets.
3. "Treat the local distributors as long-term partners, not temporary market-entry vehicles." Create an atmosphere fostering appropriate goals, such as customer acquisition and retention, new product sales, and collaborative inventory management and replenishment.
4. "Support market entry by committing money, managers, and proven marketing ideas." Invest in product modifications to meet the needs of local markets and personnel support.
5. "From the start, maintain control over marketing strategy." Product managers should visit distributors and channel members to learn about the local market.
6. "Make sure distributors provide you with detailed market and financial performance data." Develop relationships and contracts that share detailed market data and financial performance.
7. "Build links among national distributors at the earliest opportunity." Just as in the United States, distributors meet

and build relationships to share experiences. Help all parties improve their success in marketing efforts.

Once corporations understand that they can control their international operations through better relationship structures, rather than simply through ownership, they might also find longer-term roles for local distributors with a regionalized approach to global strategy.

When preparing go-to-market strategies in other countries, product managers should remember two iron rules of international business. First, the seller is expected to adapt to the buyer (when *you* are selling, you will need to do the adapting). Second, the visitor is expected to observe local customs. These rules compel an understanding of the different types of cultures that exist in different parts of the world. Richard Gesteland, in his book, *Cross-Cultural Business Behavior*, provides a thorough discussion of four types of cultural continua, as shown in Figure 12.1.[7] The book provides clear explanations and case examples of working with business people throughout the world.

The first continuum deals with the business perspective ranging from deal-focused to relationship-focused. Distributors from relationship-focused cultures want to build a trusting relationship with a manufacturer prior to commencing business, and these distributors can perceive a deal-focused presentation as aggressive and pushy. The second continuum is from formal to informal. Informal business managers typically come from relatively egalitarian cultures (like the United States) and sometimes make the mistake of not respecting the formality present in other cultures. The third continuum is from rigid-time to fluid-time. Cultures that are driven by "the clock" may inappropriately perceive cultures at the other end of the continuum as lazy, resulting in tense and uncomfortable meetings. The final type of continuum is from expressive to reserved. Reserved cultures demonstrate conservative communication both verbally and nonverbally, and can therefore "clash" with people from expressive cultures. It is important for product managers who are establishing relationships with

Deal-focused	Relationship-focused
←	→
North America	Arab countries
Great Britain	Most of Africa & Latin America

Informal	Formal
←	→
Australia	Most of Europe
U.S., Canada	Mediterranean Region

Rigid Time	Fluid time
←	→
Nordic & Germanic Europe	Latin America
North America	Africa

Reserved	Expressive
←	→
East & Southeast Asia	Mediterranean Region
Nordic & Germanic Europe	Latin America

(Condensed from Richard Gesteland, *Cross-Cultural Business Behavior*, 3rd edition, Copenhagen Business School Press, 2002.)

Figure 12.1   Example cultural divides in international negotiations.

international channel partners to understand and appreciate the cultural differences, so that trust can be established and negotiations can run smoothly.

Checklist: Preparing for Globalization

· As your company begins multinational moves, your job should start with global thinking rather than global sales.
· Embed both domestic and international standards into products and services.
· Look for common needs among globally strategic markets and standardize the core product.
· Identify the appropriate level of country adaptation required for your product.
· Anticipate global competition.

Interview with Mark Phillips, General Manager, Patient Monitoring Solutions— Asia

Q: *Discuss how you became a product manager for GE Healthcare in Asia.*

A: I joined GE Capital (GE's finance business) directly out of university into an entry-level information technology leadership training program. The program was a great experience, but the biggest take-away for me was that I did not want to be in back-office operations. At that point, I started to look for ways I could leverage my experience and training in IT to get more involved in the front line of the business. Fortunately, GE Healthcare was starting up an information technology unit focused on creating clinical IT solutions for hospitals. I joined GE Healthcare as a marketing manager and eventually worked my way to a product management position in Asia.

Q: *Describe your primary responsibilities.*

A: Being based in Shanghai, I am charged with managing my products not only in China but throughout all of Asia. It's probably easiest for me to sort of "bullet point" what I do. Primary responsibilities include:

· Define go-to-market strategy for the product line. This includes product launches, pricing, positioning, selecting key shows and conferences to attend, and planning key customer events and company sponsored road-shows.
· Enable sales and marketing teams in each region by providing training, marketing tools, and sales tools.
· Define growth opportunities and develop business cases for new products in the region.
· Encourage executive-level selling. By this I mean I support regional sales and marketing teams by getting involved in the sales cycle of key deals in each region (defined by size and strategic significance).
· Create and maintain luminary accounts in each country. Luminary accounts are those leading customers who can provide market leading insight to our product development team, conduct clinical research using beta versions of our products, and act as advocates or key thought leaders around new technologies in their region.

- Provide market updates, competitor actions, and customer feedback to product development teams. This happens on an informal basis weekly and once per year in a formal multiyear product strategy that is developed for the region.

All of these responsibilities are measured by a number of metrics; however, the two key measures are sales and contribution margin for the product line. All of the actions above should enable the region sales and marketing teams to increase sales, and more importantly, to differentiate the product line enough to command price premiums.

Q: *What do you feel are the similarities and differences between a domestic product manager (where all operations are in one country) and a country product manager (where you locally market a global product)?*

A: A domestic product manager often manages a product that has been specifically designed for his or her market. The products are designed to serve the domestic customer needs and combat the domestic and key global competitors. Product managers outside of the domestic market, often "catch" these products "as is" and are charged with the task of launching them in international markets. This involves many challenges. Here again, I'm going to give you my "laundry list" of bullets.

- While both domestic and international product managers face global competitors, the international product manager must also face local players. Combating local competitor—that specifically focus on local market needs—creates an additional battlefront that domestic product managers do not face. Local players often have a better cost position, move faster, and are very focused on local needs. This creates big challenges in value markets, where price is a major driver, or in markets with complex or specific needs, such as Japan.
- Diverse markets. People refer to Europe or Asia as markets in a similar way they refer to the United States. However, the United States is, for the most part, a homogenous market. Asia and Europe are a mix of several cultures and economies, each with their own unique characteristics. In Asia for example, there are huge socioeconomic disparities across the region coupled with diverse culture, language, and political systems. Asia itself spans numerous time zones and countries. There is usually not a "one size fits all" strategy for Asia. This diversity of GTM (go-to-market) strategies makes the international product manager's role much more complex.

- There is an added task of localizing marketing materials that have been designed for a different country and culture. This can include basic translation to actually having to have your own photo-shoots to ensure "local faces" are included in your collateral. This cuts in to your local GTM budget, which is often based on a global benchmark of GTM spending. Domestic product managers do not have to cover this extra cost and thus can apply the funds to more strategic activity.
- Size matters. While international product managers may represent markets that are growing faster than domestic markets, the domestic markets are usually larger. Thus, it makes getting the features and functions needed for local markets very challenging against the needs of the larger domestic markets.
- Dealing with upstream teams in another time zone. This means early morning and/or late night conference calls to get the support you need. Product managers in Europe may have to stay up a little later than usual; Asia product managers are often squeezed at both ends of the day, creating challenging schedules.

Q: *Do you think the differences you mentioned above are greater for a B2B or a B2C product?*

A: The differences exist in both B2B and B2C products. However, I believe the issues are more acute in the B2C business, as you are often dealing with a wider swath of the population, rather than a specific set of industry buyers.

Q: *What job changes have you experienced in the past 5 years?*

A: While the charter for international product managers is largely focused on downstream activities, I find that in being based in Asia—a fast growing, dynamic market—more of my responsibilities involve upstream-like activity. I have been spending more and more time looking at ways to get involved in the upstream process, so that I can better advocate for the needs of my region. Being closer to the market, I feel the pressure and winds of change more than the upstream teams that are based in another country (in my case, the United States). Rather than wait for them to come around, we take actions in the regions, such as researching OEM [original equipment manufacturer] options and taking on local development projects using local funding to prove a product idea can work.

Q: *What changes do you anticipate in the next 5 years?*

A: I think that gradually more and more upstream activities will be moved out of the country in which the corporate headquarters is located into a more distributed, decentralized model. High-end or sophisticated product engineering and R&D will likely remain in the domestic market, but more of the traditionally "upstream" marketing activities will be moved to the "downstream" countries.

Q: *What will be the primary challenges for product managers in the next decade?*

A: China is going to change the face of the global competition in very much the same way Japan did from the 1950s to the 1980s. Even though China has had a communist political system for the last century, the system does little to suppress the very entrepreneurial nature of the Chinese people. They are smart, aggressive, have an outstanding work ethic, are open to outside ideas, and can operate in a very low-cost environment. Today, China companies are very strong in the "low-end" or value markets—and their quality and reach are getting stronger. Already, we are seeing Chinese companies purchasing global players in the computer and television industries. It is just a matter of time before it happens in others. As product managers, we are going to have to adapt our strategies to deal with the China competitive arena. We are going to have to learn how to act faster, be more global and local at the same time, and operate with much better cost efficiencies.

Q: *What advice can you provide to current product managers?*

A: Let me think. There are several things that come to mind.

- Be a leader. Do not think of yourself as a product manager; rather, think of yourself as the CEO of your product line. (1) Always think of top line all the way to the bottom line. Never ask for a feature or new product without understanding the financial impact, from both revenue and cost perspectives. (2) Reach beyond your role's traditional boundaries. As a global product manager, you may be responsible primarily for downstream activity, but the more you understand about the manufacturing and design of your products, the better you can drive the needs for your market. Step up and take on local manufacturing initiatives or projects. Actively look for improvements that challenge your global counterparts to do better.
- Get more than your fair share. International markets have unique needs and are often smaller than domestic markets; however, they

have great growth rates. All global companies yearn for growth. Focus on being a growth engine as your competitive advantage when competing for R&D dollars for the products you need.

- When building business cases for the products you need, work with other regional product managers. You are most likely facing similar challenges. One example is Eastern Europe, China, and India. All three regions have large value segments. Often the key characteristics are similar; thus, by adding other markets to your business case, you increase your chance for success.
- Beware of voice of sales and voice of marketing when gathering market and customer feedback. I have often found the perception of local sales or marketing persons can be quite different from what the customers have to say. Spend time with customers, watch how they use your product, and ask them directly about your company's products and about competitive products.
- Segment your voice of customer feedback. Luminary feedback is great, and luminary accounts are great anchors on which you can drive market innovations. However, the bulk of the market is generally quite different from the top customers in each market. Needs of luminaries can be quite advanced—more sophisticated than the needs of the bulk of the market. Ensure you gather Voice of Customer from a diverse range of customer segments, then prioritize that feedback based on where the biggest opportunity is.
- Don't get caught sleeping at the wheel. Use your network and online services to keep abreast of the market. Always keep your networks fresh, both inside and outside of your company. These human networks are often the best way to hear of coming competitor moves, such as new products, partnerships, or mergers that have the potential to make huge changes in the competitive landscape. In addition, with all the great online tools available today that cover industry alerts, there is no excuse for not keeping up with the latest market action.

Notes

1. The information in this paragraph was derived from Jack Neff, "Unilever reorganization Shifts P&L Responsibility," *Advertising Age* (February 28, 2005): 13.
2. Salah S. Hassan, Stephen Craft, and Wael Kortam, "Understanding the New Bases for Global Market Segmentation," *The Journal of Consumer Marketing* (2003, Vol. 20, Iss, 4/5): 454.

3. Douglas B. Holt, John A. Quelch, and Earl L. Taylor, "How Global Brands Compete," *Harvard Business Review* (September 2004): 68–75.
4. John Galvin, "The World on a String," *Advertising Age* (February 2005): 13–19.
5. Alex Taylor III, "Can America Fall in Love with VW Again?" *Fortune* (May 16, 2005): 130.
6. David Arnold, "Seven Rules of International Business, *Harvard Business Review* (November–December 2000): 131–137.
7. Richard R. Gesteland, *Cross-Cultural Business Behavior*, 3rd edition (Copenhagen Business School Press, 2002).

Chapter Thirteen

What Product Management Is and Is Not

Product management has long been viewed as an effective organizational form for multiproduct firms. The advantages are numerous and frequently documented. First, it provides a dedicated champion for a product, brand, or service. Second, a healthy internal competitive environment can be created. Third, by championing a number of offerings, a firm can more quickly respond to shifting customer loyalties. And finally, an opportunity is provided to readily assess candidates for promotion to higher management levels.

Nevertheless, the effectiveness of product management is contingent upon several factors. If we expect product mangers to truly champion brands, they must be engaged in both day-to-day decision issues and in developing the strategic future paths of their offerings. Although some companies have created a hierarchical product management structure to do this, effective product management in the future will result from a horizontal decision-making process. Product managers will play a major role in most product-related decisions, while relying on specialists to carry out many of those decisions. The emphasis will be on matching customer needs with corporate capabilities through the development of specific products and services.

As stressed throughout this book, the ability to attract and retain high-profit customers is a distinguishing characteristic of successful businesses, and many companies struggle with how to attain that goal. To succeed, firms employ many different strategies, including competency management; customer retention programs; strategic leveraging; global marketing; project management; big, hairy, audacious goals (BHAGs); e-commerce; and supply-chain management. Yet all the tools and techniques espoused by management gurus have not replaced the importance of a solid organizational structure to guide an organization in accomplishing corporate goals. One such organizational structure that has withstood the test of time in many situations is the product management structure. In this type of structure, product managers oversee a set of defined products or services that face different competitors and different customer constraints than many or all of the other products and services in the company. Determining if product management is the optimal structure for a particular company involves a number of considerations, including the company's culture; how much technical knowledge is required to design, launch, and support specific products; and whether the company's products require distinctly different approaches to "going to market."

Once a structure is established, clarifying the roles of company personnel with whom product managers routinely interact is important. The product manager is a generalist who must rely on numerous functional specialists to develop and market the product line. The product manager is the liaison among the functional departments within the company as well as among the company, the sales force, and the customers for all product-related issues. As a result, some understanding of mutual expectations is appropriate.

On an ongoing basis, product managers exchange information with the sales force. They need to plan for current and future product activities that benefit the company as a whole. And they represent the voice of the customer at internal meetings on the product line in question.

An evolution has occurred in product management over the past few decades. Rather than declining in number and importance, as had been forecast in numerous articles, product management (especially "nontraditional" product, market, and service management) has prevailed by encompassing customer management and value chain analysis, evolving into a more holistic position. The overall responsibility of a product manager is to integrate the various segments of a business into a strategically focused whole, maximizing the value of a product by coordinating the "production" of an offering with an understanding of market needs. To accomplish this, a product manager needs a broad knowledge of virtually all aspects of a company, along with very focused knowledge of a specific product or product line and its customers. Product managers manage not only products, but projects and processes as well.

Procter & Gamble has been credited with the creation of the product management concept. In 1931, Camay soap was languishing, while Ivory soap was thriving. A Procter & Gamble executive suggested that an individual manager be assigned responsibility for Camay, in effect pitting the brands against each other. This brand-management system was so successful that it was copied by most consumer packaged goods companies.[1]

Product management is a matrix organizational structure in which a product manager is charged with the success of a product or product line, but has no direct authority over the individuals producing and selling the product. Much of the work of a product manager is through various departments and cross-functional teams, almost as if the product manager were operating a business within a business (see Business Brief 13.1).

The product management approach has both advantages and disadvantages. On the plus side, a product manager provides dedicated attention to a product line. This results in better information about the customers, competition, and strategic potential for that group of products. In addition, since the product manager must necessarily interact with the various operational units of a company, the position can provide a good training ground for young executives. On the other hand, a consequential criticism of the product management structure is that it is a "fast-track" or "stepping-stone" position, overemphasizing short-term results. It promotes the perception that product management skills are more transferable

Business Brief 13.1   The life of a consumer-brand product manager.

[Author's note: This Business Brief was published in the first edition of *The Product Manager's Handbook*. I tracked down Tracy Carlson to see how her career had unfolded since this 1989 article, and her interview is contained at the end of this chapter.]

Tracy Carlson, senior product manager for Lever Brothers' Wisk™ detergent, spends an inordinate amount of time with stains. In an effort to move her brand to become the best-selling liquid laundry detergent in the country, she has to convince consumers of the superiority of her product over Procter & Gamble's Tide™. Like her counterparts at other consumer-product companies, Carlson is responsible for nearly every aspect of her product.

More than being simply champions for their brands, product managers are viewed in some ways as running their own little businesses. They not only oversee product development, but also monitor advertising and promotion, as well as negotiate to obtain shelf space from retailers. With current product proliferation, manufacturers concede that there are few lasting competitive advantages from which to attain market dominance. Therefore, sensitivity, intelligence, and intuition are important traits for product managers facing these battles.

But the real challenge of the job for product managers like Carlson is often simply getting the product onto shelves. A glut of new products has made retailers reluctant to open shelf space without generous inducements from manufacturers. The inducements include paying for in-store displays, fees for mentioning the product in store advertising circulars, and compensation for the increased processing costs of warehousing the new products.

Carlson will not reveal the Wisk™ marketing budget, but she said that, in general, the proportion of consumer-products budgets for trade and consumer promotions has risen from less than half to as much as three-fourths, with the balance going to advertising.

Source: Condensed from "High Stakes for Product Managers," *The New York Times* (December 4, 1989): D1–D7.

than product and industry knowledge. In addition, product management can cause conflict, because the product manager has limited functional authority over many parts of the development, marketing, and sales of the product, but may nevertheless have bottom-line responsibility. Finally, product managers might focus on the product almost to the exclusion of the customer.

Despite its limitations, product management (or some variation of it) has found its way into virtually every type of industry, going well beyond the traditional consumer-product brand-manager position. Even within fast-moving consumer packaged goods companies, product management has evolved. Due to the increasing level of internal brand cannibalization and competition for resources, along with media fragmentation and a higher level of retail and consumer sophistication, product management is being stretched into different "shapes."

Product Management Today

Product management as an organizational form has moved into a variety of business-to-business firms, as well as into service organizations such as financial institutions and hospitals. Most large banks have product managers for credit cards, deposit services, trust operations, and commercial cash management services.[2] Property and casualty insurers have begun to utilize product managers for highly competitive, rapidly changing lines, such as workers' compensation and auto insurance.[3]

Hospitals also have experienced success with the product management structure. A study published in the *Journal of Health Care Marketing* reported that hospitals with product-line management outperformed those without it on virtually all performance indicators, including occupancy rate, gross patient revenue per bed, average profit margin, and return on assets.[4] Not surprisingly, the implementation of product-line management increased with level of competition and hospital bed size. Other health care studies found that product-line management in hospitals offered the benefits of increased accountability, elimination of duplication of services, and a better market orientation. The limitations included a possible increase in costs (because functional management was not eliminated) and an increased need for more timely and accurate data.[5]

Although traditional product management has had its successes, companies have increasingly modified their approach to product management to incorporate a focus on the customer.

This has taken many forms. Some service firms have created what is in fact segment management (although the product manager title might still be used). For example, hospitals might have a product manager for women's services. Financial institutions might have a small-business product manager or an "affluent market" manager. Deregulation in financial services has contributed to this latter phenomenon. Interest-bearing checking accounts, money market funds, affinity credit cards, and an explosion of other product offerings attempt to appeal to increasingly smaller market segments. This, along with the availability of more sophisticated technology, has changed the focus of product management at banks.

> [In one year alone], banks launched about 700 new affinity programs, and customers opened 7.5 million new affinity accounts. The aim of product proliferation has been to satisfy an increasingly divergent set of customer needs. To keep track of these divergent needs, banks have invested in customer information file (CIF) technologies that permit segmentation across many dimensions, only one of which is product. The data generated by CIFs have accelerated the growth of market-segment-focused strategies.[6]

Segment management has been successful at several banks (see Business Brief 13.2). Simply shifting the emphasis from products to segments, however, will not eliminate some of the problems that can exist in a matrix organization. A matrix organization is one in which people report directly to a specific function area, but report indirectly (through a "dotted-line" relationship) to other functional areas. Both—or neither—can result in an enhanced understanding of customers and an ability to satisfy their needs. It requires a commitment to make it work.

First, a clear understanding must exist of the basic rationale for product management as an organizational form. Product management is generally most successful for companies with several products having similar manufacturing but different marketing requirements, particularly when the same product cuts across several divisions or customer groups. Second, top management must be committed to the product

Business Brief 13.2   Segment management in financial services.

Banks that have traditionally used product managers have generally assigned them to groups of deposit products, home equity loans, mortgages, insurance, and so on. Unfortunately, these products are not always complementary, and they might even be considered indirect substitutes by consumers. Therefore, banks such as Sovran Financial and Bank One/Texas have experimented with segment management.

Sovran Financial Corp., a holding company for four Middle Atlantic banks, reorganized its marketing structure to replace product management with a market segment emphasis. Sovran had attempted a relationship-marketing strategy before the structure change, but found it difficult to implement with an organization by product. Therefore, in 1988, it reorganized

by individual market segments, such as the "affluent market." The segment-management design allowed Sovran to capture what it referred to as "share of wallet," which increased from 38% to 46% in Virginia and from 44% to 62% in Tennessee.

At Bank One/Texas, one of the product managers is the small business–market segment manager, responsible for developing marketing programs to support the branches and sales force in bringing in new small businesses to the bank. This position has enabled Bank One to package products appropriate for a specific segment's needs.

Source: Condensed from Eric Berggren and Robert Dewar, "Is Product Management Obsolete?" *Journal of Retail Banking* 13 (Winter 1991/1992): 30; Lauryn Franzoni, "Product Managers: Finding the Right Fit," *Bank Marketing* 23 (May 1991): 28+.

management organization and provide the structure and tools to make it work. If it is fundamentally a project coordinator position, it will not have the results discussed in this chapter. And, finally, the right people must be selected and developed for the job.

Regardless of the organizational changes product management may undergo in the future, successful product managers must thoroughly understand the needs of various segments within the market, appreciate the corporate competencies available in the company, and be able to leverage these competencies to meet market needs. In other words, the ultimate goal of the product manager will be customer satisfaction obtained by being a cross-functional leader in the firm.

The Product Manager's Job

The product manager's job is to oversee all aspects of a product or service line to create and deliver superior customer satisfaction while simultaneously providing long-term value for the company. To accomplish this, various day-to-day and short- and long-term activities are necessary. Ideally, day-to-day activities provide the foundation for the job of the product manager and usually absorb 40% to 55% of a product manager's time; 20% to 30% of the time is devoted to short-term activities; and 15% to 25% is allotted to long-term tasks. (This, of course, varies depending on the time of the fiscal year, the relative proportion of new versus mature products managed, as well as a host of other variables.) These percentages are goals. Unfortunately, the reality is that many product managers spend too much time "putting out fires," to the exclusion of strategic planning (Figure 13.1). Time management is crucial for all businesspeople, and even more so for product managers.

A recent national survey of product managers showed that a significant proportion of product managers spent much time responding to sales force requests and expediting products through other departments, but wished they could spend less time on those activities. This same survey found that product managers spent little time developing long-range strategy for products and

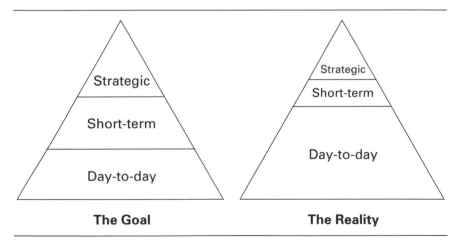

Figure 13.1   The product manager's balance of activities.

contacting customers to understand future needs and applications, but wished they could spend more time in these ways.[7]

Day-to-Day Duties

On a day-to-day basis, the product manager might have the following responsibilities:

· Maintain a product fact book.
· Motivate the sales force and distributors.
· Collect marketing information, including competitive benchmarks, trends and opportunities, and customer expectations.
· Act as a liaison between sales, manufacturing, research and development (R&D), and so on.
· Control the budget and achieve sales goals.

Short-Term Duties

On a short-term (e.g., fiscal year) basis, the product manager might have the following responsibilities:

· Participate in annual marketing-plan and forecast development.
· Work with advertising departments and agencies to implement promotional strategies.
· Coordinate trade shows and conventions.
· Initiate regulatory acceptance.
· Participate in new-product development teams.
· Predict and manage competitors' actions.
· Modify product and/or reduce costs to increase value.
· Recommend line extensions.
· Participate in product-elimination decisions.

Long-Term Duties

On a long-term (strategic) basis, the product manager might have the following responsibilities:

· Create a long-term competitive strategy for the product.
· Identify new-product opportunities.
· Recommend product changes, enhancements, and introductions.

Historically, the product manager's job has varied somewhat between consumer and B2B firms. Consumer product managers typically managed fewer products and spent more time on advertising and sales promotion. The target markets were generally larger (millions rather than thousands or hundreds), with a greater potential for diversity. Business product managers tended to be more involved in the technical aspects of the product or service and spent more time with engineering and the sales force.

However, the gap between the two types of product managers is narrowing. Fragmentation of consumer markets has escalated, resulting in greater product proliferation and parity products, for which consumers perceive little distinction in features or quality and usually make purchase decisions based on price. Trade satisfaction is becoming more critical as mass merchandisers and other "big box" retailers, such as Wal-Mart, Home Depot, and Office Max, continue to gain momentum. As a result, consumer product managers are finding themselves more involved with sales staff and the trade (e.g., retailers). On the B2B side, product managers are finding a growing need to introduce advertising to their firms and to establish a more solid position against an ever-increasing number of competitors. Market (as opposed to product) knowledge has become a key determinant of successful differentiation.

Product Management Tomorrow

Product management will continue to evolve to meet the needs of the market and of the particular company employing it. Consumer-goods product managers, for example, will find it necessary to be more involved with the trade as retailers gain more knowledge of and "influence" with consumers. Consequently, they will need to think more in terms of category management. *Category management* involves looking at a line (i.e., category) of products as it might be evaluated by a market segment (i.e., specific retailer or end-users). To accomplish this, product managers might need to work together as a category team. Or a category manager position might be established to oversee all products and product managers related to a given market segment.

Another trend that might affect the future role of product managers is the use of product management teams. As companies continue to escalate their involvement with team-based decisions, product management teams (PMTs) will appear in some companies. Global companies will have cross-border product business teams responsible for leveraging capabilities throughout the world. These will be "virtual teams," which do not meet regularly on a face-to-face basis and are not located in the same country. Although project teams have been very successful in new-product development, the appropriateness of ongoing teams in charge of existing products will have to be carefully considered and structured before implementation.

Product management has been evaluated, criticized, and applauded since its first introduction. Several writers have questioned whether product management will be a premier organizational structure in the future or whether it has become obsolete. Brand management, the most common form of product management in consumer goods companies, has perhaps come under the heaviest attack for several reasons. The availability of market data is unprecedented, causing brand managers to become overwhelmed. At the same time, senior managers demand more data to justify marketing decisions in the face of growing competition and a saturated market demand. Brand managers are being put under more scrutiny, with more and more decisions requiring higher management approval before progress can be made. Disillusionment with the system is high.

In other industries where product management has had a shorter history, the role is being viewed as a functional solution to several organizational problems. In particular, the approach is being implemented to provide the necessary match between the market's needs and the firm's ability to translate its core capabilities into products that satisfy these needs. Regardless of the industry, product management is, and will continue to be, a viable organizational form. However, modifications will occur. Three variations to the original product management structure will likely play a role in the future for several companies. These variations—product management teams, more specialized focus, and a business unit manager approach—will be explored further.

Product Management Teams

The use of product management teams (PMTs) to make product-related decisions has grown recently. The specific role of the team, as well as its effectiveness, still is unclear. To put PMTs into perspective, it is useful to look at the evolution of teams in corporate America over the past decade or two and to provide some general categorization of teams.

The widespread use of teams started in the 1980s, with the growth of quality circles used primarily in the auto and steel industries to combat Japanese competition. In general, workers and supervisors met intermittently to discuss quality problems and provide suggestions for incremental improvements. However, they rarely provided breakthrough thinking and began to lose their appeal. Nevertheless, the interest in teams continued, with the groups evolving into either worker teams or project teams:

> The teams most popular today are of two broad types: work teams, which include high-performance or self-managed teams, and special-purpose, problem-solving teams. Problem-solving teams, in particular, differ from quality circles in important ways. Where quality circles are permanent committees designed to handle whatever workplace problems may pop up, problem-solving teams have specific missions, which can be broad (find out why our customers hate us) or narrow (figure out why the No. 3 pump keeps overheating). Once the job is done, such teams usually disband.
>
> While problem-solving teams are temporary, work teams, used by about two-thirds of U.S. companies, tend to be permanent. Rather than attack specific problems, a work team does day-to-day work. A team of Boeing engineers helping to build a jet would be [an example of] a work team.[8]

The differences between the structure of the two types of teams are also worth noting. The project teams are frequently cross-functional, comprised of individuals representing the various operative areas related to the specific mission of the team. The work teams, although occasionally multifunctional, are more likely to have members who are similar in job function, with the authority to make decisions about how daily work is done.

The trouble with some PMTs being created today is that they combine the two structures, in effect developing an ongoing cross-functional team without a specific mission, yet without the ability to make decisions on daily workloads. This isn't meant to imply that teams cannot exist within a product management structure. Rather, a product manager should be prepared to work with numerous problem-solving teams on an ongoing basis, rather than with one ongoing team.

Teams are critical in product-deletion decisions, issues related to establishing a consistent corporate image among all products in the company, work flow and scheduling, and new-product development. Each of these teams is likely to have different members and involve different time periods. The product manager takes on the role of integrator across these teams, as they relate to the product line in question, and she is responsible for managing a bundle of projects at different stages of completion.

The company also plays a role in assuring that the various teams work together. If teams have to build consensus among both functional and team bosses, as at DEC, a great amount of time can be lost. On the other hand, empowering problem-solving teams to make immediate decisions can be both motivating and time-saving.

> [DEC announced in July 1994 that] it was abandoning its matrix team structure. Under the old system, workers in functional areas—engineering, marketing—also served on teams organized around product lines like minicomputers or integrated chips. The teams spent endless hours in meetings trying to build a consensus between the two factions in the matrix: the functional bosses and the team bosses. Its

sheer organizational weight left DEC a laggard in the fast-moving technology sector.

Boeing has an organizational structure similar to DEC's but with a critical difference. Its structure encourages teams to work together and seize initiative. Says Henry Shomber, a Boeing chief engineer: "We have the no-messenger rule. Team members must make decisions on the spot. They can't run back to their functions for permission." This kind of freedom allowed Boeing to use teams to build its new 777 passenger jet, which flew its first successful test flight this summer [1994] with fewer than half the number of design glitches of earlier programs.[9]

More Specialized Focus

Given the growing responsibilities assigned to product managers, some companies are questioning whether there is simply too much for one individual to handle. As a result, movement has occurred toward narrowing the focus of the product manager. The type of focus is company- or industry-specific. A number of fast-moving consumer-goods (FMCG) companies, for example, have split the product manager position into two areas of specialization. One manager focuses on consumer issues, and the other focuses on trade issues. Del Monte followed this type of reorganization in 1993. "The intent is to become more of a specialist," said Christine Di Fillippo, brand manager of tomato products at Del Monte.[10]

The ability to deal with the trade is likely to continue to escalate in importance. Although retail giants have existed for a long time, their clout has increased due to the emergence of powerful information systems that provide them with more data on consumers than manufacturers have. Consumer-goods manufacturers are finding it necessary to organize around their customers (the retailers), invest in technology, and act more as a partner than was typical in the past. Vendors to Wal-Mart have to respond to a barrage of demands to get their product sold (or even on the shelves). Companies are also increasingly including retailer input at the early stages of product development. Black & Decker solicited input from several retailers, including Home Depot, when it introduced the DeWalt line of power tools. The president of Black & Decker's power tools group emphasized their involvement: "We talked to them about the name. We talked to them about the color. We talked to them about the warranty."[11] Their input was valuable not only in terms of product design, but also as a visible sign of their involvement as a partner.

Other FMCG companies have restructured to allow the brand manager to focus more specifically on product issues, with advertising handled under a corporate umbrella. There is some logic to this approach when a company brand identity is more important to the market than the brand image of the line or item over which the product manager has control. However, unless the product has unique technical demands, the position of product manager might not be necessary in this situation, and a functional organization could suffice.

Some highly technical companies have taken a similar route, having product managers focus on the engineering and technical aspects of a product, with most marketing decisions handled by a separate function. In this case, the product manager may become a technical or applications expert with the job of helping the salespeople, while the other individual is responsible for understanding the market and communicating product benefits to them. The risk of separating marketing from development is that the product manager loses contact with the customer and becomes too close to the product to be objective.

Whatever attempts are made at specialization to make the product manager's job more manageable, it's critical to remember why the position was created in the first place: to better understand the product and its competition, so that customer needs are satisfied.

Business Unit Manager

Other companies have reorganized into what are essentially business units, with the product manager responsible for the general management of the product line. This type of team arrangement elaborates on the PMT concept but, in a sense, allows a more specialized focus on the product as a business.

Under this type of structure, the product manager assumes more responsibility for all of the business functions related to the product, going well beyond the marketing and planning.

> While the product manager has always worked in a spectrum ranging from marketing specialist to general manager, the business unit structure places greater emphasis on the general management side.
>
> Jennifer Kan at Specialty Brands is part of this new kind of team and has new responsibilities over areas such as finance and inventory. "Companies seem to be searching for the next generation of organizations, trying to figure out what will work best in the upcoming years," she said.[12]

If product managers are to be held fully accountable for the success of their products, it's reasonable to expect them to be given sufficient authority to facilitate success. The business unit manager structure makes that possible. However, it also requires that the person hired for the position has the experience, reputation, and respect to carry it out.

Other Trends

At least two trends are likely to impact the future of product management, particularly in larger firms. One is the growth of global megabrands. The other is the dramatic metamorphosis of distribution channels and logistics management.

The globalization of brands is occurring in both consumer and business arenas. Kelly Services, a temporary worker agency, has both domestic and international locations. Coca-Cola, Sony, and Levi Strauss are brand names recognized throughout the world. Companies are realizing that they have to accept this movement toward global brands as inevitable.

> Major brand companies frequently inform the media that globalization is their most pressing challenge. The year 1990 saw a series of acquisitions and (more commonly) mergers because companies felt the need to expand in order to compete in a global market: Hoffman La Roche and Genetic or Merck and Du Pont in pharmaceuticals; AT&T and NCR in computers; Matsushita and MCA in entertain-

ment electronics; Whirlpool and Philips in white goods; Asahi and Elders IXL in beer. Procter & Gamble's chairman Edwin L. Arztz offered these words at the company's general meeting in 1990: "The acquisition strategy will be driven by globalization, which will be the principal engine of growth in sales. It's not optional. That's the way business will be done."[13]

What does this mean for product managers? Many product managers will be challenged to understand the market needs for their products beyond American borders. The transition for some companies will be minor, if few changes are required to the product or its marketing. In other cases, extensive marketing research, product adaptation, and promotional modifications will be unavoidable. The product manager may also be required to work with company personnel located at plants or offices in other countries, sometimes coordinating virtual teams through videoconferencing, fax, and other electronic means. These cross-border business teams will be responsible for leveraging corporate capabilities throughout the world.

The proliferation of different channels for both consumer and business products, from club stores to distribution alliances to direct marketing, might pressure manufacturers to offer broad and varied product lines. In addition to these diverse ways of reaching customers, logistics management also includes the relationships with suppliers to get the right parts and products to your company as effectively and efficiently as possible. These factors can have a profound and strategic impact on the success of a product manager's offering.

> Many manufacturers have traditionally shipped product out to their dealers and distributors with the attitude, "Now Mr. Distributor, just go out and sell it." The dealer or distributor was considered to be the customer, without much thought about what happened to the product beyond that point. [14]

Product managers must realize the impact of the distribution channel (both in and out of the company) in affecting the success of the product line. The implication for the product manager is the need to solicit input from a wider spectrum of "customers," including suppliers, purchasing staff, and logistics and transportation personnel.

Concluding Remarks

Product management is here to stay. The position is challenging, demanding, and rewarding. Product managers will be given more responsibilities as the challenges of going to market increase. Some companies will experiment with product management teams, a narrowing of job focus for product managers, or a business unit approach, but the companies for whom the structure is most successful will hire, groom, and empower product managers to create products with both internal integrity from a design perspective and external integrity from a customer perspective.

Regardless of the organizational changes product management goes through in the future, successful product managers will have a thorough understanding of the various segments within a market (including global segments), an understanding of the "core competencies" available to the company, and the ability to leverage these competencies to meet market needs. In other words, the product manager of the future will have the ability to attain customer satisfaction by serving as a cross-functional leader in the firm.

Checklist: What Product Management Is and Is Not

· To ensure that you focus on the long-term value of a product; do not view your product manager role as a "fast-track" or "stepping-stone" position.
· Be careful not to lose sight of the customer as you strive to create competitively superior products and services.
· Expect the role of product manager to continue to evolve to meet current business challenges. Category management and the use of product management teams will be tested by companies striving to improve competitive performance.

- Balance your activities among day-to-day and short- and long-term activities to avoid the trap of constantly "putting out fires."

Interview with Tracy Carlson, Founder, The Larger View

In the first edition of my book, I provided some information from the *New York Times* about Tracy Carlson's life as a senior product manager for Wisk™ Detergent (see Business Brief 13.1). I decided to try to track her down for the third edition of my book. Tracy currently manages her own brand-strategy consulting firm, The Larger View, working with a range of clients from large firms like Rubbermaid to small start-ups. Based in Boston, she is also beginning to work in the emerging field of brand and marketing strategy for colleges and universities.

Q: *In the first edition of my book, I provided some information from the* New York Times *about your life as a senior product manager for Wisk™ Detergent. Let's talk about your career both before and after that point. How did you get started at Unilever?*

A: I started at Unilever right after getting my MBA at Wharton in 1984. At the time, consumer packaged goods was the place to be for marketers. Luckily for me, the then British VP of Marketing at Lever Brothers, Andrew Seth, was willing to take a chance on someone with a great education (Yale, Wharton) but a nontraditional background (French teacher and French/Russian translator who'd managed a small business).

Lever Brothers was a terrific opportunity for a marketer: very entrepreneurial, very unstructured, with lots of autonomy and big budgets, as our focus was building volume and share. We were given as much responsibility as we could handle, and I moved fast: from Assistant to Associate Product Manager in less than a year, then to Product Manager a year later—all on big important brands. By the time I left, after 6 years with the company, I'd managed three of the company's largest and most important brands.

Q: *Tell me about your biggest successes.*

A: One major success was a complete restage/reintroduction of Wisk™ laundry detergent for Unilever in 1988–1989. Wisk™, the first liquid laundry detergent, had lost category leadership to P&G's new entry, Tide Liquid™. Without investment in developing a competitive formula and package, it had become a price brand, reliant on money-losing pre-prices. When I managed the brand, we were able to redo everything, from product formulation, fragrance, and package to pricing and advertising—in the process, getting Wisk's infamous ring-around-the-collar ads off the air. In test market, we doubled share and volume, then expanded nationally, where we succeeded in regaining category leadership and restoring profitability to the brand.

The most personally satisfying expression of this, however, came when the manager of our St. Louis manufacturing facility told me that successfully repositioning Wisk™ had meant his plant workers had more stable jobs. Steady, higher volume on the brand meant more and steadier jobs, replacing the cycle of temporary hirings and layoffs to cope with wild volume swings. His local bottle supplier had also added a new line to meet demand—creating new well-paying manufacturing jobs in a blighted neighborhood. Having a real impact on the everyday lives of real families felt terrific.

Another success was successfully growing profits for Hellmann's/Best Foods Mayonnaise despite declining category sales and new competition from private label brands, which had never occurred in the category before. We were able to sharpen our marketing efforts, sustaining volume and increasing profits, while also developing a new understanding of pricing relationships and effective new advertising that focused on emotional benefits instead of functional benefits.

Q: *What was most satisfying and least satisfying about your product management jobs?*

A: Generally speaking, it was wonderfully satisfying to have a fast-paced, demanding job with a lot of responsibility and variety—one that tapped a lot of skills. In addition to getting hands-on experience with key functional areas of marketing (advertising, marketing research, promotion etc.) with tangible results, it was also satisfying to have good people skills recognized and rewarded. As a product manager, you have lots of responsibility coupled with very little authority: You have to get things done through people. It was also great to mentor junior people: I'm still in touch with people who worked for me over 15 years ago.

I'd like to cite one additional experience that was personally satisfying: When Ed Arzt, CEO of Procter & Gamble, Unilever's main competitor, cited advertising I had championed on Dove Beauty Bar™ as an example of an excellent way to evolve an ad campaign. I later heard it was featured in P&G's fabled "Copy College."

The least satisfying aspect of product management was dealing with internal politics, particularly micro-managing by senior management. Tremendous quantities of time, money, energy, and enthusiasm were squandered because senior management would interfere with what was best for the brand. Endless fire drills to produce absurd amounts of butt-covering data, for example, or dictating advertising direction based on personal taste, despite incontrovertible research findings.

Q: *What have you been doing since leaving Unilever?*

A: I have currently been running my own brand-strategy consulting firm, The Larger View, for a few years. This comes after a stint directing the marketing program at a national nonprofit, a year or so at a boutique ad agency, and 3 years running the branded food/beverage division of a specialty consulting firm. These opportunities were in metropolitan Washington, D.C.—an area with virtually no consumer marketing. The consulting experience was particularly fun: working on big-picture strategic issues affecting the future of the food and beverage industry, such as the evolution of ethnic food, strategies for mid-sized players to compete among giants, or unconventional but successful approaches to category reinvention.

I'm currently working with clients like Rubbermaid on issues of positioning, advertising, and portfolio strategy. I'm also working with a start-up, Emotion Mining, a fascinating technology that measures conscious and subconscious emotions. It's a technology with tremendously exciting potential for brand marketers.

I am also moving in a new direction, working in the emerging field of branding for colleges and universities. Having worked in nonprofits before, I really like mission-driven people: You don't have to squint to see the good guys. And I love working in a nonprofit space while applying private-sector skills and discipline, helping stretch limited resources more effectively and giving them more impact.

Q: *Given your knowledge of consumer marketing, what do you think will be the primary challenges of product managers in the next decade?*

A: Several factors converge to make the job more challenging and in some ways less "controllable." Everyone knows that in most areas of consumer marketing, retailer clout means that many manufacturers have lost power, often sacrificing what's in their own long-term interests as a brand or company.

In addition, greater consumer individualism and sophistication, coupled with a changing retail and media environment, has taken place alongside a massive failure of imagination in many large companies. Products are conceived because they can be made, not because anyone really wants them, and the me-too clones follow in a heartbeat. This means there are few home runs and a glut of poorly supported products with little consumer resonance. Marketing resources are often scarcer and under greater scrutiny, resulting in less autonomy.

Consumer product managers will continue to have to deal with these challenges—none will be getting easier—though one hopes the pendulum will eventually swing back from its current tilt toward retailer power. But I think there are some bright spots. The trick is to focus on truly understanding the consumer: what his/her life is like, what problems you can solve for him or her, how to create some genuine resonance with his or her life and aspirations. Currently, this tends to happen on the fringes, where entrepreneurs with passion create products for small, highly focused audiences. Their products mean something to someone, and that catches on. Unfortunately, these companies tend to get bought up by some giant that doesn't enable the same sense of passion.

For product managers in large companies, the challenge is often to balance internal and external realities. These companies are fabulous places to acquire and practice the important skills and disciplines of consumer marketing. But they're also fairly unreal places, ones that have a culture and momentum of their own. When product managers ponder "the consumer," it's easy to think abstractly, forgetting that they're talking about developing and selling a product or service to a bunch of real people. It's also easy to go native in a big company, assuming that products or services that can be made/sold should be made/sold. At the end of the day, we haven't done consumers any favors if we've complicated their already complicated lives, shouting at them to buy our slightly tweaked version of some marginally useful thing that's been line-extended into absurdity.

Q: *What is the best advice you ever received?*

A: The best advice was, "Don't get really good at anything you don't want to do..." More seriously, I would quote a woman at Unilever who taught me how to get along with a very difficult, sexist guy in sales planning. He was very powerful, but very demeaning to women. She advised me: "Ask him about his granddaughter." And I did. I ended up developing an excellent relationship with him, and I was the only woman in marketing who did. He even went out of his way to help me. This advice made me realize that there is a way to get along with everyone, and everyone, no matter how snarly or curmudgeonly or obstreperous is a person with a real and interesting life. In a profession like product management, where you need to have good people skills, this was excellent advice.

Q: *What advice can you provide to today's product managers?*

A: Have some humility. Your success rests on working effectively with a lot of interesting and complicated people, including those within your company and those who might be motivated to buy your products. Get to know them and what their lives are like.

Enjoy what you can while you can. Product management is a terrific profession, but it doesn't last forever. The pyramid narrows, and not everyone can, will, wants to stay in line marketing. It also tends to be a profession for younger people, both because it requires long hours and because enthusiasm for what one markets is important.

Recognize that the skills and perspective you develop as a product manager can be enormously helpful elsewhere. Nearly every enterprise or organization grapples with the question of product and audience, and how to make the most effective connection given the unique context in which it operates. Moreover, other skills required to be a good product manager are in real need everywhere. These include keeping the big picture in view, building and sustaining a team, accessing data and turning it into relevant information, and being a good project manager.

Notes

1. Zachary Schiller, "The Marketing Revolution at Procter & Gamble," *BusinessWeek* (July 25, 1988): 72.
2. Jean E. LeGrand, "A Product in Need of Management," *Bankers Magazine* (November/December 1992): 73+.

3. William Wichman, "Product Management as a Marketing Strategy," *National Underwriter* (July 29, 1991): 10+.
4. G. M. Naidu, A. Kleimenhagen, and G.D. Pillari, "Is Product-Line Management Appropriate for Your Health Care Facility?" *Journal of Health Care Marketing* (Fall 1993): 8.
5. Ibid, 10.
6. Eric Berggren and Robert Dewar, "Is Product Management Obsolete?" *Journal of Retail Banking* (Winter 1991/1992): 27+.
7. Based on information from a proprietary survey conducted by the author.
8. Brian Dumaine, "The Trouble with Teams," *Fortune* (September 5, 1994): 88.
9. Ibid., 88–90.
10. Tracy Carlson, "Brand Burnout," *Brandweek* (January 17, 1994): 26.
11. Zachary Schiller, Wendy Zellner, Ron Stodghill, and Mark Maremont, "Clout!" *BusinessWeek* (December 21, 1992): 70.
12. Carlson, p. 27.
13. David Arnold, *The Handbook of Brand Management* (Reading, MA: Addison-Wesley, 1992: 226).
14. Linda Gorchels, Edward Marien, and Chuck West, *The Manager's Guide to Distribution Channels* (New York: McGraw-Hill, 2004: 45).

Chapter Fourteen

Introducing Product Management and Managing Product Managers

Shifting from a functional (silo) organizational structure to any of a variety of team or matrix-based organizational forms (including product management) requires careful planning. Job descriptions must be written to help the product managers understand their new roles, and other departments must understand what to expect from the new positions. Product managers must rely on the support and performance of many others in the organization to achieve product performance goals, although they have no control over those functions. A clarification of objectives is imperative for the successful introduction of a product management structure to an organization. Unfortunately, many companies introduce the title "product manager" because their competitors have such a position (or they read about it in a magazine article), but they lack an understanding of what the position entails.

Four steps are involved in initiating product management. First, the company must assess whether product management is the appropriate organizational form and, if it is appropriate, decide what reporting structure (hierarchy) it will have. Second, the company must clearly specify the responsibilities of product managers, as well as of other integral members of the system. Third, the characteristics of successful product managers must be identified, with suitable personnel recruited for the product management openings. And, fourth, a system must be in place for developing and evaluating product managers. Each of these steps is discussed in detail in this chapter.

Assessing the Need for and Structure of Product Management

Product management can be an appropriate organizational structure when a company's product line has grown to the point where a functional structure no longer works. There might be more products than a single marketing manager can handle, even though these could flow into a common market through the same channels. Or, the company's products might be so different from each other in terms of competition and customer groups that they must be handled differently. Or, technical or sophisticated product knowledge might be required to meet the needs of the market. In this case, the product manager might be involved in the development and marketing of a product line across various divisions or markets (Figure 14.1).

On the other hand, subtle variations might be appropriate under different circumstances (Table 14.1). If the industry's

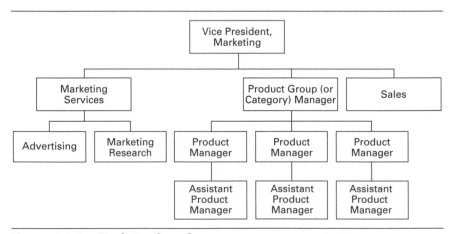

Figure 14.1   Traditional product management organization.

Table 14.1 Appropriate Organizational Structures for Various Product/Market Types

Product/Market Characteristics	Possible Organizational Structure
Many products going to a limited number of market segments. The products require focused attention to be fully successful.	Product management
Company sells to a variety of market segments with preferences for various product sets. The products might not require elaborate customization, but the "bundling" of products is unique to the market segments.	Market or segment management
The same situation as above, but there is also a need to develop some new products for various market segments.	Segment management with "special products" managers
The company sells to a few large customers with differing needs from the rest of the customer base.	Key account management
New-product efforts are time-consuming and critical for the company, to the point where a special position is created exclusively to handle new products.	Product development manager or new-products manager, possibly (although not necessarily) part of a technical department

products are primarily "parity" (essentially the same) in the minds of the customers, a traditional product manager structure might result in pressure to create artificial differences simply for the sake of differentiation. In this case, a market or segment management approach might be preferred. Market managers are used when a company needs to develop different markets for a single product line. Focus is on developing the *market*, rather than on taking the product to market. The market manager would "bundle" and/or adapt combinations of a company's products to fit the needs of select market segments. A need also may be present to have "special products" managers in conjunction with segment managers.

A variation of market management is key account or national account management. With the emergence of "big box retailers," "category killers," and other large customers, key account managers have been given the responsibility of working with major accounts to determine how products can best be adapted to meet their needs. If product managers are spending an inordinate amount of time handling special requests for major customers, a key account position could focus on the "special requests" and work with the product manager on product adaptation.

The Impact of New-Product Development

The last major consideration in organizational structure is related to new-product development. Although most product managers spend a significant part of their time on new-product development activities, some companies choose to have a separate new-product manager position to handle the specifications, design, and development of products, with the product managers following through with the marketing activities after commercialization. Although this is less common, it is an organizational form that can fit certain needs.

Implementing a Global Structure

Product managers should generally be familiar with the global environment for their products, if they deal with global suppliers, customers with global locations, or competitors with foreign operations. For multinational companies, there's an additional level of complexity. Companies must decide whether a single product manager has global authority for a product, whether product managers should interact with country managers, or whether there should be country-specific product managers. At a minimum, the product manager will be involved in cross-cultural teams charged with leveraging the skills of different parts of a global company located in different parts of the world. As Whirlpool CEO David Whitwam said in an interview with *Harvard Business Review*:

> The only way to gain lasting competitive advantage is to leverage your capabilities around the world so that the company as a whole is greater than the sum of its parts. Being

an international company—selling globally, having global brands or operations in different countries—isn't enough.

Let me use washing machines as an example. Washing technology is washing technology. But our German products are feature-rich and thus considered to be higher-end. The products that come out of our Italian plants run at lower RPMs and are less costly. Still, the reality is that the insides of the machines don't vary a great deal. Both the German and the Italian washing machines can be standardized and simplified by reducing the number of parts, which is true of any product family. Yet when we bought Philips, the washing machines made in the Italian and German facilities didn't have one screw in common. Today, products are being designed to ensure that a wide variety of models can be built on the same basic platform. Our new dryer line has precisely this kind of common platform, and other product categories are currently being designed in the same way.[1]

Reducing Hierarchy

Most product managers are part of a marketing or marketing and sales department, usually reporting to a marketing or product management director, a marketing or product management manager, or a vice president of marketing. Product managers frequently have no one reporting to them. In larger firms, however, product managers might have assistants and associates reporting to them, as well as authority over some functional subordinates. Some product managers have eight or more people reporting to them directly. If staff will be positioned under the authority of a product manager, it's usually best to provide information processors, coordinators, or analysts, rather than proliferating pyramids of assistants and associates, thus creating a hierarchy within a hierarchy.

Hierarchies are designed to prevent mistakes, but they also diminish individual responsibility, creativity, and risk-taking opportunities. That's why so many management gurus have espoused variations of the horizontal corporation, with an emphasis on providing better products and services for the end-customer. Product managers and product management teams are consistent with this philosophy, if they are linked to customer satisfaction (as they should be) and given the authority to make relevant decisions regarding their product lines.

Specifying Responsibilities of Product Managers and Others in the Firm

To minimize the potential for miscommunication and misunderstanding, and to increase the chances of a successful product management structure, management must thoroughly explain to key managers exactly how the organizational concept will work and what the underlying rationale is for moving to it. It's important to specify not only the roles of product managers, but also the roles of the individuals with whom they commonly interact. Let's take a hypothetical example of a company with three product managers, a marketing services manager, a marketing research manager, and regional sales managers. (All these people might report to a marketing director or a vice president of marketing and sales.)

Typically, the product managers would recommend and establish strategic guidelines for their products, obtain market information about their customer segments and products, provide input to sales for the closing of selected accounts, and play a major role in product or service development, modifications, and elimination. The marketing services manager would support the product managers by providing communication materials and handling company-wide promotional and public relations activities. The marketing research manager would contract out or conduct marketing research activities required to fully understand customer needs and competitive capabilities and provide input into company growth and acquisition opportunities. The regional sales managers would provide the day-to-day motivation and management of the sales force and support the product managers in the introduction of new products.

Many product managers (particularly in B2B companies or in the service sector) are hired for their technical expertise with a specific product or service. Therefore, the roles of the product management function and the related operational functions must be clarified. For example, the product manager might supply customer and competitor data in support of a recommended new product, but leave the actual design to the design staff.

Although these descriptions of responsibilities would not be appropriate for every organization, it's important to think through and define the related responsibilities and overlaps. Providing a summary of role responsibilities before introducing product management will reduce uncertainties about the organizational structure.

Where product managers are positioned in a company also can significantly influence their role, regardless of the responsibilities put in writing. A critical issue for management is to establish a balance between the product managers' administrative and entrepreneurial functions. Product managers with a relatively low perceived status cannot become true change agents. On the other hand, product managers with a relatively high perceived status should have the skills and earned respect required to perform effectively.

A major service-sector firm, introducing product management for the first time, created a task force charged with establishing a model of product manager responsibilities along with the responsibilities of 10 support areas (plus senior and business unit management) as they related to product management. The product managers were charged with many of the specific activities listed in this chapter. An abbreviated summary of the responsibilities of the 10 support areas is listed in Figure 14.2. Once the structure of product management is installed, management must select the right people and monitor and coach their activities to make sure they stay on track.

Characteristics of Successful Product Managers

No ideal profile exists of a successful product manager. However, several traits, skills, and experiences are frequently identified as related to product management success. Frequently cited traits looked for in product managers include an entrepreneurial attitude, leadership, and self-confidence. Acquired abilities should include organizational, time-management, and communication skills. Sales proficiency and techni-

Senior Vice President

- Setting overall direction and priorities of the organization
- Allocating overall resources

Business Unit Manager

- Approving annual product business plans and budgets
- Determining product resource allocation

Product Development

- Conducting feasibility studies of new products/major enhancements
- Coordinating the development and introduction of new products

Market Research

- Measuring, tracking, and reporting product market shares
- Conducting product research as requested

Marketing and Communications

- Developing and coordinating product-related marketing and sales communication
- Assisting in the development of marketing plans
- Executing marketing plans

Sales

- Prospecting for new business opportunities
- Closing sales

Operations

- Providing routine customer support and service
- Providing product operational efficiency

Corporate Relations

- Identifying new business opportunities and retention strategies
- Coordinating corporate business development plans

Personnel

- Developing and implementing a product manager professional development plan
- Conducting product manager specialized skill training

Quality Assurance

- Assisting in the development and monitoring of quality standards
- Providing process improvement evaluations

Figure 14.2   Responsibilities established by a major financial services company.

cal competence also are important in many industries. The importance of prior experience depends on the particular needs of the product management position. If highly technical, engineering-oriented knowledge is required, a background in engineering is appropriate. If an understanding of customer applications is desired, a sales background in the industry is appropriate. If knowledge of large-market trends and competitive positioning is important, marketing research and/or advertising experience are desirable.

The appropriate characteristics of a product manager also depend on the culture of the organization and the expectations placed on the position. Some product managers provide (and are expected to provide) a coordinator role; others may be more directive; and still others take on a leadership role.

Product managers who are coordinators primarily function as administrators to assure that deadlines are met and requests are carried out. Coordinative product managers are more likely to deal with budgets than plans. Product managers who are directive not only coordinate projects but also develop product plans. Product managers who are leaders are more entrepreneurial and become more active in the strategic planning of products and services for the company.

Part of the difference among desired product manager characteristics depends on whether they work for consumer or industrial product manufacturers. A study of senior marketing executives from Australian companies with a product management organization found differences in management expectations between consumer and industrial firms. Marketing executives from consumer goods firms tended to view product managers as coordinators or implementers of strategy to a greater degree than was true for industrial firms. On the other hand, a greater importance was placed on forecasting and competitor intelligence for industrial product managers than was true for consumer product managers. This is partly because of the wealth of syndicated data available about consumers that is absent in many industrial channels.[2]

This same study highlighted some problems with the product management concept (PMC).

Those companies who expressed dissatisfaction with the PMC were asked in an open-ended question to explain their reasons. The range of reasons embraced the following: product managers spent too much time on day-to-day matters and not enough on planning and searching for new opportunities; product managers were not sufficiently entrepreneurial; product managers did not have enough authority over the sales department and had poor communication with the sales force (the most frequently mentioned responses); there was poor understanding of [the] product manager role; product managers were inexperienced; and there was an authority-responsibility mismatch.[3]

Developing and Evaluating Product Managers

Product managers need a variety of knowledge, including product and industry knowledge, business knowledge, and interpersonal and management knowledge. Since beginning product managers typically spend most of their time gathering and organizing information on the product, its customers, and the competition, product knowledge is paramount. As they gain experience, the focus shifts to more comprehensive business knowledge, including finance, marketing, and strategic planning. At the same time, they develop team-building, negotiation, communication, and leadership abilities. Companies use both formal and informal approaches to developing product managers, as discussed in Business Brief 14.1.

Many companies believe it takes from 3 to 5 years to develop an effective product manager. According to Bill Meserve, a principal at the management-consulting firm of Temple, Barker & Sloane Inc., training and motivation are critical at this time, and career development must be an obligation: "The formal approach used at one 3M division is based on a written career development document and scheduled annual reviews, which are separate from performance appraisal. Primary responsibility for monitoring career development rests with senior marketing management or a separate marketing council."[4]

For product managers to be effective, they need to build bridges throughout the company and be cross-functional lead-

Business Brief 14.1   Skill and knowledge development for product managers.

Product managers typically had job descriptions listing their duties and responsibilities, such as competitive analysis and new product development. But discovering—and enhancing—the skills and knowledge required can be challenging. Identifying competencies is a process of discovery. Many companies start by analyzing top performers to uncover "secrets" to their success, and/or compile general information from outside sources. An *internal* analysis is useful for industry-specific competency requirements, whereas the *external* analysis allows a broader benchmarking perspective. In either situation, the competencies should be truly related to effective performance as a product manager.

The process of developing product managers can be formal or informal. Unilever has a relatively formal program using its Marketing Academy, a global pseudo-university for its employees focused on enhancing marketing capabilities. The curriculum forms the focal point of how the organization develops brands,

and it ties training into business objectives. The approach also increases the transfer of knowledge. Resources consist of books, booklets, an intranet, and workshops and courses.

Given the importance of cross-functional knowledge and the need to create the right culture and atmospheres, informal processes are also important. Paula Sneed, Senior Vice President of global marketing resources for Kraft Foods, found that listening to and appreciating colleagues at all levels during her career at General Foods and Kraft—a tool she referred to as a *mentoring mosaic*—provided a significant developmental component.

Source: Linda Gorchels, *The Product Manager's Field Guide* (New York: McGraw-Hill, 2003) provides a product manager competency model, along with alignment exercises for each competency. Anonymous, "Unilever: The Marketing Academy," *Brand Strategy* (May 2004): 28. Anonymous, "Dreaming Big, Preposterous Dreams Gives Vision for Success," *Chicago Tribune* (October 25, 2005): 5.

ers. Therefore, in the selection and development of product managers, this ability to transcend functional lines must be considered. The downfall of several product or brand management systems was the establishment of a product manager as caretaker of the product, with an emphasis on "safe" results. Product managers were charged with immediate results, rather than with the creation of long-term customer value. When this happens, product managers focus on improving their own position rather than that of the company's product. According to William Weilbacher in his book *Brand Marketing*:

> In the end, the brand manager is forced by the brand-management system to pay more attention to career management than to brand management. Brand championship and brand advocacy are replaced by actions that make the brand manager look good to management, no matter what the long-term effect upon the brand or the perceptions of the consumers who buy it.[5]

Appropriate evaluation criteria depend on the performance expectations of management. Sales and profit goals are fairly common measures of performance. However, if profit is a measure, it's important to distinguish between profit contribution and bottom-line profit. Profit contribution is the amount of product revenue remaining after subtracting all of a product manager's direct, controllable, or relevant expenses. This contribution to overhead (CTO) figure is a fairer assessment of performance than is fully allocated profit, because CTO minimizes the concern over the validity of the allocation methodology. Obsessive attention to allocating overhead against each product often consumes effort that could be better spent elsewhere. This isn't meant to imply that total overhead doesn't need to be covered. The CTO goal is established to cover anticipated overhead allocations but doesn't hold product managers responsible for overhead increases beyond their control.

Some companies implementing quality management principles have opted to minimize individual performance measures and focus on company performance. This does not have to be an either/or decision. Metrics can be designed to measure both individual and corporate performance. Companies can weigh these metrics differently, depending on their corporate philosophies on performance measurement.

In addition to financial measures, product managers may be evaluated on some combination of other factors, such as:

· Successful introduction of new products
· Market share defense or growth
· Customer satisfaction indexes
· Attainment of company-specific goals

Checklist: Introducing Product Management and Managing Product Managers

· Recognize product management as an organizational business form, not as an isolated job function.
· If you have specific groups of customers who require unique products, or if you must combine standard products in unique ways to meet the needs of these customer groups, consider segment management as an alternative (or in addition) to product management.
· Prevent product management from being done in the absence of market management. Otherwise, you run the risk of being production-driven rather than market-driven.
· Develop an information system of cost, business, and market data according to the relevant products or product lines.
· Clarify the roles of product managers and the roles of those with whom they routinely interact.
· Push product managers to evolve from being solely product specialists to being cross-functional leaders.
· Establish performance goals that reflect company expectations and provide the tools (budgets, people resources, approval authority) to achieve these goals.
· Select product managers with the skills appropriate for the culture, expectations, and responsibilities for your company. Provide additional training as required.

Interview with Therese Padilla, Co-Founder, Association of International Product Marketing and Management

Q: *In a nutshell, could you describe the AIPMM?*

A: AIPMM, the Association of International Product Marketing and Management, is a worldwide association dedicated to the careers of product managers. From the AIPMM's perspective, product management should be considered one of the most important roles in any organization. We support and advocate for more product management education, certification, and provide a community for product managers to collaborate.

Q: *What was your background prior to this position?*

A: Although I was a business major, I showed more interest in the programming and development side of high technology in the late '70s. I spent the better part of the '80s writing programs and databases, until I landed at the Peter Norton Group (now Symantec). There, I was able to use my business skills as product manager of the Norton Anti-Virus product. I continued to progress as a product manager specializing in the anti-virus, Internet security fields and moved on to being a director of product management and finally a VP of marketing. In the late '90s, I became aware of a need for an association to help, promote, and support individual product managers, and co-founded the AIPMM in 1998.

Q: *You've advocated certification for product managers. Can you talk a bit about that? What is the "body of knowledge" you encourage product managers to acquire? Are there different skill sets for B2B, B2C, and high-tech and service product managers?*

A. Most people who manage products take on their roles using what they know about the fields from which they came—they didn't go to school to learn product management. Moreover, many do not have business-management experience, including strategic and financial skills. Most were appointed either because they picked the short straw or they showed some project management ability. In order to advance product management as a viable and important role in an organization, the role should be more clearly defined. AIPMM's mission is to standardize the role and have our certification test the knowledge of those who participate. Even though industries and applications of product management might change, there is an essential skill set that applies, and we believe the certification test covers this. As far as the body of knowledge AIPMM recommends, we follow the product life cycle. However, our focus is on the individual. We decided early on not to map the process of the certification to a particular methodology of PLM. It's mostly a result of my belief that all these processes are transitory.

I remember in the '70s there were hundreds of books on Japanese-style business management. Today, new product development (NPD), for example, has about three or four major competing methodologies; Stage-Gate R, Agile, Voice of the Customer, and others. These are specific processes that would have to be adopted by the entire organization—and let's face it, they will come and go. I believe the core competencies of the product manager transcend any trendy process the organization adopts. AIPMM simply asks the questions: Does the product manager know how to make a profit or how to work through a difficult company? Do they know what they don't know, how to think on their feet, and get the information they need? And most of all, do they have the makings of the next CEO? The core competencies come from the fact that a product manager is a manger who has broad general knowledge and skills in several areas, who must work through the organization. I believe you call it a "generalist."

The body of knowledge includes:

- Product Life-Cycle Management (Discovery – Development – Delivery)
- Business management
- Financial management
- People management—most importantly, how to work through and with people (including cross-functional skills)

Q: *What changes in product management have you observed over the last 5 years or so?*

A: I'm still surprised by one change I haven't seen: That so few product managers have complete access to financial data within the organization. Companies are still unwilling to provide their product managers with this critical information they need to make decisions. To answer the question, though, I have seen more organizations (and it's generally the more successful ones) implementing their own product management training and, in some cases, creating a business process. It is clear those companies that compete heavily and succeed have created a more substantial product management organization within the company.

I've also seen more companies hire a tandem team (a product manager and assistant product manager). In this way, they are recognizing the dual role of the senior strategist and the junior tactical specialist.

Q: *What changes do you expect over the next 5 years?*

A: I expect that, with the number of universities and specialized programs for product management, we will continue to see the product management role growing within more organizations. I think we will see industries that typically let new product development drive future revenues like fashion, the automotive industry, and even computer software, utilizing product management in a more thoughtful or strategic way. I believe organizations will see solid product management as a way to gain revenue growth as well as sustain better product life-cycle management.

Q: *What will be the primary challenges for product managers in the next decade?*

A: The biggest challenges will come from globalization and effective cross-functional management. The ability to manage across continents and cultures will test the effectiveness of the product manager. Also, I see too much emphasis on new-product development as a means of growing an organization or delivering on revenue. I personally challenge product managers to look deeper into wringing out more profits from better positioning, better partnerships, and better planning.

Q: *What advice can you provide to current and prospective product managers?*

A: I frequently advise them to continue to develop their business management skills, to keep up with technology, and to stay keenly aware of the market and conditions. And for heaven's sake, enjoy the ride! Product management, in my opinion, is one of the greatest careers. The diversity from working with customers to working with talented development teams is exceptional—not to mention the fierce competition and extensive travel. This is not a career for the faint of heart or those seeking a pencil-pushing job.

For more information about the Association of International Product Marketing and Management, refer to: http://www.aipmm.com/.

Notes

1. Regina Fazio Maruca, "The Right way to Go Global," *Harvard Business Review* (March/April 1994): 137.
2. P.L. Dawes and P.G. Patterson, "The Performance of Industrial and Consumer Product Managers, *Industrial Marketing Management* (February 1988): 73–84.
3. Ibid., 83.
4. Bill Meserve, "The Changing Role of Product Management," *Electronic Business* (January 9, 1989): 146.
5. William Weilbacher, *Brand Marketing* (Lincolnwood, IL: NTC Business Books, 1993: 123).

The 3M ScotchCart®II Cartridge[1]

The 3M ScotchCart®II cartridge was a broadcast cartridge tape for prerecorded radio messages introduced in 1986 by 3M's broadcasting and related products department. Product manager Bill Parfitt developed a marketing plan for it that highlighted the tactics most appropriate for increasing the cartridge's sale volume. According to Parfitt, "You must have a marketing plan to follow to be effective. With a plan, you are 90% proactive and 10% reactive. Without a plan, you are 90% reactive and 10% proactive. Even if a plan is not required, do one. It will save a tremendous amount of work."

The marketing tactics called for sales support products/activities, flexible pricing policies, trade shows, and print advertising.

Sales Support

3M's toolbox of support items for the sales force was extensive. Some of these were provided routinely, while others were developed and made available on an as-needed basis. The product reference guide was an important piece of information for the sales force. It contained a brief product description, an opening sales statement, and opening and follow-up questions. The next page of the reference guide contained common problems broadcasters might experience with tapes—and the resulting consequences—to enable the reps to customize the 3M product to the customer's needs. Although not all items are used with each product, many of these were provided for the ScotchCart®II Cartridge.

As part of the marketing tactics, Parfitt made sure the sales force was informed of marketing activities before they were seen by the customer, and they always received a sample of giveaways in advance.

3M supplied the following materials to its sales force:

- Comprehensive product/application/market manuals
- Information on special accounts
- History timelines
- Complete pricing, including special pricing
- Brochures
- List of key accounts or new prospects
- Advertisement reprints
- Buying-pattern information
- Article reprints
- Market-research data
- Technical bulletins
- Competitive brochures, ads, PR, etc.
- Competitive comparisons
- Glossary of industry terms
- Promotion outlines
- Video training tapes
- Product reference guide
- Yearbooks
- Newsletters
- Directories
- Complete set of policy pages
- Flow charts
- Complete dealer information
- Market-application charts

Flexible Pricing Policies

Radio stations, the target market for these 3M products, including the ScotchCart®II, were under pressure to conserve working capital while also needing to acquire sophisticated, technologically advanced equipment. 3M responded with several extended payment plans. The standard lease offered 336-, 48-, or 60-month pay-for-use plans on total purchases exceeding $5,000. The options available at the end of the lease included purchasing the equipment for the estimated market value, renewing the lease, or returning the equipment. The prime rate lease purchase plan provided financing for a 12- to 36-month term, with the title to the equipment transferring automatically upon completion of the final payment; the interest rate for the program was based on the current prime lending rate published each day in *The Wall Street Journal*.

In addition to the lease program, 3M used price actively in gaining customers both directly and through distribution. Special prices were developed for customer-special versions, partially based on the added value to the customers. Monetary incentives were also used to encourage dealers to switch their broadcasting customers from a competitive product to a 3M product. A 5% switcher/finder's fee was allocated for this purpose.

Trade Shows

Trade shows were also used as a tactic for gaining awareness and preference for the product. Parfitt started by compiling a list of shows relevant to the potential market for the ScotchCart®II and then obtaining performance data on the shows.

Several decisions had to be made regarding the potential attendance at the trade shows. Should inquiry cards or brochures be provided? How many? Should giveaways, incentives, or contests be part of the plan? What types? Should a preshow mailer be sent to potential attendees? Who would be responsible for each activity?

Recognizing that trade shows are more than three-dimensional ads, Parfitt put together a trade show plan. For an example of the type of planning tool that can be used, see Figure A.1. This information not only highlights the activities that need to be controlled for an effective trade show, but it also lists the individuals responsible for making them happen.

Print Advertising

The advertising for the ScotchCart®II cartridge was designed to emphasize that the product lasted longer than the competition while delivering consistently high performance. In the ads, the product was centrally positioned with significant features pointed out through the use of arrows. *Business Marketing* evaluated the first ad of this series in its Copy Chasers column:

> 3M, always a strong contender in any advertising judging, caught our eye with an excellent invitation to "Discover the secrets to a longer life" for its broadcast cartridges (tape cartridges carrying prerecorded radio station messages, commercials and the like). The product cutaway and call-outs tell the entire product feature story, backing up the promise in the headline.[2]

Two other ads in the campaign continued the use of consistent layout and message. All carried the headline on top, the product cutaway in the center with call-out features on each side, two columns of copy at the bottom, with the 3M logo in the bottom right corner.

In order to get approval on the marketing communications expenditure required, Parfitt used supporting effectiveness ratios from an Advertising Research Foundation study. A formula built on this information was presented in *Business Marketing* for estimating return on promotional investment. The ROPI formula is:

$$\text{Leads} \times \text{Inserts} \times (45\%) \times \text{Market share \%}$$

$$\times \text{Average sales amount} = \text{Sales}$$

The 45% figure in the formula is based on the results of two studies. The Inquiry Handling Service Inc., in analyzing 10,000 leads from 15 different business-to-business companies found that 21% bought some company's product within six months and 31% were still budgeting to buy within the year. A prior Advertising Research Foundation report (Report No. 25) cited similar ratios of buyers. The number of leads per insert is based on the uniqueness of the product, the effectiveness of the insert, and similar variables; your best estimate of the figure can be obtained from your own company's past experience. The market share and average sales amount can be obtained from internal documents.

According to James Obermayer,

> The rules for the ROPI are simple: 22% or slightly more of inquirers will buy within six months; around 45% of them will buy someone's product within one year. Furthermore, your company's share of those sales will usually be your market share in the industry.
>
> For example, suppose each insertion (magazine insertions or direct mail waves) produces 30 leads and the media plan calls for 12 insertions. We expect 45% of those leads to buy within a year. Knowing or estimating market share at 36%, and knowing the average sale produces $950 revenue, we forecast total sales of $55,404 from the leads generated by the ads. From that point, it's very easy to predict cost per raw lead and a cost per closed lead.[3]

Several techniques were built into the program to help track the campaign. Bingo cards (reply cards inserted into a publication for readers to request literature from companies whose products and services are advertised) were used where appropriate. In other cases, steps were taken to ensure that inquiries were routed to the product manager.

Conclusion

The marketing tactics for the ScotchCart®II as well as other 3M products were based on an integrated approach to plan-

Description	Responsible	Projected Completion Date	Date Completed
Set objectives			
Gather show information			
Show selection			
Contract for space			
Exhibit design			
Exhibit construction			
Freight			
Drayage			
Set-up			
Electrical			
Plumbing			
Telephone			
Furniture rental			
Janitorial service			
Photography			
Guard service			
Florist service			
A/V equipment			
Presenters/models			
Inquiry cards			
Literature			
Equipment			
Badges			
Rooms			
Directory copy			
Suite			
Invitations			
Preshow promotion			
Booth staffing			
Prizes			
Giveaways			
Budget Projection			

Figure A.1 Trade show responsibilities.

Description	Responsible	Projected Completion Date	Date Completed
Show evaluation form			
Inquiry follow-up			
Postshow follow-up			
Audit and pay-related invoices			
Miscellaneous			

Figure A.1   continued

ning. Objectives were established to guide the implementation of the plan. All possible promotional vehicles were considered as viable elements of the marketing communications. Pricing was built into the plan rather than simply being an after-the-plan reaction. And finally, sales promotion, in the form of free sampling, was incorporated to help the market gain rapid experience with the product.

As for other product managers, the message is clear. The first step is to identify the problems and opportunities for a given product that should trigger planning items for the next fiscal year. These problems and opportunities must then be converted into objectives for the marketing plan. Based on the objectives, a target market must be selected for the product and a positioning strategy developed to differentiate the product from the competition in the minds of that target market. Finally, specific tactics (pricing, marketing communications, logistics, product support) need to be acted on to solidify the positioning in the customers' minds and accomplish the fiscal-year objectives.

Notes

1. The information in this section is adapted with 3M permission from a workshop conducted by Bill Parfitt, June 7, 1991, and 3M promotional materials.
2. "Copy Chasers" column, *Business Marketing* (March 1989): 90–92.
3. James W. Obermayer, "Marrying Communications to Sales Dollars," *Business Marketing* (July 1998): 71.

Appendix B

Sample Job Descriptions

This appendix contains actual job descriptions from companies in a variety of industries.

Job Description in a Biotechnology Firm

Title: Senior Product Manager, NDA Purification
Reports to: Director, Product/Marketing Management
Duties:

1. Develop long-term marketing plan for business/customer focus area (includes many product lines), determining what products to add to the line and the short-term and long-term marketing mix that will result in maximum growth of the product line (i.e., promotions needed, publicity, training and support, pricing, image of product).
2. Prepare and give group presentations on marketing and sales strategy and proposed new product development, including return on investment (ROI) calculations, competitive analysis, customer needs, critical success factors, market analysis, sales justification, and other components outlined in the standard business plan template.
3. Initiate and negotiate contracts and licenses for new technologies, products, or kits using standard process and coordinating, as appropriate, with research and development,

legal, corporate development, and manufacturing departments after corporate approval.

4. Initiate and follow up on original equipment manufacturer (OEM) opportunities by meeting with OEM supplier and meeting with the legal department to discuss and approve terms and give sales estimates. Identify potential products and customers to purchase company products on an OEM basis. Discuss and approve pricing with OEM sales staff.

5. Prepare annual marketing budget for the business area. Responsible for keeping spending within budgetary limits.

6. Evaluate the marketing side of possible new technologies presented by corporate development and other groups, completing the evaluation checklist in the company intranet. Identify potential technologies needed for the strategic direction of the product line for corporate development to pursue. Negotiate licensing terms, as needed.

7. Provide leadership, training, coaching, and/or mentoring to one or more product managers, including giving input into hiring, development, and evaluation processes for these staff.

8. Give final approval on pricing guidelines for distributors and direct customers, within pricing strategy and pricing policies. Ensure that pricing has been approved by the appropriate internal group.

9. Attend trade shows as marketing representative, as needed. Responsible for setting trade show theme and managing booth on-site. Work with trade show coordinator on booth happenings and logistics.

10. Approve final language used in catalog. Train others in features and benefits to be used for catalog text, as needed. Work with external staff on overall product image plan for catalog.

11. Ensure that all goals and objectives of the marketing and sales plan for the business area are met by continually monitoring and reporting on product trends, competitive trends, sales trends, financial changes, and other problem areas. Recommend and lead alternative actions as needed to meet overall objectives of short-term and long-term position.

12. Understand and comply with all elements of the company quality system outlined for the position.

Qualifications:

1. B.S. in appropriate scientific area or B.S. in marketing with concentrated training in appropriate scientific area; seven years in marketing position, including at least three years in product or marketing management or sales.
2. Proven ability to effectively communicate with several types and levels of staff and external contacts, both in writing and verbally. Effective presentation skills.
3. Ability to effectively work simultaneously on many priorities, which change frequently.
4. Thorough knowledge of all financial components of product and marketing management, including product contribution margins, profit and loss statements, budget processes, and return on investment calculations.
5. Thorough knowledge of contracting and licensing process. Ability to effectively negotiate terms and conditions for licenses and contracts with outside parties.

Job Description in a Biotechnology Firm

Title: Product Manager, Cell Regulation
Reports to: Manager, Product Management
Duties:

1. Responsible for product logistics of assigned product line, including entering information into company system (and accuracy of information entered by others), printing labels, finalizing pricing, completing packaging, and preparing literature and distributor/branch notifications for all new products. Pricing involves analysis of pricing of similar company and competitor products and recommended process to marketing managers and group leader for review and approval. Packaging involves determining appropriate packaging after review and input from research and development staff and recommendation and approval by marketing managers.
2. Notify branch office staff, distributors, and internal staff of new product introductions by sending internal notification, standard forms, and sales summary (as reviewed by senior product manager or marketing manager).
3. Implement trademark searches for approved trade names.
4. Develop monthly progress reports on all products within area of responsibility, including sales for product line, trends, monthly advertising and promotion schedule, and competitive information by the third day of each month. Follow monthly report format.
5. Input information into computer system and run sales analysis on product line, as requested. Demonstrate proficiency with senior product manager review.
6. Coordinate responses to daily faxes and e-mails. Mail and send daily replies.
7. Assist group with annual marketing plan, strategic plan, and budget.
8. Provide quotes to customers as needed (after review by product marketing manager).

9. Proofread catalog section for accuracy in text, pricing, trademarks, and so on.
10. Prepare monthly analyses of spending activities and provide them for the marketing managers.
11. Assist more experienced product managers with focus groups. Specifically, recruit participants, arrange logistics, and pay attendees (if needed).
12. Assist others in identifying outside sources for contract and OEM licensing. May prepare draft marketing issues for inclusion in contract/licensing.
13. Assist with special projects (i.e., conducting customer surveys by telephone or Internet).
14. Attend weekly product manager meeting.
15. Understand and comply with all elements of the company quality system outlined for the position.

Qualifications:

1. B.S. in appropriate scientific area, or in marketing with concentrated training in appropriate scientific area. One year in marketing related position or utilizing marketing skills.
2. Strong written and verbal communication skills, including technical writing.
3. Ability to work simultaneously on many priorities, which change frequently.

Job Description in a Consumer Product Firm

Title: Assistant Product Manager, Clothing
Reports to: Product Manager, Clothing
Purpose: Responsible for the promotional clothing business for the company family of brands. Responsibility covers executing all merchandising and design functions, communicating product availability, and timely task completion.
Duties:

1. Work with product manager of clothing, marketing and sales departments, outside design resources, and vendors in all aspects of line development, including line planning, color, product selection, fit styling, product sourcing, and manufacturability.
2. Develop detailed line plan for each brand.
3. Secure sourcing for each product to maximize customer value and profit objectives.
4. Analyze product costing and establish product pricing for promotional products to balance corporate gross margin goals with market demand and positioning.
5. Develop initial product forecasts to determine profitability of each line and examine impact of adding additional products to the line.
6. Initiate timetable for development of promotional product lines to ensure introduction during the appropriate time frame to maximize sales and minimize carrying costs.
7. Present promotional clothing line to management, sales force, and other internal departments.
8. Interface with subsequent departments to minimize production/development problems and determine product needs.
9. Coordinate the distribution of samples to sales force and ensure the development of all coordinating sales tools, including but not limited to catalogs and dealer flyers.
10. Prepare booking analysis for promotional products on a quarterly basis to aid in planning the introduction of future products.

Secondary Duties:

1. Execute the development of special product for promotional and team needs.
2. Communicate with sales force to determine seasonal product, price, and forecast needs.
3. Maintain boards of promotional products for each line.
4. Distribute line information to applicable internal departments, including sales, marketing, international, and the company stores.
5. Interface with all appropriate vendors to communicate product development timetables and initial forecasts. Initiate new product development.
6. Maintain product plans and cost/detail sheets for each product.
7. Input travel/budget needs to product manager, clothing.
8. Additional duties as assigned by product manager, clothing.

Qualifications:

1. B.S. or B.A. degree in business administration/merchandising.
2. Minimum two years retail and/or product development experience.
3. Outstanding communication and presentation skills.
4. Well-developed organizational and human relations skills.
5. Ability to establish and maintain multiple priorities.
6. Ability to function in a team environment.
7. Working knowledge of forecasting techniques, percentages, and mark-ups.
8. Working knowledge of computer programs including Excel and Word.

Physical Requirements:
Domestic and international travel required.

Job Description in an Industrial Capital Equipment Firm

Title: Product Manager, Drying and Air Systems
Department: Paper Group
Reports to: Director, Product Management
Summary: Provide overall management of the designated products. Provide product direction and vision. Responsible for implementing product development process, reducing product cost, and ensuring worldwide product standards. Work with sales, marketing research, production engineering, product analysis, and central standards departments, as well as manufacturing site, field service, and applications groups.
Duties:

1. Has single-source responsibility for developing and implementing global product strategy and market positioning for the designated product, in each grade.
2. Coordinate selection of products for development. Organize and coordinate product development process for the designated product. Coordinate product development work and research activities.
3. Responsible for costs, features, performance, reliability, maintenance, and manufacturability. Work with capital manufacturing and purchasing to achieve cost objectives. Develop and document global design, safety, and performance standards.
4. Work with sales and service organizations to maximize product performance and achieve revenue objectives. Ensure that customers are satisfied with product performance. Use market feedback for product improvements and new product development process.
5. Supervise the market assessments, competitive evaluations, product development activities, identification of customer needs and perceptions, management of product database, and preparation of sales and marketing materials and product training programs. Continuously monitor competitive offerings, maintain knowledge of competitive features, and incorporate competitive features, as appropriate.

6. Direct planning of each product development activity and assist in the preparation of the strategic plan for the designated product.
7. Establish and maintain an effective staff, evaluate employee performance, administer group wages, determine workforce requirements, maintain global communications, and promote group training and technical competence.
8. Help establish and manage group operating budget and keep product development costs on each product's activities within the plan limits.

Job Description in a Telecommunications Organization

Title: Product Manager/Team Leader
Department: Product Marketing
Division: Marketing
Status: Exempt
Reports to: Product Marketing Manager
Supervises: Associate Product Managers
Summary: Manage, promote, direct, plan, and coordinate activities for specific product line and ensure synergy with related product line managers on the team to ensure that product line objectives are accomplished within prescribed time frame and parameters.
Quality Statement: Promote total quality management. Demonstrate and encourage the importance of internal and external customer satisfaction and quality work.
Duties:

1. Responsible for managing, promoting, directing, and controlling related product line, which includes but is not limited to the following duties:
   - Establishing product line direction for existing products, including product line extensions and additional target markets;
   - Marketing/promoting product line;
   - Supporting and training sales staff;
   - Devising sales channel strategies;
   - Tracking revenue and margin;
   - Pricing markets and targeting strategies and discount structures;
   - Initiating measures for product cost containment and cost reduction (due diligence with engineering and operations);
   - Tracking industry trends, product segment growth, market share;
   - Ensuring synergy and cohesive approach to execution and communication by the team members to support the overall product family objective.

2. Establish clear pricing strategies, discount structures, and guidelines for all sales channels and target markets.

3. Prioritize engineering development and promotional projects for the product line.

4. Manage product line direction through an ongoing assessment of current products, pricing, and position; systematically develop and evaluate opportunities for new products and/or line extensions; and identify new target markets (jointly with industry marketing) and related strategies.

5. Document concept for new products and/or line extensions to meet existing or anticipated market needs and present to manager and/or research and development committee as appropriate, according to the established product development process. Develop market opportunity document; document product specifications required (PRD); initiate and prioritize the project within engineering; track product development through project engineering; plan, develop, and communicate strategy for product launch and initial forecast; track sales, costs, and margin and effects on existing product line revenues; and conduct continued product promotion.

6. Develop, execute, and maintain product and product family business plan that provides current market information, including sales and gross profit margin history, year-to-date (YTD) actuals and projections, key market positioning, sales channels and competitive strategies, pricing, market share, product life cycle plans, and evolution plans.

7. Initiate and participate in the development of all marketing collateral, including Web site and catalog pages, product releases, brochures, advertisements, video, PC presentations, special premium items, and flyers. Establish sales promotions and special incentive programs.

8. Support sales force through joint sales calls to key accounts; proposal/bid volume pricing and development assistance; and trade show support and conference calls. Develop and conduct product, market, and application training. Communicate product line updates and key information in weekly update; e-mail to sales force and key employees.

9. Establish final pricing on the product, including list price, discount structure, and special price incentives, on a global scale.

10. Maintain an awareness of the competition and other market forces affecting the product line, through effective networking and mainstream research. Provide key competitive information and product comparisons to market research team for the timely maintenance and publication of the competitive product information manual, adding information as required and ensuring accuracy and accessibility to key employees.

11. Provide and/or present monthly, quarterly, and annual product line update reports as directed.

12. Provide supervision, training, ongoing guidance, and mentorship to assigned personnel in accomplishing their objectives and fulfilling their responsibilities. Monitor their progress and participate in performance review process for assigned personnel, as appropriate. Interview potential candidates and assist in hiring decisions.

13. Assist in leading the day-to-day activities of the department to achieve both the corporate and departmental objectives.

14. Encourage continuous process improvement by developing ways to maximize each team member's involvement in all process improvements.

15. Assist in special projects and/or perform additional duties that are assigned.

16. Demonstrate and encourage a cooperative and congenial working relationship, within and outside the company.

Qualifications:

1. Bachelor's degree in marketing, business, or a technical field, or an equivalent combination of education and technical/professional experience.

2. Three years of product marketing experience in telecommunications or a related technical industry.

3. Demonstrated ability to lead and organize cross-functional meetings, committees, and people in a professional manner.

4. Demonstrated aggressive, persuasive, and creative problem-solving skills.
5. Excellent verbal and written communication, presentation, organization, and time-management skills.
6. Proficient use of word processing, spreadsheet, presentation, and e-mail software.

Job Description in a Mid-Sized Industrial Firm

Title: Manager/General Aftermarket
Department: Marketing
Reports to: Director of Marketing
Purpose: Serve customers and develop products and markets by assessing customer needs, establishing and implementing tactical market plans, developing and/or finding sources for required products, and establishing longer-term strategic plans.
Duties:

1. Service existing accounts and establish new accounts by planning and organizing a daily work schedule that maintains contact with existing and potential customers and establishes new customers.
2. Facilitate the sale of current products through existing channels by establishing promotional programs, recommending advertising venues, participating in trade shows, calling on customers with field sales representatives, evaluating sales-call results, and providing a liaison role with other product and market managers.
3. Pursue new-product and market opportunities by comparing company products, services, and capabilities to those of competitors regarding markets, price, new products, delivery, advertising, and merchandising techniques. Gather current information on total and served market, market share, and growth opportunities.
4. Increase aftermarket sales by developing and/or finding sources of new products to position company for growth.
5. Determine product pricing by reviewing costs, anticipating volume, and utilizing competitive market research data.
6. Provide liaison in new products by coordinating product development and sourcing programs. Establish and follow up on completion date requirements.
7. Evaluate existing distribution channels in relationship to company capabilities and current and potential competitive position.

8. Resolve customer complaints by investigating problems, developing solutions, preparing reports, and making recommendations to management when necessary.

9. Suggest advertising and sales promotion programs by reviewing and evaluating current and previous company programs' effectiveness and programs offered by competitors.

10. Keep management informed by submitting activity and results reports, such as call reports and monthly significant developments. Prepare short- and long-term product sales forecasts and special reports and analyses. Answer questions and requests.

11. Maintain inter-and intra-departmental work flow by fostering the spirit of cooperation.

12. Contribute to team effort by accomplishing related results and completing special projects as assigned by management.

Index

Note: Boldface numbers indicate illustrations; italic *t* indicates a table.

About the CD

Product managers are busy people. Busy people looking for shortcuts. So, when people asked me for electronic versions of the worksheets in my book so that they could more easily adapt them to fit their needs, it was a Eureka moment! While the worksheets and templates are not complex, it can be time-consuming to retype the material to be able to reformat to fit a specific company or product line. And since no approach fits all needs, I decided to offer the worksheets in Word (and a few in Excel) to simplify the customization process. (However, I did not provide standard financial forms, since companies provide them to product managers in their own formats.)

The CD contains all 10 of the worksheets from the book, as well as a few figures that I converted to worksheets specifically for this CD. In addition, I added a few items from *The Product Manager's Field Guide*—providing you with a total of more than 20 worksheets, templates, and checklists to adapt, amend, adjust, and manipulate to your heart's content. Happy morphing!